The Economics of Poverty and Discrimination

BRADLEY R. SCHILLER

University of Maryland

Prentice-Hall, Inc., *Englewood Cliffs*, New Jersey

Library of Congress Cataloging in Publication Data

Schiller, Bradley R
  The economics of poverty and discrimination.

  Includes bibliographies.
    1. Poor—United States. 2. Poverty.
  3. Discrimination—United States. 4. Economic
  assistance, Domestic—United States. I. Title.
HC110.P6S27   331.5'4'0973   72-5407
ISBN 0-13-232017-7

© 1973
by Prentice-Hall, Inc.
Englewood Cliffs, New Jersey

10 9 8 7 6 5 4 3 2 1

Prentice-Hall International, Inc., *London*
Prentice-Hall of Australia, Pty. Ltd., *Sydney*
Prentice-Hall of Canada, Ltd., *Toronto*
Prentice-Hall of India (Private) Ltd., *New Delhi*
Prentice-Hall of Japan, Inc., *Tokyo*

Printed in the United States of America

Contents

III   Public Programs and Policies

IV   Summary and Conclusions

Preface

Poverty and discrimination are popular subjects. They arouse the attention and interest of students, policy makers, and taxpayers alike. Mention "welfare," for example, and almost every taxpayer will have a firm opinion on how to improve the "welfare mess." After only a moment's hesitation, most people are ready either to deny or decry the existence of poverty or discrimination in the United States and to offer policy solutions.

Unfortunately, the popularity of these subjects far exceeds understanding of them. In spite of extended and often heated discussions of poverty and discrimination, very little consideration has been given to the nature and sources of these social ills. As a result, popular discussions, and even public policy, are most often based on very superficial views of what poverty and discrimination are, why these phenomena exist, and what policies will eliminate them. In this context, it is hardly surprising that we often perceive only limited progress in our public efforts to combat these ills.

This book provides no unchallengeable and definitive solutions to the problems of poverty and discrimination. It does attempt, however, to approach a more comprehensive understanding of the nature and causes of these problems. It proceeds on the assumption that to do something effective about poverty and discrimination, one must know something about them. Accordingly, the first half of the book focuses on the causes of poverty. A variety of alleged causal factors are discussed in some detail, and many popular "explanations" of poverty emerge considerably scathed. However, not every causal discussion results in unambiguous conclusions. While this may frustrate many readers, it must also be recognized as necessary. Social phenomena rarely lend themselves to quick and easy explanations. Where they are sought, more misunderstanding usually follows.

Building on the analysis of the early chapters, Part III focuses on existing and proposed public programs to alleviate or prevent poverty and discrimination. The programs are examined both on the level of their internal performance and in the broader context of general antipoverty strategy. A special effort is made to relate what we know about the causes of poverty to the programs designed to eliminate it. The book concludes with a discussion of prospects and desirable directions for future public policy.

It would be naive to treat poverty and discrimination as purely economic phenomena. While the title of the book is intended to convey a particular perspective on the ensuing discussion, it is not meant to imply a strict disciplinary exclusiveness. On the contrary, frequent, and often extended, explorations are made into other disciplines, most notably sociology. These will be most apparent when the cultural and racial aspects of poverty are considered.

Finally, it must be made clear from the outset that neither poverty nor discrimination are exclusively racial concerns. Poverty is not all black, nor is discrimination always exercised in a racial context. While the subject of discrimination does receive much attention in this book, it tends to be confined within the context of its causal relationship to poverty. It is recognized that the elimination of either poverty or discrimination does not imply the elimination of the other. While antidiscrimination and antipoverty policies may be mutually supportive, they are only rarely identical.

The ultimate objective of this book is to lay the foundations for a clearer understanding of poverty and discrimination and for a keener perspective on related public policy. The human and economic cost of both phenomena are greater than Americans need or want to bear.

Bradley R. Schiller

Acknowledgements

Among the many persons and institutions who helped make this book possible, I wish to especially thank Dudley Dillard, who provided the necessary institutional flexibility and atmosphere at the University of Maryland, and my tireless research assistant, Tom Anderson, who unearthed needed data and references. Gratitude is also due Professors Henry Aaron, Christopher Clague, and Sandra Christensen, and to the reviewers, Professor Neil J. Smelser of the University of California at Berkeley and Professor John J. Kain of Harvard University, all of whom suggested important improvements in the text. Financial support for the research was provided through the Project on Discrimination at the University of Maryland, while additional assistance was made available by Pacific Training and Technical Assistance Corporation. Greatest appreciation is reserved for my wife, however, whose patience, sacrifice, and hard work made this book a reality.

I The Scope of Poverty

1   The Nature
of Poverty

Most Americans no longer accept the existence of poverty as inevitable. Indeed, most of us are surprised to learn that millions of Americans remain inadequately fed, clothed, and housed. As a nation we desire and sometimes strive to relieve the material hardships of those who are poor. We also deplore the waste of resources that poverty engenders—especially in the areas of welfare, crime, and civil disorder. Two questions remain, however: (1) Why are so many Americans poor? and (2) What policies will eliminate their impoverishment?

In seeking to answer these questions, we must recognize their interdependence. What we believe to be the dimensions and causes of poverty will have a determining influence on the policies we pursue. By the same token, how effective those policies are will depend in part on how accurately we have identified the roots of impoverishment.

Different historical phases of antipoverty activity in America illustrate the interdependence of causal perspectives and policy prescriptions. In colonial times poverty was viewed as a curse on those of disreputable character. Impoverishment was seen as the companion to and punishment for vice. Accordingly, early antipoverty prescriptions focused on religious training, corporal punishment (to drive out sin), and physical expulsion. Very little was done to help the poor become more self-sufficient or even to alleviate their suffering.

It was not until the depression of the 1890s that many people seriously began to question the proposition that poverty resulted from sin and slovenliness. The march of unemployed and poor men—Coxey's Army—on Washington, D.C., in 1894 helped stimulate fresh perspectives on the origins of poverty. But it was not until 15 million Americans simultaneously experienced unemployment in the depths of the Great Depression that a really new perspective on poverty took hold. Only as millions of otherwise responsible and industrious individuals fell abruptly into joblessness and poverty did the

American public begin to speak of poverty as being outside the control of the individual. Awareness grew that poverty might be the consequence of social and economic forces rather than of immorality and vice.

From one point of view, our experience with depressions and poverty may have been too brief. With the passage of time and the return to prosperity, poverty lost its middle-class constituency. With this loss, views toward those who are poor have become less generous. There has been a tendency to return to theories of poverty that characterize earlier eras. Thus, many observers again question the ambitions, motivation, ability, and the entire cultural orientation of those presently poor. To some extent the character of the poor is again being interpreted as different and apart from traditional American mores and ethics. This interpretation has acquired particular significance in discussions of the nation's expanding welfare crisis. An editorial from the Tulsa, Oklahoma, *Tribune* typifies the residual hostilities and resentments that persist:

> Relief is gradually becoming an honorable career in America. It is a pretty fair life, if you have neither conscience nor pride. The politicians will weep for you. The state will give a mother a bonus for her illegitimate children, and if she neglects them sufficiently she can save enough of her AFDC payments to keep herself and her boyfriend in wine and gin.[1]

Current American attitudes toward the poor, then, are best described as ambivalent. The disquieting suspicion that external social and economic forces are at the root of poverty continues to stir the public conscience. At the same time, however, the egocentric conviction that the poor are less deserving still lingers close to the surface. Only as unemployment rates reach crisis proportions—as in the early 1970s—does the former perspective clearly gather significant strength.

Against this background of uncertainty about the dimensions and causes of poverty, it is not remarkable that public policy often appears contradictory and ineffective. Until we reach a consensus on the dimensions of the problem, we cannot muster the necessary political support for public action. Where the causes of poverty remain the subject of intense debate, we cannot expect our efforts to meet with success. Accordingly, a serious effort to do something about poverty must begin with certain fundamentals. We must first decide what we mean when we refer to so many Americans as being *poor.* Then we must determine how many persons fall into this category and why they are there.

ECONOMIC DEFINITIONS OF POVERTY

Despite all the time that has been spent on poverty research, no consensus has been reached on the answers to some basic questions. Most profound of all is

---

[1] Quoted in Edgar May, *The Wasted Americans* (New York: Harper & Row, Publishers, 1964), p. 7.

our continuing inability to specify exactly what is meant by the term *poverty*. It is facile and perhaps satisfying to say that poverty is simply a lack of money. And, of course, such a response is essentially correct; poverty *does* mean a scarcity of money. But when we examine this definition more carefully we must recognize a certain vagueness about the nature of poverty. Exactly what is meant by a *lack of money*? Do we mean no money, no income, no assets, and no credit, that is, a complete and devastating inability to acquire the basics of life? Or do we mean simply a shortage of cash? And if any one or all of these criteria, then how do we measure and define each one? Do we speak of a scarcity of money with reference to certain goods we think should or must be obtained, or do we mean a scarcity relative to the amount of money, assets, income, or credit that others have? Clearly, there is room for a great deal of ambiguity and discussion even if we can agree that poverty is, in essence, a lack of economic resources.

To achieve a workable and acceptable definition of poverty, we may begin by noting that there are two basic economic approaches to the concept of poverty. The first of these is the humanitarian approach, which deems some particular amount of goods and services as essential to an individual's or a family's welfare. Those who do not possess the economic wherewithal to obtain these goods and services are considered poor. In the least humanitarian of the so-called humanitarian approaches this bundle of economic goods and services consists of the minimum caloric intake essential to human existence. Additional frills are tacked onto this basic diet according to the generosity of the analyst.

This, of course, is the fundamental problem with the humanitarian approach to defining poverty: once the bare-bones, life-sustaining minimum caloric diet has been exceeded, there is no agreement as to how many additional frills can be included in the definitional bundle of basic goods and services. In the 1890s no one felt particularly poor if he did not possess electric lights, yet today a family without electricity most likely is considered poor. Thus, we include a provision for electricity in our minimum poverty-defining budget. But consensus is far more difficult to achieve on a table lamp, much less on a television, a car, or a six-pack of beer. How many of these items will we include in a poor family's budget?

How different opinions can be on this subject is illustrated by the controversy over the Nixon administration's proposed Family Assistance Plan. The National Welfare Rights Organization, a spokesman for welfare recipients, calculated that $6,500 a year was required to provide the basic economic needs of a family of four in the United States in 1971. President Nixon, on the other hand, concluded that $2,400 was adequate. Even more extreme, the state of Mississippi has indicated that $708 per year would do.

These differences serve to focus attention on the most perplexing issues of who is to determine the basic needs of individuals, and on what basis that determination is to be made. Quite obviously, each person's conception of what a family needs will be conditioned by his own economic position and his familiarity with the poor. Faced with these dilemmas, some observers have suggested an alternative approach to defining poverty. We may call this second method the egalitarian approach.

The humanitarian approach presumes the ability to construct an *absolute* measure of poverty. As a practical matter, however, we have seen that such a measure is vague and subject to the views of those formulating the yardstick. The egalitarian approach is simply more explicit about this subjectivity. In essence, it states that a person is poor when he falls into some specified lower end of the income distribution. For example, an egalitarian might say that a person or family with less than one-half of the average income is poor. A person's poverty is defined relative to the incomes of others; if his standard of living is substantially below the average, then he is deemed poor.

As we have said, the egalitarian approach is, in one respect, simply a more explicit approach to an absolute measure of poverty. In constructing an absolute measure, we have seen the necessity of basing our calculations on notions of a "proper" standard of living. By subtracting the frills from that standard, we arrive at a poverty measure. The egalitarian method proceeds in a similar fashion. In fact, it can be shown that one approach leads easily to the other.

Take, for example, the family income distribution in the United States for 1970 presented in Table 1.1. It can be seen that under 2 percent of all American families earned less than $1,000, 4.6 percent less than $2,000, and so forth. Only 4.6 percent of American families earned more than $25,000.

TABLE 1.1 Cumulative Family Income Distribution, 1970 and 1935-6

Income in 1970 dollars	$1,000	$2,000	$3,000	$4,000	$5,000	$10,000	$15,000	$25,000
Percentage of families with income less than specified amount								
In 1970	1.6	4.6	8.9	13.9	19.1	50.9	77.7	95.4
In 1935-6	13.4	31.3	47.3	65.3	77.8	94.6	-	-

Source: U.S. Bureau of the Census

Suppose then, that after very intricate and tedious calculations of minimal shelter, food, and clothing allowances, we determined that $3,000 was the minimum amount of income needed to provide a bare but decent standard of living in American society. That is to say, suppose we determined that $3,000 represented a fair and equitable poverty line. Given this figure and the data in our table, we could then state with equal validity that any family in the lower nine percent of the income distribution was poor.

Or, to reverse the sequence, we could say that anyone in the lower nine percentiles of the income distribution is poor and then check our table to determine the absolute measure of poverty implied thereby. Quite obviously, either definition of poverty implies the other, and both must proceed from some common base of what constitutes a minimum or decent standard of living.

If the distinction between the two definitions of poverty is so blurred, why do we emphasize the differences in approach so much? It would appear that much ado has been made about nothing. However, our deliberations have not been wasted. There are very important differences in the relative and absolute measures of poverty when consistently applied over time.

Suppose we wanted to compare the number of Americans who are in poverty today with the number who were poor in 1936. Franklin Roosevelt spoke of one-third of the nation as being "ill-housed, ill-clad, ill-nourished." Apparently he regarded an income of about $2,000 as a threshold of poverty (see Table 1.1). By Roosevelt's definition, only 4.6 percent of the American population was poor in 1970. From an historical perspective, then, we could conclude that the incidence of poverty in the United States had declined markedly over a period of thirty years.

But what would we conclude about the course of poverty between 1936 and 1970 if we had instead applied the egalitarian concept of poverty to the comparison? If we were consistently to regard the lowest fifth of the American income distribution as poor, then by definition we would find that 20 percent of the population was poor in 1936 and continues to be so today.

This example illustrates the basic weaknesses of the egalitarian, or relative, measure of poverty. First of all, it perpetuates poverty in the statistical sense that some fixed proportion of the population is always regarded as poor. If the lowest fifth of the income distribution is regarded as poor, then the poor will certainly be with us always because the income distribution will always have a lowest fifth. Secondly, a relative measure of poverty by itself tells us nothing about how well or how poorly the people at the bottom of the income distribution actually live. Yet we want to know not only how many people are in poverty but also how desperate their situation is. In a similar vein we may want to know how much money poor families need to bring their incomes up to an acceptable standard of living. For these reasons we will employ an absolute measure of poverty throughout the remainder of this book. Those who wish to do so can easily translate our standards into relative measures of income distribution.[2]

The contrast between relative and absolute measures of poverty highlights a basic policy issue. Is our primary policy concern with the misery of those who command low incomes, or are we more concerned with the unequal distribution of incomes? While income distribution and poverty are intrinsically related, they

---

[2] Victor Fuchs of the National Bureau of Economic Research has formulated an alternative measure of relative poverty. By his definition, those with incomes less than half of the national median are poor. This "Fuchs point" eliminates the perpetual character of other relative measures but is not as flexible as the poverty standard formulated in this chapter.

can be approached separately. Poverty could be eliminated, for example, by making *everyone* better off. This policy would leave the size distribution of incomes unchanged. On the other hand, direct redistribution of incomes from rich to poor could speed the elimination of poverty and might be a goal in itself.

NONECONOMIC MEASURES OF POVERTY

To some observers poverty is just as much a state of mind as it is a state of one's pocketbook. In this most subjective of views, a person is not poor unless he *feels* poor. The Kentucky backwoodsman is sometimes seen not as impoverished but as enjoying the rich benefits of a bountiful and uncluttered natural world. He is not to be pitied, but rather idealized. To lift him out of financial destitution would be to corrupt him.

While Henry Thoreau forcefully expressed this distinction between monetary and spiritual richness, his views are not easily translated into statistical or policy-making terms. Short of surveying all destitute persons as to their spiritual contentment and materialistic anxieties, Thoreau's distinction permits no census of the poor. That is not to say that his perspective does not merit reflection, but rather that it does not provide an adequate guide to policy formulation. Accordingly, we are led to use other criteria for identifying the poor and to conclude from their political agitation that the poor are not wholly content.

More recent observers from other social disciplines have construed similar definitions of modern poverty. Generally, they focus on the hopes, expectations, and aspirations—the entire "culture" in some cases—of those without material means. To these observers, poverty is to be without money, without spirit, without hope for a better life. Poverty is thus understood to be complete material and spiritual deprivation. While these concepts have considerable merit in their own right, they are not easily observed, much less quantified. While they contribute to an understanding of poverty in many cases, they add little to its definition or measurement. Moreover, they are likely to create more disagreement on poverty measures than already exists. Accordingly, we will rely on economic and strictly observable criteria in defining and measuring poverty.

THE CONCEPT OF MINIMUM NEEDS

In the previous section we mentioned some of the difficulties inherent in specifying the minimum or essential needs of a family. We emphasized that such a specification necessarily embodies the subjective views of the analyst. Nevertheless, having selected an absolute measure of poverty, we must identify the components of that measure.

To approach our specifications as scientifically as possible, we want to begin by determining what are the absolutely basic ingredients of human subsistence; presumably everyone will agree that our poverty measure should include at least these components. Such a list will include minimum food, clothing, shelter, and fuel requirements as determined by appropriate experts. To this list of basic minimums we may choose to include means of transportation, some recreation, and whatever additional goods and services we deem appropriate, if not absolutely essential. The sum total of our efforts, assuming consensus can be achieved, will be a shopping list of what we consider to be basic goods and services. Those persons who cannot obtain all the items on our list we will consider poor, those who can as not poor.

Suppose for the moment that nutritionists, physiologists, and other assorted scientific experts could actually detail the minimum subsistence requirements we have outlined. Such a list might be like the one in Table 1.2. Note that each functional requirement is expressed in its generic measure. To this list of social and biological minimums we might add additional food, clothing, or entertainment, depending on our sense of generosity. In this way we could construct a complete specification of what we deem to be the minimum acceptable (or poverty) standard of living.

TABLE 1.2 Hypothetical Minimum Human Needs

Category	Amount
Minimum food requirements	2,471 calories
Minimum fuel requirements	37 kwh
Minimum shelter requirements	60 board feet
Minimum clothing requirements	4 pounds
Minimum transportation requirements	7 miles

But consider carefully the list we have compiled. To begin with, how are we to translate 2,471 calories into more familiar staples like peanuts, bananas, and chewing gum? As anyone who has ever dieted well knows, there are an infinite number of ways in which a person can consume the requisite number of calories. Or, consider the clothing requirement. The specification "four pounds" tells us nothing at all about the appropriate type of clothing or even whether we should shop at Saks Fifth Avenue or a Salvation Army store. Similar problems arise with every item on our list.

As if this vagueness of detail were not a serious enough problem, let us return to the generic specifications. While there is some conceptual foundation for speaking of "minimum" food, shelter, clothing, or fuel requirements, there is admittedly no firm basis for specifying what these minimums are. People do survive on varying amounts of calories; the warming and protective value of clothing cannot be adequately gauged in pounds; and the need for shelter varies enormously. Consequently, any claim to scientific precision, even in the generic specifications of our poverty standard, is pretentious and misplaced.

While the specification of a poverty standard is an imprecise endeavor, it is not necessarily useless. The achievement of consensus as to the components of a poverty standard may be a formidable task, but it may not be impossible. If we can achieve some sort of reasonable compromise, our basic objective of specification will have been attained.

We return, then, to our position that an absolute standard of poverty can be defined in terms of a shopping list of goods and services. Poverty is thus understood as the inability to obtain the goods and services sufficient to meet socially defined minimum needs. Momentarily sidestepping the issue of specification, our only remaining conceptual problem is to consolidate that list of goods and services into more convenient and observable units.

UNITS OF MEASURE

In a market economy, the ability of an individual to obtain needed goods and services is determined by his *purchasing power*. The producers and sellers of goods require some form of payment before they willingly yield up their wares. Accordingly, we may be able to simplify our poverty standard by expressing that measure, not in terms of a list of necessary goods and services but instead in terms of the purchasing power required to obtain those same goods and services. This simplification will greatly enhance the usefulness of our measure, since we will be able to inquire merely whether a person has a specific amount of purchasing power rather than a cumbersome list of essential commodities.

The obvious and familiar measure of purchasing power in a market economy is money, so it should come as no surprise that we express our poverty standard in dollars and cents. The necessary conversion requires that we price all the goods and services in our list, then sum to determine the total amount of money involved. That total is our gauge of poverty, for it represents command over the goods and services we have specified.

Not only is such a summary measure more convenient but it also facilitates the compromise which produced the standard itself. Suppose, for example, that Mr. Blixen believes that 1,437 calories and 1.57 pounds of clothing are the absolute daily minimum needs of one person. You, on the other hand, contend that 2,113 calories and 0.86 pounds of clothing are necessary (a difference equivalent to giving up your shirt for a banana split). Given your respective resolutions, you and Mr. Blixen are unlikely to reach a compromise on the generic specifications of minimum needs. However, what if current market prices indicate that your "needs" require $4.37 to fulfill, while Mr. Blixen's budget is $4.35. In *monetary* terms, it is obvious that you are not far away from a potential compromise and that agreement on the *generic* components of a minimum budget might be postponed indefinitely.

While we do need the food, shelter, and other items on our shopping list daily, it is not necessary to have the right amount of cash every day. To shop each day for that day's minimum requirements of shelter, fuel, clothing, and food would be extraordinarily inconvenient at best and downright impossible at worst. Our real interest lies in ascertaining that a person has an adequate flow of cash so that he can provide himself with the basic necessities as the need arises. Hence, our poverty standard will incorporate the basic needs of an individual for some particular span of time and will be expressed in terms of the amount of money needed during that period to make the required purchases. Whether that individual then elects to shop monthly, weekly, or daily is immaterial to our concern with poverty.

The best single indicator of a person's purchasing power over a period of time is his *income* during that period. Income is the flow of cash to a person over time, and thus it represents what he will have available to acquire goods and services. But here, too, there are complications. While income does represent purchasing power, it is not the sole determinant of purchasing power. Two other factors, namely assets and credit, can render a person's command over goods and services much larger than his current income. Where credit is available, goods and services can, in effect, be borrowed. No current income is necessary, just a promise to make repayment when time and circumstances permit (or the creditors demand).

A similar situation holds true with assets. Here again, a person may acquire goods and services without an income, in effect by trading one good for another. In the most common instance, a person may sell a particular asset to acquire a desired commodity. Or he may trade the asset for the commodity or even combine the features of credit and wealth at a nearby pawnshop.

Notwithstanding these complications, we will accept income as the best guide to purchasing power and thus to a person's ability to acquire necessary goods and services. At the same time, we take notice of the fact that other forms of purchasing power may exist and that in some individual cases may be important.

Poverty Thresholds

We are now in a position to identify what may be called a *poverty line*. We have established the process by which that line may be formulated; all that remains is to apply the process. But lest we become too complacent about our theoretical achievements, it should be noted that a nearly identical procedure was formulated at least as early as 1890. At that time Charles Booth, an English sociologist, estimated the goods and services necessary to maintain a family in what he called a "state of chronic want." He then priced those commodities and concluded that a weekly income of approximately 24 shillings or less was necessary to achieve the condition he described. At about the same time,

American economists estimated that from $400 to $600 per year was necessary to attain this condition in the United States.

Since Booth's time our standards of living have grown enormously. So also have the number of proposed poverty lines, each varying with the circumstances of the time and the perspectives of the architect. While it is not necessary to review the history of those lines, each of which had significance in its own time, it is of interest to examine two of the most recent formulations.

The CEA Line

In 1963 the president's Council of Economic Advisers (CEA) officially sanctioned a poverty line of $3,000 per annum for a typical American family. The council's estimate is probably the most familiar of poverty lines and continues to be used in poverty discussions. While their estimation effort itself was an important step in the development of poverty statistics and policy, we shall see that their estimate was not without serious faults.

The rationale behind the council's poverty line estimate was similar to that which we have already outlined. The council accepted the notion that food requirements constitute the foundation of any poverty budget. Accordingly, they set out to determine what were the minimum nutritional requirements of a typical American family. These requirements had been estimated by the Department of Agriculture for the Social Security Administration, which was already developing a poverty measure. The estimates indicated that three minimally adequate meals a day would cost the typical family of two adults and two children exactly $2.736 a day. Now, the very precision of that nutrition estimate should be suspect. We have already suggested the difficulties inherent in specifying minimum nutrition requirements, converting those requirements into real commodities, and pricing those goods in the market. To pretend that this process could yield an estimate as exact as $2.736 a day is to strain one's credibility.

The council adopted a more pragmatic approach to arrive at the *total* budget for a poor family. You will recall that the frills added to a starvation diet were the prime source of arbitrariness in the budgetary process. Some people said ice cream was essential, others insisted on beer and pretzels. These problems were circumvented by simply observing how much money low-income families actually spend on such frills. Consumer studies indicated that such families spend approximately two-thirds of their incomes on nonfood items; hence, on commodities that include clothing, shelter, fuel, and goods that might be considered as less than essential to human subsistence. Using this observation as a benchmark, the council then multiplied their basic food budget by three to determine how much total income a poor family needs. The results of their calculation are depicted in Table 1.3. The council then rounded off the total budget estimate to the 3,000 figure. Using this measure, the council found that there were 33,400,000 poverty-stricken persons in America in 1963.

TABLE 1.3 The CEA Poverty Budget (1963)

Food budget	$2.736 per day × 365 days = $ 998.64
Nonfood budget	2 × food budget = 1,997.28

Total budget = $2,995.92

Michael Harrington has warned us "not to allow statistical quibbling to obscure the huge, enormous, and intolerable fact of poverty in America."[3] This is a warning we must take seriously, especially when over nine and one-half million families may be involved. Accordingly, we would do well to overlook some of the imperfections in the council's estimation procedures and concentrate on the mass of poverty they identified. Whether the "true" size of the poverty population in 1960 was then 33 million, 33.5 million, or even 35.23 million would not seem to be of much consequence.

But one glaring error in the council's estimation procedure prevents us from accepting their results. To appreciate the nature of the council's error, let us look at three families from the 1960 income distribution:

The husband in Family 1 is thirty-seven years old and supports six children and a pregnant wife on his income of $ 3,200 a year.

Family 2 consists of a soon-to-be-retired couple, both in their mid-sixties. The wife does not work and the husband's earnings amount to $2,800 per year. They own their home, having made the final mortgage payment last Christmas.

Family 3 consists of a struggling graduate student, his working wife, and their three-month old child. They both work at the college carry-out in their spare time. Their combined earnings including overtime and tips amounts to $2,400 a year.

How did these three families place in the council's census of poor Americans? Family 1, consisting of eight and one-half persons, was officially classified as nonpoor. Families 2 and 3 were counted as poor, since their incomes were under the $3,000 limit. But how many people would be willing to accept the council's classification of these families? Family 1 is clearly desperate, while Family 2 is living a quiet and perhaps comfortable life. Our graduate-student family is not exactly affluent, but they are not desperate on $200 a month.

The source of the council's error should be obvious at this point. The council calculated a poverty budget for a *typical* family of two adults and two children. But not all families consist of four persons, nor do all four-person families have consistently "typical" needs. As our illustration has made clear, the council's definition of a poverty line must *at a minimum* be adjusted for varying family size. A further refinement should take into account gross differences in family needs even among families of the same size.

[3] Michael Harrington, *The Other America* (New York: The Macmillan Company, 1962), p. 10.

The SSA Index

These basic refinements of the council's poverty line were undertaken by Mollie Orshansky of the Social Security Administration (SSA). She first adjusted for size of family; then she adjusted for varying family needs based on whether or not the family lived on a farm, whether the family was headed by a man or woman, and how many children there were. Using these four variables she identified 124 types of families and meticulously calculated an appropriate poverty budget for each one. And while Miss Orshansky's estimates were not faultless, they represented a significant improvement over earlier estimation attempts.

For the "typical" family of four identified by the Council of Economic Advisers, the SSA poverty budget and the council's own budget were very similar. The SSA adjustments, however, counted many more large families and fewer smaller families as poor due to different family needs. Our earlier examples illustrate the difference. Miss Orshansky found that Family 3, that of the struggling graduate student, needed only $2,275 for a minimum budget. Hence, they were not counted as poor under the SSA index. Family 2, the soon-to-be-retired couple, required a minimum of only $1,855 and was living quite comfortably on their income. Family 1, however, the population expanders, needed at least $5,100 per year to meet essential needs and were classified as poor by the Social Security Administration index.

The Current Poverty Index

Despite the considerable sophistication of the 1963 Social Security Administration poverty index, it was not presented as either perfect or unchangeable. It was recognized that, as prices and our standards of living continued to rise, the SSA poverty lines would require repeated upward adjustments. Over time our concept of what is essential to modern-day living will be enlarged, and to buy the necessary ingredients will also cost more. Accordingly, the current poverty index is an expanded but straightforward extension of the one formulated by Miss Orshansky.

According to Miss Orshansky's earlier calculations, an average nonfarm family of two adults and two children required a minimum of $3,130 in 1963. In 1970, after seven years of mild and not so mild inflation, that index stood at $3,968. We are saying that it cost $3,968 in 1970 to buy those goods and services that cost $3,130 in 1963. The increased dollar amount of our definition does not imply in any way an increased standard of living for the poor. It adjusts only for rising prices. If we wanted to increase the standard of living of those whom we define as poor—and not many affluent persons are so inclined—then we would have to raise the index by more than the inflation adjustment, that is, to a figure higher than $3,968.

A current poverty line that adjusts only for changing prices leaves the standard of living of the poor unchanged. But the income and living standards of the rest of the population will continue to advance as the American economy grows. Hence, poverty lines adjusted only for inflation imply a growing disparity between the status of the poor and that of the rest of the population. If we refuse to raise our expectations of what the poor require, then we will have to confront the consequences of a widening inequality.

Despite the limitations of current poverty line adjustments, we will adhere to present standards. Accordingly, a 1970 income of less than $3,968 will qualify a family of four for inclusion in our count of the poor. How this standard applies to other family sizes and types is summarized in table 1.4. It may be seen that poverty lines for farm families are considerably lower than for nonfarm families. This difference is attributable to the fact that the cost of living is less for farm families and that they produce much of their own food.

TABLE 1.4 Poverty Standards, 1970

Size of Family	Poverty Standard	
	Nonfarm	Farm
One member	$1,954	$1,651
Two members	2,525	2,131
Three members	3,099	2,628
Four members	3,968	3,385
Five members	4,680	4,000
Six members	5,260	4,490
Seven or more members	6,468	5,518

Source: U.S. Bureau of the Census.

To enumerate the persons below either the 1963 or the updated poverty index is a simple and straightforward task and will be undertaken in Chapter 2. Unfortunately, the clinical nature of the statistical operation tends to impress the observer very little with the real impoverishment that the numbers represent. Consequently, it is worthwhile to dwell for a few moments on the standard of living that a poverty budget implies.

The austerity of the poverty budget was well described by B. Seebohm Rowntree, an English sociologist, in 1901. The essence of his description is still valid today:

A family, living upon the scale allowed for in this estimate, must never spend a penny on railway fare or omnibus. They must never go into the country unless they walk. They must never purchase a half-penny newspaper or spend a penny to buy a ticket for a popular concert. They must write no letters to absent children, for they cannot afford to pay the postage. They must never contribute anything to their church or chapel, or give any help to a neighbor which costs them money. They cannot save, nor can they join sick or Trade Union, because they cannot pay the necessary subscription. The children must have no pocket money for dolls, marbles, or sweets. The father must smoke no tobacco and must drink no beer. The mother must never buy any pretty clothes for herself or for her children, the character of the family wardrobe as for the family diet being governed by the regulation, 'nothing must be bought but that which is absolutely necessary for the maintenance of physical health, and what is bought must be of the plainest and most economical description.'[4]

That Mr. Rowntree's description of poverty living remains appropriate can be seen by looking first at the food component of the current poverty budget for a family of four. Our $3,968 budget allows approximately 91 cents per person per day. That is 91 cents for breakfast, lunch, dinner, and any snacks—an amount less than what one good lunch costs in most places. This means that the homemaker must plan, buy, and prepare a nutritious meal for her family of four for approximately $1.21. When even hamburger costs up to 90 cents a pound in urban areas, it is devastatingly clear that this poverty family is not eating either very well or very much. And if they have aspirations to eat out on occasion, their only hope is to save money by eating lots of hot dogs and boiled eggs at home. Then, if they are lucky, they will have enough money to go out and order a hot dog, perhaps in the park.

You may respond that this is a gross exaggeration of how the poor live. You may even know of a poor person who once ate a sirloin steak. And in a sense you are right. We have described how a poor family would act if they spent only their food allowance on food. In fact, poor families do not follow our carefully budgeted allowances. They tend to forego other items and spend some of their nonfood allowance money on better and more palatable meals—maybe even an occasional beer to wash down the grits and pick up their spirits. And it is this process which comes closest to describing what it means to be poor. Every day a poor person or family must choose between an adequate diet of the most economic sort and some other necessity because there is never enough money to have both. Consequently, some of the poor eat steak and walk around with holes in their shoes.

For those who may not be impressed by the impoverishment of the budgets we have described, we also note that the above descriptions apply only to those families who actually command a budget of $3,968. Most poor families have less, often markedly less, than that. In 1970 the typical poor family had an income of only $2,900. For these families, even having the opportunity to choose between minute steak and hole-worn shoes would seem like affluence.

If the prospect of existing for a short time on a poverty budget or less is not disquieting enough, consider the prospect of subsisting at that level on into the indefinite future. A poor family must not only adjust to a subsistence budget

[4] B. Seebohm Rowntree, *Poverty: A Study of Town Life* (London: Longmans, Green & Co., Ltd. 1901).

but must also be prepared to remain at that standard of living. That is why a more affluent person cannot adequately grasp the significance of poverty by adopting a subsistence budget for a brief time. The affluent person knows that his experiment can and will be terminated shortly. The poor person possesses no such luxury. As was reported on a similar experiment by Tolstoy, "poverty is not the lack of things; it is the fear and the dread of want. That fear Tolstoy could not know."[5]

Let us then be clear about what our poverty index implies. The line we have drawn separating the poor from the nonpoor does not indicate what is enough—it only asserts with confidence what is too little. As Robert Hunter observed in 1904, "to live up to the standard . . . means no more than to have a sanitary dwelling and sufficient food and clothing to keep the body in working order."[6] Those who fall below the line are unquestionably poor by contemporary standards. Nevertheless, many of those who have incomes above our standard cannot be regarded as rich or even as moderately well-off. While we will concentrate our discussion on those persons we have defined as poor, we would do well to remember that there are a great many more people whose standard of living is only marginally higher than that of the poor.

REFERENCES

COUNCIL OF ECONOMIC ADVISERS, "The Problem of Poverty in America," in *Economic Report of the President,* Washington, D.C.: Government Printing Office, 1964.

HARRINGTON, MICHAEL, *The Other America.* New York: The Macmillan Company, 1962.

HUNTER, ROBERT, *Poverty.* New York: The Macmillan Company, 1904.

LARNER, JEREMY, and IRVING HOWE, eds., *Poverty: Views from the Left.* New York: William Morrow & Co., Inc., 1968.

MILLER, S. M., and S. M. LIPSET, eds., *Poverty and Stratification.* Boston: American Academy of Arts and Sciences, forthcoming.

ORNATI, OSCAR, *Poverty Amid Affluence.* New York: The Twentieth Century Fund, 1966.

ORSHANSKY, MOLLIE, "Counting the Poor: Another Look at the Poverty Profile," *Social Security Bulletin,* January 1965.

_____, "Consumption, Work, and Poverty," in *Poverty as a Public Issue,* Ben Seligman, ed. New York: The Free Press, 1965.

_____, "Who's Who Among the Poor: A Demographic View of Poverty," *Social Security Bulletin,* July 1965.

[5] Conversation quoted in Robert Hunter, *Poverty* (New York: The Macmillan Company, 1904) p. 1.

[6] Ibid., p. 7.

REIN, MARTIN, "Problems in the Definition and Measurement of Poverty," in *Poverty in America,* Louis Ferman, Joyce Kornbluh, and Alan Haber, eds. Ann Arbor: University of Michigan Press, 1968.

ROWNTREE, B. SEEBOHM, *Poverty: A Study of Town Life.* London: Longmans, Green & Co., Ltd., 1901.

STEIN, BRUNO, *On Relief: The Economics of Poverty and Public Welfare.* New York: Basic Books, Inc., Publishers, 1971, Ch. 1.

U.S. CHAMBER OF COMMERCE, *The Concept of Poverty.* Washington, D.C.: U.S. Chamber of Commerce, 1965.

2   The Poor

Having established a measure of contemporary poverty, we are now in a position to proceed with a census of the poor. We not only want to consider how many Americans fail to exceed the austere budget standards we have set but also to delineate certain characteristics of these impoverished individuals and families. We shall also review briefly how the number and characteristics of the poor have changed over time.

What we know about the extent of poverty helps to determine the interest and resources we devote to its elimination. If we were to discover that economic want affects only a few thousand individuals in the United States, presumably antipoverty concern would occupy a very low position on our scale of public priorities. On the other hand, if poverty were found to be the condition of a majority of Americans, we can suppose that its eradication would be of foremost public concern. What one considers a "large" or "small" poverty population is essentially a question of individual predilections, of course, but at least a specification of the number of poor persons will provide a common basis for discussion and policy planning. That awareness of the dimensions of poverty is not yet widespread is demonstrated by a recent poll of college seniors, whose estimates of the size of the current poverty population varied from 120,000 persons to 60,000,000 persons. Clearly, agreement on the importance of America's poverty problems would be difficult to attain in the face of such diverse perspectives.

The Poverty Count

As noted in Chapter 1, there were some 34,000,000 persons in poverty as recently as 1963. According to our definition of poverty, that is the number of persons whose income in 1963 was less than the minimum standard needed for their particular family size and type. This tremendous number is ample evidence that poverty in America deserves special public concern. Nearly one out of five

TABLE 2.1   The Poverty Population, 1970

	U.S. Population	Persons in Poverty	Poverty Rate
All persons	202,556,000	25,522,000	12.6%
white	176,566,000	17,480,000	9.9
black	22,768,000	7,650,000	33.6
Aged persons	20,050,000	4,709,000	24.6
Children (under 18)	69,995,000	10,493,000	15.0

Source: U.S. Bureau of the Census

Americans was poor in 1963. As Michael Harrington observed at the time, the number of poor Americans was simply unconscionable.

Table 2.1 updates the poverty count to 1970 and shows that the prevalence of poverty in the United States has diminished markedly in a relatively short time. In 1970 the number of poor Americans was just over 25 million, nearly one-third fewer than in 1963. At the same time, the incidence of poverty declined from one out of five Americans to one out of eight.

We may also observe in Table 2.1 that the incidence of poverty varies enormously among population groups. For example, more whites experience poverty than blacks but in far smaller numbers than the relative size of the white population would suggest. Accordingly, we may say that blacks face a far greater likelihood (33.6 percent) of being poor, although blacks still comprise a minority of the poor. The same relationship applies to the aged population and, to a lesser extent, all children. We will discuss these inequities in later chapters.

The marked decline we have observed from 1963 to 1970 in the number of poor persons is a legitimate foundation for some optimism about America's poverty problems. Quite clearly, we need not accept any given size of the poverty population as a permanent feature of American society. In later discussions, we will analyze the observed decline and assess prospects for future progress in considerable detail, but before leaving the subject of numbers, we should make at least two additional observations. First, we should realize that the recent decline in the size of the poverty population is likely to induce an attitude of public complacency toward the poor. Such an attitude is unwarranted. Unless we know the reasons for the decline, we have no basis for expecting the downward trend to continue. Accordingly, there is no justification for diverting attention or resources away from the problems of poverty. In addition, while it may not be possible to reach a consensus on what constitutes a "tolerable" level of poverty, surely we can agree that 25 million poor Americans are still too many.[1] As long as one-eighth of our fellow citizens are poor, we must not relax our efforts to reduce poverty.

[1] The number of poor persons exceeds the combined populations of Colorado, Oregon, Mississippi, Arizona, Utah, New Mexico, Arkansas, West Virginia, Nebraska, Hawaii, Nevada, Wyoming, Idaho, Montana, District of Columbia, Delaware, South Dakota, North Dakota, Rhode Island, Vermont, New Hampshire, Maine and Alaska!

A second constraint on our optimism concerns the meaning of the numbers themselves as we have presented them. The numbers we have used to depict the size of the poverty population tell only part, perhaps only a small part, of the poverty story. They fail to tell us how malignant a disease poverty is, or how widespread is the affliction. To understand this failure, we must examine the concept of income mobility.

Income Mobility

Consider again the number of persons who were poor in 1963. Our total indicated approximately 34 million. The number itself is based on a statistical sample undertaken by the Census Bureau. Of course, there are problems with any estimate based on samples. The individuals sampled may not be representative; they may not be willing or able to tell the truth. But these are straightforward statistical problems, and we learn to solve them, or at least live with them. They need not detain us here.

In evaluating our census of the poor, however, we must pay some attention to a related problem. Suppose your family's income was $7,000 in 1963. You have one brother, your mother is a housewife, and your father is a plumber. Based on your father's income, we can reasonably exclude your family from our count of the poverty population.

But suppose further that in August your father dislocated his wrist while bowling. He recovered but was not able to turn a wrench for the remainder of the year. Although he earned $250 a week during the first seven months of the year, his earnings dropped to zero after his accident. Moreover, because his accident was not work-related, your father was not eligible for medical insurance benefits. From that point on, your family began to taste poverty. Your allowance disappeared, your mother was suddenly doing babysitting and ironing, the family vacation was cancelled, and in the fall you and your brother had to drop out of school.

Regardless of whether or not your family recovers, we are faced with a serious conceptual and statistical problem. Should we restrict our census to those families who were poor throughout 1963, or do we want to include all families who experienced impoverishment at least part of the year? In the extreme, you might even want to include yourself because you were out of money and hungry on Sunday night. More reasonably, suppose we agree to count as poor those people who experience impoverishment for a significant part of the year, and something only a little better for the rest of the year.

Even so, we have omitted some, perhaps many, of these families from our poverty count. There is no easy resolution of this problem. Conceptually, we must decide how much experience with poverty qualifies a family for the poor population. Statistically, we must find an appropriate measure of that experience. That our answers to these problems are of acute importance for policy decisions is apparent when we look again at the changes in the poverty count between 1963 and 1970. Our figures show that the poverty population declined from 34 million to 25 million in seven years. What they do not tell us is whether the people who were poor in 1970 are the same people who were poor seven years earlier. But it matters a great deal whether poverty is a malignant affliction for some identifiable part of our population or if, instead, it is a communicable disease which strikes different families every year. The one situation implies, for example, the need for concentrated birth control programs or old age assistance, while the other argues for pervasive workman's disability and unemployment insurance.

We are not prepared to resolve these issues at this stage of our discussion. Later in this chapter, when we have reviewed the characteristics of the present poor, we will be in a better position to address these questions.

CHARACTERISTICS OF THE POOR

While the statistics we have reviewed might justly support the statement that poverty in America is still of massive proportions, we must take care in our use of descriptive adjectives. The poverty that we have observed is certainly not like the mass poverty that still exists in most of the world today. Whatever the differences in the depth of deprivation experienced in earlier times and in other countries, an outstanding dissimilarity between modern American poverty and the poverty of India or Sicily is that in America, to be poor is to be markedly distinguishable from the majority of the population.

If you lived in India, you would not have to make an effort to uncover the poor—they would be everywhere all the time. In America the situation is dramatically different. Except for an occasional panhandler on a downtown street, most of us never come into direct contact with the people we have enumerated in our census of the poor. The poor in America are a minority, albeit a sizeable minority, and they are largely unseen and unheard by the affluent majority. As a consequence, very few of us know anything substantial about the characteristics of the poor—we rely instead on gross generalities and largely unfounded stereotypes.

We have already previewed some of the most salient characteristics of the poor in our census. In this section, we continue that examination and attempt to deepen our familiarity with the 25.5 million poor individuals we have counted. The formulation of intelligent policies to combat poverty demands not only that we know how many persons are poor but also whether they are young or old, infirm or employed, and whether they live in Abbeville, Louisiana, or Winchester, Oregon.

A complete statistical profile of the poor would demand more effort and patience than most people have. In addition, such an array of statistics would tend to smother any meaning the numbers might possess. Therefore, we will examine the composition of the poverty population only as it relates to three

FIGURE 2.1 Age and Family Status of the Poor, 1970 (Source: U.S. Bureau of the Census)

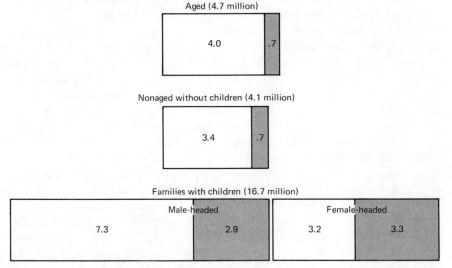

Aged (4.7 million)

4.0 | .7

Nonaged without children (4.1 million)

3.4 | .7

Families with children (16.7 million)

Male-headed | Female-headed

7.3 | 2.9 | 3.2 | 3.3

Note: Shaded areas represent black population.

major and policy-relevant characteristics: age and family status; geography and residence; and labor force status. Within each category, we will observe also the number of whites and blacks.

Age and Family Status

Michael Harrington has said that this is no country for old men—that our society is obsessed with youth and tries to ignore age.[2] Statistics on the number of aged poor confirm his observations. Figure 2.1 shows that the aged comprise a sizeable minority of the poor. In 1970 they accounted for one-fifth of the poverty population, and one out of every four aged persons was poor.[3]

Who are the aged poor? Approximately one-third are couples, many of whom own, or have an equity in, their own modest homes. The other two-thirds are primarily widows, some living in their own homes, but more often living in rented rooms in old hotels and apartment houses. They are just as likely to be found in metropolitan areas as in smaller cities and rural communities. Their income sources are few and consist primarily of public or private retirement payments, such as Social Security. Their savings are negligible.

[2] Michael Harrington, *The Other America* (New York: The Macmillan Company, 1962), p. 101.
[3] We employ the term *aged* here to refer to persons over the age of sixty-five.

Although the aged command the barest sort of material existence, poverty is not their only misfortune. Most of the aged poor live isolated and lonely lives and suffer chronic poor health. While we cannot hope to explain the American ethos that has led to the social deprivation of the aged, we should not ignore it.

The second population group depicted in Figure 2.1 refers to nonaged persons without children; that is, without children under the age of eighteen. Statistically they comprise a relatively small proportion of the poor (under 10 percent). Although these retired and soon-to-be-retired men and women are slightly younger than the aged poor, the social and material circumstances of each group are very similar; the only significant distinction is age. What is perhaps most disheartening about this subpopulation of the poor is that they have so much misery to look forward to. They have no tangible prospect for a better life; they simply get older and poorer.

The aged and aging poor, for whom there are now few alternatives, represent failures of our politico-economic system. The existence of such clusters of poverty serves to underscore the importance of doing something about material deprivation while there are still a variety of remedies available. From now on, while not forgetting the aged poor and their problems, this book will focus primarily on those who are still young and able enough to escape the demeaning poverty of the aged.

A second reason for concentrating our attention on the younger generations of the poor is the sheer size of this group. As Figure 2.1 clearly indicates, families with children constitute the dominant subgroup of the poor population, accounting for approximately 70 percent of the American poor in 1970.

Contrary to a popular impression, a majority of families in the younger poverty group have a male head-of-household (father). Nevertheless, families without a male head-of-household are a substantial minority of the younger poor population and a majority of the young black poor.

Of the 16.7 million people in the youngest poverty classification, over 10 million are children under eighteen years of age. Hence, children alone comprise fully 40 percent of all poor persons in the United States. We might well reflect on how equitable such a distribution of poverty is and what kind of preparation for adulthood an impoverished childhood provides. Will poor children later become poor adults? If so, we may confidently predict that poverty has a great future in this country.

Geography and Residence

In an increasingly urban nation, it is not surprising to find a high proportion of poor families in metropolitan areas.[4] In 1970 over one-half of all

---

[4] The term *metropolitan area* essentially refers to cities of at least 50,000 persons and their surrounding communities.

TABLE 2.2   Residential Distribution of the Poor, 1970

	White		Black	
	Number (in thousands)	Poverty Rate	Number (in thousands)	Poverty Rate
Entire United States	17,480	9.9%	7,650	33.6%
Metropolitan Areas	9,017	8.0	4,129	25.9
In Central Cities	4,770	10.8	3,228	26.2
In Suburban Rings	4,247	6.1	901	25.0
Outside Metropolitan Areas	8,464	13.2	3,520	51.6
Nonfarm	7,017	13.0	3,018	49.0
Farm	1,447	16.6	502	55.0

Source: U.S. Bureau of the Census.

the poor lived in metropolitan areas, most of them in the central city. In general, the residential distribution of poor families resembles the residential distribution of all families. However, there does exist a tendency for the poor to be overrepresented in large central cities and in rural areas and underrepresented in suburban communities.

The racial distribution of poverty among metropolitan and nonmetropolitan areas is very similar; that is, poor whites are just as likely as poor blacks to reside in metropolitan locations. However, a marked racial difference is apparent *within* metropolitan areas. While poor whites are likely to be found in either central cities or suburban communities, poor blacks are confined almost exclusively to the cities. It is important to note, though, that the high number of poor blacks in central cities is a result of the greater degree of urbanization among the black population rather than a higher likelihood of poverty in the cities. Indeed, a black person in a rural area is more than twice as likely to be poor than his counterpart in an urban metropolis.

Nonmetropolitan areas include smaller cities, rural communities, and farms. While nearly one-half of all the poor live in such localities, very few poor persons actually live on farms. Farm poverty is a serious problem in the sense that the incidence of poverty among farmers is very high (almost 17 percent for whites and 55 percent for blacks), but because the entire U.S. farming population is relatively small, poor farmers constitute less than 10 percent of all the poor. In this case, we must distinguish between the incidence of poverty among a particular group and the prevalence of that group within the entire poverty population.

Because the economic resources and social conditions of different regions in the United States vary tremendously, it is important to know the geographical location of the poor. Slower economic growth or less opportunity in a region is likely to create a regional concentration of poor families and require special programs. Were the poor all concentrated in Appalachia, for example, particular antipoverty policies would be appropriate.

Outside of the South, poverty is fairly proportionately distributed across the country for both whites and blacks (see Table 2.3). Thus, a person is as likely to be poor in New England as he is in the Corn Belt or in the West. In each of those areas, the incidence of poverty among whites is around 7 to 9 percent and around 22 percent for blacks. While there are fewer poor persons in the West than in the northeastern or northcentral states, that disparity conforms to general population patterns.

TABLE 2.3   Regional Distribution of the Poor, 1969

	Number (in thousands)		Poverty Rates	
	White	Black	White	Black
Northeast	3,216	938	7.2%	22.1%
Northcentral	4,433	1,028	8.6	22.4
South	6,237	4,930	12.1	41.0
West	3,188	319	9.8	20.7
Entire population	17,074	7,215	9.5%	32.3%

Source: U.S. Bureau of the Census.

It is apparent from Table 2.3 that the South[5] contains a disproportionate number of poor persons. Less than a third of the total U.S. population lives in the South, but nearly one-half of the poor reside there. This excess of poverty results not only from a high concentration of blacks in the South, but also from the fact that the South is simply poorer and less urban than any other region. Hence, a southern resident, regardless of his color, is much more likely to be poor than his northern counterpart, and in both the North and the South, a black person is approximately three times as likely to be poor as is a white person.

Labor Force Status

The geographical and family characteristics of the poor are important considerations in the formulation of antipoverty policies, but their primary value is that they tell us something about the potential of the poor to participate in national employment- and income-generating policies. In a market economy, the relationship of a person or his family to the labor market is the prime determinant of his income. Furthermore, the willingness of society to provide for the poor is materially affected by whether or not the poor are thought to work or at least seek work. Accordingly, the last characteristic we shall observe is the labor force status of the poor.

[5] The Census Bureau includes the following states in its definition of "South": Alabama, Arkansas, Delaware, District of Columbia, Florida, Georgia, Kentucky, Louisiana, Mississippi, Maryland, North Carolina, Oklahoma, South Carolina, Tennessee, Texas, Virginia, West Virginia.

To be "in the labor force" signifies that a person is either employed or that he is actively seeking employment (i.e., "unemployed"). Also included in this category are persons who are temporarily not working because of illness, bad weather, vacation, or a labor-management dispute. All of these people are regarded as idle only momentarily, with visible prospects of returning to work. Their regular work may be full-time or part-time (less than 35 hours per week), and it must be monetarily compensated. Hence, volunteer work is regarded as activity outside of the labor force.

To be "out of the labor force" means essentially that a person does not fall into one of the above categories. These persons are keeping house; attending school; unable to work because of age or disability; or, if otherwise able to work, are not actively seeking employment. The inactivity of the last group may result from a desire to seek leisure or the fact that employment prospects are too small to merit job-hunting.

It is widely believed that the poor are essentially a lazy lot. While we will examine this contention in considerable detail in later chapters, Table 2.4 provides a preliminary perspective on the employment behavior of the poor. From the first two lines of Table 2.4, we see that the poor participate in the labor force much less than the rest of the population. Only 57 percent of all poor persons are in families where the head-of-household is working or actively seeking work. This participation rate is far less than the rate for nonpoor families and has often been used to confirm the belief that the poor consciously avoid work, but the statistics in this case are very misleading.

We must recall that the poverty population includes a disproportionately high number of persons over the age of sixty-five. Because we generally anticipate reduced labor force activity from the aged, we should inquire

TABLE 2.4   Labor Force Status of the Poor and Nonpoor, 1969

Population	In The Labor Force	Out of Labor Force
All Persons		
Nonpoor	91%	9%
Poor	57	43
Aged Persons		
Nonpoor	23	77
Poor	16	84
Persons in Male-Headed Families with Children		
Nonpoor	98	2
Poor	84	16
Persons in Female-Headed Families with Children		
Nonpoor	80	20
Poor	50	50

Note: Family members are classified by the labor force status of the family head.
Sources: U.S. Bureau of the Census and U.S. Department of Labor.

separately into the participation rates of the aged and nonaged poor. When this simple adjustment is made, the labor force behavior of the poor and nonpoor begin to look much more similar. Table 2.4 confirms that neither the aged poor nor the aged nonpoor participate extensively in the labor force. Moreover, differences in the behavior of the aged poor and nonpoor are very small.

When we observe the labor force status of the nonaged poor, there are some striking contradictions to typical stereotypes of the poor. First of all, poor families headed by men are very much a part of the labor force. While their participation rate is somewhat below nonpoor families, we cannot ignore the fact that 84 percent of them are either working or actively seeking employment. Poor families headed by women have a much smaller attachment to the labor force, but their participation is far from negligible, especially when consideration is given to their greater household responsibilities. Why these families are poor in spite of their extensive labor force participation will be the subject of Part II, particularly Chapter 3.

OVERVIEW

The statistical profiles of the preceding section are not intended to dull one's senses nor to obscure the many problems of the poor. Rather, they are offered as a backdrop to the analytical discussions which follow in later chapters. If any general impressions are possible, we might say that the statistical profiles of the poor are not markedly different from those of the rest of the population. For the most part, the poor population is a little older, more southern, blacker, and slightly less attached to the labor force than the rest of society. Nevertheless, the poor, like the larger society, consist primarily of whites, of younger families with children, of urban dwellers, and of labor force participants. There do exist important distinguishing demographic characteristics, but they must not be allowed to conceal the basic similarities between the poor and nonpoor populations.

The demographic characteristics we have reviewed by no means provide a complete description of the poor. Among the more obvious omissions in our profile are education, family size, and health. These characteristics are discussed in later sections, where a more complete examination of the above traits is also found. But our profiles are incomplete in another important sense. We deal in this book almost exclusively with measurable, or at least observable, phenomena. Thus, we may report how old, white, or employed the poor are, or whether they live in cities or suburbs. What we are unable to do is relate how oppressed, politically isolated, or hostile the poor may be. In *The Other America,* Michael Harrington argues that today's poor are "more isolated and politically powerless than ever before." Although we are not in a position to evaluate that statement, we must recognize that such forces may be critical considerations in the lives of the poor.

REFERENCES

U.S. BUREAU OF THE CENSUS, *Current Population Reports,* Series P-60. Washington, D.C.: Government Printing Office.

U.S. DEPARTMENT OF LABOR, *Special Labor Force Reports.* Washington, D.C.: Government Printing Office.

II The Causes of Poverty

Introduction

The poor do evidence some characteristics that are different from the larger society. We may not conclude, however, that these distinguishing characteristics are necessarily the *cause* of the poverty we observe. For example, while the poor are, on average, slightly older than the rest of the population, we cannot claim that aging per se is a cause of poverty; clearly, it is not. Nor does the fact that the poor are, on average, more often black than the nonpoor demonstrate that race itself is a cause of poverty. These characteristics are referred to as demographic correlates of poverty. They may or may not have causal significance.

In Part II we attempt to identify the major causes of poverty with the aid of three major classifications: labor market forces; demographic forces; and institutional forces. These classifications are not necessarily exclusive, and, in fact, two or more different causes will often be operative in any given situation. Nevertheless, they do provide a convenient and meaningful analytical framework.

Demographic forces generally represent the traits that an individual carries with him into the labor market. They come closest to resembling the personal characteristics discussed in Chapter 2. Essentially, they define the relative employment and earning potential of an individual relative to all other prospective workers and constitute what economists now call *human capital.*

Labor market forces, on the other hand, are primarily useful in determining how much income any given quantity of human capital will command. They indicate how many persons (or how much human capital) will be employed, in which occupations, for how long, and at what wage rates. Whereas demographic forces indicate what qualities individuals bring to the labor market, labor market forces themselves indicate what incomes those individuals will take out.

Institutional forces are those nonmarket barriers that exclude some people either from the acquisition of human capital or from equal access to the labor market. In such cases, the individual may be willing or able to obtain the employment and income required for nonpoverty status but is prevented from doing so on the basis of nonmarket criteria. In other words, a variety of discriminatory practices single out certain individuals and groups for unfavorable treatment.

We may generalize further and say that labor market and institutional causes of poverty involve forces that are external to the individual. Demographic forces, on the other hand, are largely subject to the actions of an individual or his parents. Hence, we may say that the former categories of causation refer to social actions and forces, whereas the latter category refers to individual action. This distinction is critical to perspectives on poverty policy. It has been acknowledged historically that society has a greater responsibility for the impoverishment of an individual in those instances where his poverty is the result of social forces. Where poverty has been thought to be the outcome of purely individual actions, society has always been less disposed to render aid.

In assessing the significance of any particular demographic, labor market, or institutional force, we will be interested in two dimensions of causation: with respect to each force, we will inquire as to its effect either on the *extent* or on the *distribution* of poverty. The extent of poverty refers to the total number of persons who are poor, while the distribution of poverty refers to the particular people who are consigned to impoverishment. Some forces may influence the size of the poverty population without affecting the selection of individuals so included. Other forces may markedly affect the distribution, but not the total extent, of poverty. Some forces may, of course, influence both the extent and distribution of poverty. Therefore, we are asking what forces determine how many individuals will be poor and which determine who is to be included in that total.

3   Subemployment

The brief statistical profiles of Chapter 2 have already suggested that the poor have a strong attachment to the labor force. Aged, female-headed, and especially male-headed poor households appear to participate in the labor market to nearly the same degree as do the nonpoor. This seeming contradiction to the commonly accepted assumption that labor force participation provides a sure escape from poverty is the subject of this and the following chapters.

CAPITALIST IDEOLOGY

It is a basic tenet of capitalist ideology that an individual must contribute to the output of the economy in order to share in its productive benefits. We anticipate that if an individual aspires to material comfort, he will offer his talents and services to the competitive market. If he chooses not to contribute, then it is deemed justifiable on the grounds of both equity and productivity to deny him a share of the goods produced.

In a purely competitive capitalist economy, it is clear that the unemployed will not eat, or at least they will not obtain sustenance by conventional routes. By the same token, among those who are employed, individual productivities will determine how much and how well each person eats. Accordingly, in assessing the relationship between poverty and labor force status, we may conveniently examine two groups of individuals separately, the nonworkers and the workers.

We should not approach our inquiry, however, under the impression that capitalist ideology is rigidly enforced. Adherence to the "no work, no bread" doctrine is by no means complete; in fact, the number of exceptions nearly exceeds the number of conformities. Among the exceptions to our ideological tenets are wives, with or without children; children who are often legally barred from employment; the aged, whom we often compel to retire; the infirm, who cannot work; and college students, whose productivity is assumed and deferred. Indeed, the number of people eating but not working approaches 100 million.

Aside from such obvious exceptions as infants and the infirm, we may ask why society allows, even encourages, such widespread dependency. Clearly, maximum production, especially when it is based on desperate incentives, is not the only goal we pursue. Rather, we recognize that other social objectives compete with those of production. While maximum output from maximum labor force participation remains a foundation of capitalist ideology, that goal is severely and willingly compromised in practice. Issues that we must reflect on in the course of our analysis are (1) who makes the exceptions to society's work ethic, and (2) on what basis are such exceptions made?

The Nonparticipants

People who do not participate in the labor force must have an alternative source of support. For most nonparticipants, this support comes from their immediate families, and they depend on the work effort of a relative. A good many others are past traditional working ages and depend on often inadequate retirement incomes. But not all families are retired or contain a working member, and it is these latter families who are most likely to be poor. Indeed, the median family income, including welfare, of men aged twenty to fifty-four, who do not participate in the labor force is less than $150 per month. Very few such men are able to sustain their families above a poverty line.

Why do such men fail to participate in the labor force? Is it because they prefer idleness and impoverishment, or is it because they are physically unable to work or locate a job? A 1967 U.S. Department of Labor study suggested that a good many such persons were "dreamers and drifters who were able to adjust both financially and psychologically to nonworker status." No data were available, however, to support that allegation. More recent studies have shown that very few men with family responsibilities desire to "dream and drift" rather than work. More likely, these nonparticipants are either too sick or disabled to work. A considerable number of others have not looked for jobs because they are convinced that no employment opportunities are presently available for them.

Even more important to observe is the fact that even most so-called nonparticipants do work if and when they are able. As their physical condition and/or the economic outlook improves, nonaged nonparticipants are most likely to resume their search for employment. Indeed, one of the outstanding characteristics of the poor is their extraordinarily high rates of mobility between different labor force statuses. The poor are constantly moving in and out of the labor force and from employment to unemployment and back again. A poor person out of the labor force one week may well be working or looking for a job the next week.[1]

To note that nonparticipation is likely to be a temporary condition is not tantamount to denying its causal importance for poverty. On the contrary, we have observed that nonparticipation is a condition that many poor male heads-of-household experience. We must next determine what forces prevent these men from fuller participation in the economy and thus from the likelihood of escaping poverty.

The Unemployed

That unemployment, like nonparticipation, might lead to poverty is a chain of causation few people question. After all, to be unemployed means that one is out of work and actively seeking employment. Can we assert with confidence, then, that unemployment is a major cause of poverty? Some seeds of doubt about this association between unemployment and poverty are sown by those who compare unemployment totals with the size of the poor population. In 1970, for example, there were an average of about 4 million persons unemployed, while there were over 25 million poor persons (see Table 3.1). Moreover, not all of the 4,088,000 unemployed were from poor families. From an aggregate perspective, unemployment thus appears to account for only a small fraction of poverty at best. Nevertheless, we need not reject the hypothesized relationship between poverty and unemployment on the basis of these aggregate comparisons. On the contrary, a closer scrutiny of the numbers reinforces, rather than contradicts, our first impression.

To compare the total number of poor people with the average number of unemployed is quite unfair. First of all, the poverty population includes not only heads-of-household but also all their dependents. Since the unemployment

TABLE 3.1 Unemployment and Poverty Statistics, 1969

	Unemployed	Poor
Average, all persons	4,088,000	25,522,000
Average, heads-of-household*	1,300,000	4,048,000
Number of heads-of-household who experience unemployment during year	4,550,000	900,000

*Figures for poor heads-of-household exclude aged population
Sources: Bureau of the Census and U.S. Department of Labor.

[1] In fact, there are six times as many prime-age men outside the labor force at some time during the year than there are outside the labor force all year long. Nonparticipation is obviously a temporary condition for the father of a poor family.

figures do not include dependents, the comparison is obviously unbalanced. Looking more closely at the figures in Table 3.1, we find that only 1,300,000 of the unemployed were nonaged heads-of-household. At the same time, there were only 4,048,000 nonaged poor *families,* and thus that many poor household heads. Accordingly, on this more detailed basis, it appears that unemployment may contribute to the low economic status of as many as 25 percent of all nonaged poor families.

While the comparison between unemployed and poor heads-of-household suggests a markedly stronger relationship between poverty and unemployment than did the gross comparisons, our analysis is not yet complete. Just as nonparticipation is likely to be a temporary condition for the poor male head-of-household, so we must recognize that unemployment is likely to be a transitory state for most of the poor. Accordingly, there will be many more persons who experience unemployment during the year than there are unemployed at any given time. In fact, the turnover in the ranks of the unemployed exceeds 300 percent. This means at least three times more persons experience unemployment during the year than are unemployed at any one time. Hence, there are more heads-of-household who experience unemployment than there are poor heads-of-household. On this basis, then, unemployment emerges as a possibly dominant explanation of poverty.

Can we say, though, that all of these household heads who experience unemployment are poor? No, a great many of these unemployed persons, aerospace engineers, for example, enjoy incomes sufficiently high while working to stave off poverty when jobless. Others are fortunate enough to have wives or other dependents in the labor force who can provide alternative incomes. Reasonable estimates indicate that less than one-fourth of those who experience unemployment have family incomes below our poverty standards. While many of the other unemployed may be near our poverty threshold, they are presently counted as nonpoor. Hence, we may conclude that approximately 25 percent of all nonaged poor heads-of-household, or about 900,000 nonaged families, experience a direct income loss as a result of unemployment.

THE PROCESS OF ECONOMIC DETERIORATION

Just how unemployment leads to poverty is evident when the relationship is viewed over time. Whereas a few days or a week of unemployment will not significantly diminish a family's income, several weeks of joblessness will begin to undermine a family's economic foundations. Accordingly, we expect to see more and more people slip into poverty as the duration of unemployment status lengthens. This process is confirmed by Table 3.2, which portrays the various methods families use to meet expenses as the duration of unemployment increases.

TABLE 3.2 Methods Used by Families to Meet Living Expenses, by Duration of Unemployment, 1961 (percent distribution*)

Method	Duration of Unemployment	
	5 to 25 weeks	27 weeks or more
Used savings	49.1%	39.9%
Borrowed money	23.7	18.8
Moved to cheaper housing	8.8	12.0
Received help from friends	18.0	22.5
Received public or private charity	14.7	31.9

*Sum of percents is more than 100 because many families resorted to more than one method.

Source: Adapted from Stanley Lebergott ed., *Men Without Work* (Englewood Cliffs, N.J.: Prentice-Hall, Inc., 1964), p. 144.

In Table 3.2, the income sources of short-term and long-term unemployed families are compared. It can be seen, for example, that among the short-term (up to twenty-six weeks!) unemployed, 49 percent of the families have savings from which to draw in order to meet their everyday living expenses. As the duration of unemployment surpasses 27 weeks, however, the number of families with savings or available credit declines. As unemployment continues and the families become more desperate, they begin to sell their homes, to seek aid from friends, and, most striking of all, to fall back on public or private charity.[2]

INDIRECT LOSSES FROM UNEMPLOYMENT

While it is already clear that unemployment constitutes a direct and increasingly serious threat to a family's economic welfare, we have not yet completely described the dimensions of that threat. So far, we have considered only the immediate income loss to those who suffer unemployment, but there are indirect effects that further strengthen the causal link between unemployment and poverty and extend the resultant hardships to still more persons.

When unemployment rates are high in a particular area, job-seekers are apt to become increasingly frustrated in their efforts to secure employment. Jobs are scarce and available to only a select few. Faced with one employment rejection after another, job-seekers are likely to give up the search. This erosion of confidence was expressed by a young man who described his search for a job as follows:

I'll tell you, man, I go to Catholic Charities, to the youth center,

---

[2] We note in passing that in 1969 the average duration of unemployment for *all* the unemployed, poor and nonpoor, was eight weeks.

> down by the employment people—a couple of weeks ago I try to buy a job—I talk to social workers . . . you go from place to place, you know, and you get tired. I guess you get bored. Guys say no work, no nuthin', and then you say, "to hell with it. Let the job come to me."[3]

Not surprisingly, this young man is called a "discouraged worker." Because he no longer seeks work actively, he is not counted as among the unemployed; he belongs to the ranks of the nonparticipants previously discussed. Yet it is clear that the two categories are not wholly separable. Instead, the extent and likely duration of unemployment in an area has a significant effect on the size of the nonparticipating population. Accordingly, many discouraged workers must be counted among the casualties of unemployment.

No one knows the exact number of discouraged workers among the poor. We do know, though, that a household head cannot maintain both his discouraged status and his family for long. The family must eat, and the head of the household will be compelled to locate some work, any work, just to keep body and soul together. Accordingly, we may expect other family members, particularly wives, to be affected by the process of discouragement. Where unemployment is prevalent, a wife's chances for employment are likely to be even smaller than her husband's. Hence, the family may decide that her job search is fruitless and that her productivity will be highest in the home. If she could find employment, however, the odds that her family would escape poverty would triple, for working wives are one of the surest escape routes from poverty.

Considerable statistical attention has been directed recently toward the phenomenon of discouraged workers. As a result, it is estimated that in 1970 there were an average of at least 700,000 such persons, mostly wives (many more persons, of course, were discouraged at least part of the year). What proportion of these individuals were from poor families we do not yet know, but the impact of this group on the size of the poverty population is potentially sizeable.

Another indirect hardship resulting from high unemployment rates concerns the type and amount of work people undertake when jobs are scarce. As we already noted, the father of a low-income family, facing a loose labor market, may have to accept whatever employment and wages are available. The work may not fully utilize either his time or his talents and is likely to be menial. But he accepts the work as a temporary measure, while waiting for better employment opportunities to emerge. When a person finds himself in this situation, we may say that he is *underemployed*. That is, he is at work, hence, not unemployed, but not working to his capacity. Commonly, the underemployed work full time at menial jobs and seek better or part time work at any job and also seek more work. In 1970, the U.S. Department of Labor estimated

---

[3] Quoted in Edgar May, *The Wasted Americans* (New York: Harper & Row, Publishers, 1964), p. 60.

that more than two million persons were underemployed in these ways. At the same time, at least 150,000 poor household heads were working part time while awaiting better employment opportunities.

The phenomena of unemployment, discouragement, and underemployment combine to form the concept of *subemployment*. Taken as a whole, the distressing impact of subemployment on a family's finances is reasonably clear; very few families have enough economic resources to maintain themselves in the face of these forces for long. What is not so obvious is that the social foundation of the family, as well as its economic foundation, may suffer from the impact of these phenomena. Can we expect the father in a low-income family to gain in self-respect or familial admiration as his employment prospects and income diminish? Do we anticipate a Charles Dickens kind of increased solidarity as the family begins to sink into impoverishment? It is more reasonable to expect intrafamily tensions to mount along with economic distress. To the extent that economic distress leads to a weakening of the family relationship or even to dissolution of the family unit, we must include family breakup as one of the consequences of unemployment. While we postpone a more thorough discussion of this relationship to Chapter 6, we note here that the potential exists for family breakup as a result of labor market forces.

Tallying the Losses

As the list of direct and indirect consequences of unemployment grows, the crushing burden of a loose labor market on the economic status of the poor becomes apparent. The size of this burden can be approximated by asking how much income the poor have lost as a result of each form of subemployment. The total answer represents the amount of income the poor would have received had they been able to participate fully in the economy. The totals, presented in Table 3.3, are striking.

We have suggested that as many as 900,000 poor heads-of-household may have experienced direct unemployment in 1970. Given the typical wages of the poor ($60 per week) and the typical duration of their unemployment (17 weeks), we may estimate the income loss to these families as approximately

TABLE 3.3 The Losses from Subemployment

Source of Loss	Number of Poor Families Affected	Aggregate Income Loss
Unemployment	900,000	$1,000,000,000
Discouragement	200,000	450,000,000
Underemployment	200,000	300,000,000
	1,300,000	$1,750,000,000
Broken families	?	?

$1,000 per unemployed family. This is the amount of additional income these poor families would have received had they not experienced unemployment. Multiplying the number of affected families (900,000) by their average loss ($1,000) tells us that the poor as a group lost close to $1 billion as a direct result of unemployment.

We estimate the number of poor persons out of the labor force due to the erosion of confidence we term discouragement to be about 200,000 individuals, mostly wives and female heads-of-household. Because these individuals were out of work all year long, their implied loss is equal to their opportunity incomes, that is, the incomes they would have received if they had been able to get a job. For poor persons, we may approximate this figure as $2,500 per discouraged worker. Multiplying the number of affected families (200,000) by the average loss ($2,500) indicates that the poor were deprived of another $450,000,000 by labor market discouragement.

The third effect of high unemployment rates, namely underemployment, deprives about 200,000 poor families, each losing some $1,500 per year. Their losses are smaller because they are employed much of the time, but these losses still add up to a significant $300,000,000 for the poor population.

On the basis, then, of some rather conservative assumptions, we may conclude that at least 1,300,000 poor families are financially stricken by subemployment in one form or another. Moreover, the implied aggregate loss to the poor approached $2 billion in 1970, *enough money to move most of these families out of poverty!* If we include the number of families broken up as a result of subemployment, the total number of affected families will probably reach 40 percent of all nonaged poor families, or 30 percent of all poor families including the aged. At the same time, the aggregate income loss will exceed $2 billion. Given the enormity of this loss, we must conclude that subemployment is a direct, and perhaps the dominant, cause of poverty.

ISSUES RAISED

The tremendous significance of subemployment to the extent and depth of poverty raises several questions. For example, to what factors may the widespread subemployment of the poor be attributed? What are the forces that subject particular groups in the population to the burdens of subemployment? Finally, what kinds of policies would reduce the incidence of subemployment or at least cut the link between subemployment and poverty?

Do the Poor Really Try?

When we seek to explain why so much subemployment exists among the poor, it is logical to entertain two general hypotheses. On the one hand, it may be the case that the poor are not serious or persistent enough in their job search activity. They may be unrealistic in their employment demands or simply too lazy to go out and secure available work. On the other hand, the subemployment of the poor may result from no fault of the poor themselves; perhaps it is simply a reflection of the fact that few decent jobs are presently available for them.

The first explanation is more convenient for the nonpoor and enjoys a distinct popularity. If the poor can be shown to be inadequately concerned about their own welfare, then the responsibility of the rest of society for their impoverishment is considerably reduced. Among those who sense a certain irresponsibility on the part of the poor is sociologist Nathan Glazer who perceives that at "the heart of the crisis is a massive change in values which makes various kinds of work that used to support families undesirable to large numbers of potential workers today."[4] In other words, the jobs are there but the poor simply refuse to take them. Unfortunately, Glazer offered no evidence to support the allegation he made. However, a later attempt by a second observer in New York City yielded the following evidence:

> No one who rides the subways can fail to see the numerous ads for electrician's helpers (about $7,000 per year), subway patrolmen (around $8,000 per year), Office Temporaries, and Kelly Girls. The New York Telephone Company urges people to join them and be trained by them. No one who walks down Madison, Lexington, or Third Avenue will miss the signs for Help. No one who has had the misfortune of staying in a hospital recently, or even visiting one, is untroubled by the shortage of auxiliary and service personnel. . . . and any one who rides taxis with any frequency is aware of the number of taxis in the garage despite the industry's efforts to recruit additional drivers. . . . One of the fascinating statistics about New York City is that fewer persons were employed in domestic service in 1968 than in 1960. This is surely not the result of diminished demand but of a refusal to accept such employment.[5]

Despite this catalogue of apparent opportunities, there seems to be little evidence to support the notion that the poor are turning down abundant job offers. At the time Bernstein related her impressions (1970) there were about 5,000 standing job vacancies, including domestic service, for unskilled workers in New York City. Confronting these vacancies were 139,000 unemployed individuals and over 200,000 publicly-assisted heads-of-household. In light of the enormous number of potential and actual job seekers, the number of available jobs for the poor is hardly significant. Even if a poor person keenly desires to secure a dead-end job, his chances to do so hardly seem encouraging.

What is astonishing, then, about the poor is not that they sometimes appear idle but that they exert so much energy trying to secure employment despite often negligible job opportunities. We have already seen evidence of this

---

[4] Nathan Glazer, "Beyond Income Maintenance," *The Public Interest,* Summer, 1969, p. 120.

[5] Blanche Bernstein, "Welfare in New York City," *City Almanac,* February, 1970, p. 6.

activity in the high turnover rates among the employed and the attendant mobility of the poor between labor market statuses. Even the U.S. Department of Labor acknowledges that "policies aimed at reducing poverty should start from the premise that most poor people are already working unless barred from jobs by labor market or other personal circumstances. Contrary to a widely held opinion, what the great majority of poor people need is not a stronger work ethic but added skills and more employment opportunities."[6] An earlier study by the Labor Department noted that the poor are active in their job search activity, that they seek primarily lower skilled jobs, and that their salary expectations are only around $60 per week.[7] It does not appear, therefore, that the poor are conspicuously indolent or unrealistic in their employment demands.

Where Are the Jobs?

If the poor are trying so hard to secure regular and decent employment, why are such jobs not available to them? Because we profess the ethic that a person should work for his keep and because the poor apparently do try to find jobs, we must determine what obstacles impede the fulfillment of our ideological objectives and the economic needs of the poor.

UNEMPLOYMENT AS A SOCIAL GOAL

Economic theory tells us that there are basically four types of unemployment: frictional, seasonal, aggregate, and structural. Frictional unemployment arises when people move from one job to another with only a slight interval of time in between. People who are frictionally unemployed normally have visible job prospects and are simply in transit, either geographically or occupationally. Likewise, people who are seasonally unemployed often face the sure prospect of renewed employment as the weather or season changes. This is not to say that their unemployment is not serious; we merely distinguish its sources from other types of unemployment.

Aggregate unemployment is markedly different from the first two types of unemployment. Not only is the nature of later job prospects uncertain, but the causes of this type of unemployment are also distinct. Aggregate unemployment exists when there is less demand for labor in the economy than there is labor willingly available. In this situation, neither a change in the weather nor a change of residence is likely to create employment for the jobless. For this reason, the

---

[6] U.S. Department of Labor, *Manpower Report of the President,* March, 1970 (Washington, D.C.: Government Printing Office, 1970) p. 119.

[7] Robert Stein, "Work History, Attitudes and Income of the Unemployed" in Stanley Lebergott, ed., *Men Without Work* (Englewood Cliffs, N.J.: Prentice-Hall, Inc., 1964), pp. 130-46.

unemployed individual has no certain prospect of later employment. Instead, he must wait, along with others so positioned, for an expansion of the demand for labor.

The shortage of aggregate demand that these unemployed individuals confront is not the consequence of unbridled market forces. Nor will the required expansion of demand emerge as the work of an "invisible hand" of the kind that Adam Smith described. On the contrary, the level of demand, and, hence, the level of aggregate unemployment, is now widely recognized as being a component responsibility of government. Fiscal and monetary policies, as integral features of a general manpower or incomes policy, largely determine the number of available jobs. Because these policies are the outcome of conscious activity on the part of a federal administration and not autonomously formulated by an invisible hand, we may say that the level of unemployment is part of society's matrix of goals. Hence, the level of demand we seek and the means by which we achieve it are directly subject to the collective will as expressed in the political process.

Of course, no one consciously and forcefully promotes a high level of aggregate unemployment for the sheer sense of achievement or beauty. Were the level of demand our only social concern, then we could confidently anticipate that aggregate unemployment would disappear. But we must recognize that the goal of aggregate full employment competes with other social objectives for the limited attention and resources of the public. As a consequence, consciously, unthinkingly, or simply by default, a nonzero level of aggregate unemployment may become a social goal. One popular basis for such a decision is discussed in the appendix to this chapter. Regardless of what we think of any particular social choice, or nonchoice, as the case may be, it is critical to our perspective of the unemployment problem that its link to the socio-political process be exposed. Then, whatever level of unemployment may exist or be sought, it becomes clear that the level is subject to realignment.

We must also recognize that the extent to which the types of unemployment mentioned earlier prevail is not insensitive to the aggregate demand decision. Structural unemployment is, in many respects, similar to aggregate unemployment. Here, however, the shortage of demand appears to be confined to only a few occupations or areas. While most people seem able to locate jobs, there may be a large number of pipe fitters, coal miners, or flight engineers seeking employment. There may be a large number of people out of work in the Texas Panhandle and Appalachia but relatively few unemployed in other areas of the country. Thus, it appears that localized or structural deficiencies in demand are more at fault than general demand shortages. Job prospects may seem better in this case, since an occupational or geographical move appears to hold promise of improved employment opportunities.

The purely structural character of structural unemployment can, however, be easily exaggerated. Can we maintain that the jobless situation of coal miners and flight engineers is impervious to the state of demand in other occupations or areas? While it is reasonable to expect some hesitancy in moving across geographical or occupational boundaries, it is unrealistic to imagine that the speed and extent of such moves are not conditioned by employment opportunities. When good jobs exist in plentiful supply elsewhere, the structural character of structural unemployment is bound to erode. People will move and change occupations as alternate prospects merit. Even in Appalachia, an area often presumed to exist in economic isolation, unemployment rates follow national patterns. Accordingly, the apparent dimensions of structural unemployment are shaped in part by the state of aggregate demand and, thus, are subject to the social decisions of which we have spoken. As Paul Samuelson has noted, "the alleged hard core of the structurally unemployed is in fact a core made of ice and not of iron. The core of ice can be melted over a period of time by adequate effective demand, or it can be solidified from inadequate over-all demand."[8]

SUMMARY

A positive relationship between an individual's employment status and his economic status is central to the American capitalist ethic. Accordingly, we are not surprised to discover that among those who work little or not at all, poverty is a relatively common occurrence. What is perhaps more noteworthy is the observation that the poor are integral members of the labor force and are constantly shifting from one labor force status to another. Therefore, we may conclude that millions of individuals are poor, not because they never work, but because they do not work as much or as often as others.

The work loss of the poor takes many forms. They may, at any given time, be out of the labor force, unemployed, or underemployed. These conditions are not independent but instead are related, in the market place, by the forces of aggregate demand. Together they constitute a condition of subemployment and may be costing the poor as much as $2 billion a year in lost income. Hence, subemployment appears to be a major cause of American poverty.

Finally, we have seen that the subemployment of the poor is not the consequence of their failure to seek employment. On the contrary, it appears that their subemployment is determined in large part by the decisions society makes regarding the utilization of economic resources. Where a nonzero level of aggregate unemployment becomes a part of society's goal structure, some individuals are simply prevented from working their way out of poverty.

[8] Paul A. Samuelson, *Economics,* 7th ed. (New York: McGraw-Hill Book Company, 1967), p. 766.

APPENDIX: THE CHOICE BETWEEN UNEMPLOYMENT AND INFLATION

The foregoing chapter presented estimates of the losses to the poor resulting from unemployment. We also suggested that the level of unemployment is the outcome of a socio-political decision. Together, these observations imply either that policy makers are willfully and consciously oppressing the poor or that they are pursuing other goals, which they deem to be more important and in conflict with the goal of full employment. Giving policy makers the benefit of the doubt, we will assume the latter explanation to be the case. We must discover, therefore, what goals are regarded as more important and how they conflict with the attainment of fuller employment.

The goal most often deemed in direct competition with full employment is that of price stability. It is widely believed that we cannot have both price stability and full employment at the same time, thereby implying that the pursuit of one objective necessarily means the abandonment of the other. Furthermore, because the potential destruction of currency and market functions that might accompany really serious inflation is widely feared, price stability is considered a foremost policy goal. As a consequence, some unemployment is tolerated as part of the cost of maintaining existing price levels.

The suggested relationship between unemployment and inflation has been formalized as the Phillips curve, depicted in Figure 3.1. To achieve successively lower rates of unemployment, higher and higher rates of inflation are encountered, resulting in a convex curve. The reasoning behind the Phillips curve is akin to arguments about structural unemployment. Nearly everyone agrees that an expansion of aggregate demand is necessary to reduce high levels of unemployment. The proponents of the Phillips curve theory argue that comparatively few benefits of increased spending actually reach the unemployed, because they have the wrong skills, are too young or old, live in the wrong places, or are simply unaware of new opportunities. Accordingly, demands for new output are met by overworking existing employees rather than by hiring new workers. Wage rates, and then prices, go up while unemployment rates change little. The greater the effort to reduce unemployment, the faster the rate of inflation.

The argument for a trade-off between fuller employment and greater price stability has a convincing plausibility. Nevertheless, there are grounds for believing full employment and price stability to be more compatible than the Phillips curve (and much political discourse) implies. Indeed, both theory and practice suggest that the relationship between unemployment and inflation is more flexible than current attitudes and policy presume.

In theoretical terms, an expansion of demand for output can be expected

FIGURE 3.1 The Phillips Curve

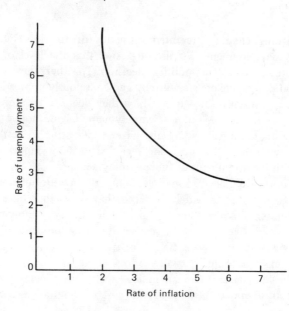

to increase the producer's demand for labor. The producer will have to hire additional workers or employ his existing labor force more fully. Other workers may not be immediately available, however, and they are likely to require training or orientation before they can contribute to output. As a result, producers probably will have to rely primarily on their existing workers for an initial expansion of output. Such reliance is expensive, however, as overtime wage rates are high; productivity is likely to decline with longer hours; and workers will feel in a better position to demand higher base wages. Hence, producers will have a large and increasing incentive to locate and train new workers as expanded output continues. As time passes, producers will substitute new labor for overtime labor, thus reducing costs.

The labor market adjustment process implies that expansion of demand will, indeed, lead to higher prices but that the stepped up rate of inflation is only a temporary phenomenon. As new workers are absorbed into the production process, the pressure on prices is abated. Hence, what the Phillips curve portrays on an aggregate level is the rate of inflation necessary to evoke the required labor force adjustment. It should not be understood to mean that the same high rate of inflation will continue once the adjustment is made. Not only is the price rise temporary, but it is an integral feature of the adjustment mechanism. Hence, we might be able to say that a 5 percent rate of inflation is necessary to reduce the unemployment rate from 4.5 to 3.5 percent, but we have no grounds for

FIGURE 3.2 Unemployment and Price Changes, 1953-1970 (Source: *Economic Report of the President,* 1971)

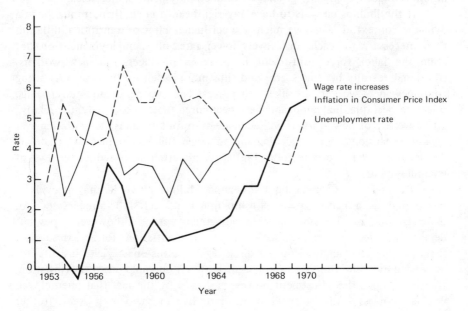

anticipating continued high rates of inflation once the lower level of unemployment is reached.[9]

On an aggregate level, then, the choice between fuller employment and price stability is misconstrued. Some inflation may be required to *reach* lower levels of unemployment. Once there, however, price stability can co-exist with fuller employment. The policy issue is not how much inflation can be tolerated indefinitely, but how great of a temporary inflation is acceptable to achieve lower unemployment. Clearly, inflation which is only transitory is less burdensome, and thus more acceptable, than permanent inflation.

On the basis of economic theory, we thus expect that different rates of inflation may exist with any given level of unemployment, contrary to popular notions about the Phillips curve. Our expectations are borne out by the American economy in the years since 1953. As Figure 3.2 indicates, for example, an unemployment level of 5.5 percent prevailed in 1954, 1959, 1960 and 1962. In those same years, however, the rate of inflation varied from 0.4 percent to 1.6 percent. Conversely, in both 1958 and 1967, the rate of inflation was 2.7 percent, but the rate of unemployment was 6.8 percent in the former

[9] High rates of inflation could continue, of course, but they would be the consequence of actions other than the initial effort to reduce unemployment. Inflationary *expectations* are often the source of continued wage-price escalation.

year and 3.8 in the latter. Quite clearly, there is no distinct and necessary rate of inflation to accompany any given level of unemployment, or vice versa.

If the Phillips curve is to have any significance at all, then, it must be in a dynamic context. That is, we might expect higher rates of transitional inflation to be necessary to reach successively lower rates of unemployment. Consider again the labor force adjustment process. As producers hire new workers, additional recruits become scarce and thus more expensive to locate. As hiring continues, new workers are likely to possess less experience and fewer skills, since the best qualified applicants have been hired first. Accordingly, the relative attractiveness of new workers will decrease as output expands, necessitating ever greater expansions of product demand to reach full employment. A trade-off develops between efforts to control inflation and attempts to reduce the level of unemployment.

The risk in formulating a dynamic Phillips curve is that it will be interpreted as a necessary relationship much like its static predecessor. An understanding of the labor market adjustment process, however, does not demand acquiescence in the face of accelerating inflation. Rather, it suggests that viewing the relationship in disaggregate terms may yield insights for improving even the transitional trade-off between unemployment and inflation. If, for example, the adjustment process is slowed by the fact that unemployed workers possess skills in small demand or live in the wrong areas, further expansion of demand might be channeled more specifically in their direction. Hence, the *pattern* of demand, both occupationally and geographically, will affect the speed of adjustment and, thus, the dynamic trade-off. Accordingly, there is no unchangeable relationship even of transitional inflation to unemployment, since the relationship depends on the capability and determination of policy makers to alter the pattern of demand as they expand it.

A similar qualification to the dynamic Phillips curve emerges when we consider the phenomenon of racial discrimination in the labor market. Even when employers are reluctant to hire black workers, their reluctance will not be impervious to economic forces. An unassisted market adjustment thus implies that more and more racial barriers will be eliminated as the economic incentive for recruiting new and able workers increases. By the same token, the extent and strength of discrimination are among the forces that determine the dynamic trade-off between unemployment and inflation. Accordingly, the government's efforts to overcome or circumvent discrimination can lead to different trade-offs. Again, there is no necessary or fixed relationship between inflation and unemployment.

The upshot of these considerations is that a fixed rate of inflation is not associated with any given level of unemployment or with efforts to reduce unemployment by any given amount. Policy makers have a variety of options available at all times to effectuate an improved trade-off between inflation and unemployment. By changing the pattern of demand or improving the functioning of the labor market, policy makers can achieve lower rates of unemployment with little pressure on prices. To formulate the goal of price stability as an alternative to fuller employment is to ignore other options and rob the poor.

REFERENCES

KOLKO, GABRIEL, *Wealth and Power in America.* New York: Frederick A. Praeger, Inc., 1962.

LEBERGOTT, STANLEY, ed., *Men Without Work.* Englewood Cliffs, N.J.: Prentice-Hall, Inc., 1964.

U.S. BUREAU OF THE CENSUS, *Current Population Reports,* Series P-60. Washington, D.C.: Government Printing Office.

U.S. DEPARTMENT OF LABOR, *Manpower Report of the President,* March, 1970. Washington, D.C.: Government Printing Office.

_____, Bureau of Labor Statistics, *Special Labor Force Reports.* Washington, D.C.: Government Printing Office.

The Choice between Unemployment and Inflation

GALLAWAY, LOWELL E., *Manpower Economics.* Homewood, Ill.: Richard D. Irwin, Inc., 1971.

HOLT, CHARLES C., C. DUNCAN MAC RAE, STUART O. SCHWEITZER, and RALPH E. SMITH, *The Unemployment-Inflation Dilemma: A Manpower Solution.* Washington, D.C.: Urban Institute, 1971.

4 The
Working
Poor

Observing that unemployment is a major cause of poverty leads easily to the suggestion that we could eliminate most poverty if we could provide everyone with employment. According to this line of reasoning, employment emerges as a sure route to at least some degree of economic security. We have already learned, however, that this route is not so certain. We know, for example, that many poor people whom we think of as "unemployed" do work a great deal. In fact, a salient characteristic of the subemployed poor is that they are repeatedly engaged in part-time or part-year work. Hence, we are in a position to reject the naive assumption that employment automatically lifts a person out of poverty.

A slightly more sophisticated view of the relationship between employment and poverty would suggest that the attainment of economic security depends not on whether one works but rather on how much one works. Therefore, we do not expect to find many part-time or part-year workers among the nonpoor. Instead, we anticipate that, by and large, economic security will be reserved for those individuals and their families who work full time throughout the year. In this chapter, we examine the relationship between increased employment and poverty and observe the plight of those who violate our anticipations.

WORK EXPERIENCE AND POVERTY

The expectation that increased employment improves one's chances of escaping poverty is fully supported by available data. As Figure 4.1 shows, there is a distinct inverse relationship between the number of weeks one works and the likelihood of poverty; as the duration of employment is extended, the incidence of poverty progressively drops. Thus, among full-time workers who are employed less than half the year, one out of four individuals is poor. On the

FIGURE 4.1 Poverty and Employment, 1970 (Source: U.S. Bureau of the Census)

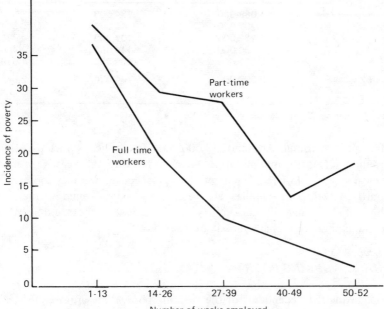

other hand, of those workers who are employed at least 35 hours per week all year long, only one out of 25 is poor.

The same relationship between the duration of employment and poverty is true for part-time workers, as Figure 4.1 also indicates. The only exception to the rule occurs among part-time workers who work all year round. Their noticeably higher rate of poverty reflects the fact that this group of workers is comprised primarily of female heads-of-household, who have large family responsibilities and few income sources.

The relationships depicted in Figure 4.1 are likely to instill the comfortable feeling that there are few full-time, year-round workers among the poor, but this impression is dispelled quickly when the numbers are examined more closely. Because year-round workers in the economy vastly outnumber part-year workers, the incidence rates do not adequately reflect the work experience of the poor. Once again, numbers and proportions convey very different impressions.

Table 4.1 summarizes the work experience of the poor in absolute numbers. It shows that there are over 1 million poor families whose heads work

TABLE 4.1   Work Experience of the Poor, 1970 (Heads-of-households)

Weeks Worked	Full-time Workers	Part-time Workers	Total
50-52	1,068,000	234,000	1,302,000
40-49	257,000	44,000	301,000
27-39	232,000	104,000	336,000
14-26	260,000	144,000	404,000
1-13	281,000	238,000	519,000
Total, 1-52 weeks	2,098,000	764,000	2,862,000
Did not work	---	---	2,293,000

Source: U.S. Bureau of the Census.

full time all year round. Another 223,000 poor family heads work part time all year round. In fact, the number of poor year-round workers exceeds the number of poor part-year workers. From another perspective, we may observe that one-fourth of *all* poor families are headed by a year-round worker, while one-third of the nonaged poor families are so headed. In short, extensive work effort and experience is characteristic for the poor.

THE HARD-WORKING POOR

Counting the dependents of the working poor, there are over five million persons in families headed by individuals who worked all year round at full time jobs. Why, we may ask, are so many people poor if their families work so much? Doesn't the existence of this paradox violate the very same principles that comprise our capitalist ideology? If we cannot guarantee economic security to those individuals who contribute their maximum work effort, what sort of admonitions or incentives can be directed to those who work less?

We may entertain two general explanations for the status of the hard-working poor. The most obvious suggestion is that their wages are unusually low. At poverty wages, very few people could work hard or long enough to attain economic security. But low wages is not the only possible explanation for the plight of the working poor. Poverty refers to the relationship between a family's income and its needs. Thus, it might also be the case that the poor simply have above average needs, due to either larger families or special expenses, for example, medical bills. In this situation, even standard wages would tend to leave the family financially destitute. The distinction between income and needs is vital for policy concerns. The one situation implies the need for labor market intervention of some kind, while the second implies the need to address nonmarket phenomena, such as family planning or health insurance.

To the extent that the poor do have larger families, they require, of course, higher wages. The full-time working head of a family of four required wages of $1.98 per hour in 1970 to attain our poverty standards. The head of a five person family needed $2.34 an hour to reach the same level, while families of six members required $2.63. Still larger families would have to command more than $3.00 an hour to maintain a poverty budget. With average blue-collar and clerical wages only slightly higher than this, it is clear that heads of large families will have to be fairly productive workers.

While it is obvious that the incidence of poverty will be aggravated by the wage requirements of larger families, it does not follow that the poor are impoverished because of their above average needs. We still must inquire whether the hard-working poor command high enough wages to support even an average (four person) family. If they do not, then the above average needs of larger families simply deepen their poverty rather than explain it.

Poor Wages

There is abundant evidence that the hard-working poor do not command wages high enough to assure economic security for an average-sized family or, for that matter, for any family. Very few full-time working poor earn as much as $2.00 an hour, and virtually none earn more than $2.50 an hour. On the contrary, the typical wage of a poor head-of-household who works all year round at a full-time job is between $1.00 and $1.50 an hour.

To work long hours all year round and still remain in poverty must be tremendously frustrating, and yet many of these families supply even more work effort. Among poor families with full-time working heads, close to half send other family members into the labor market also. Not only is the head of the family unable to provide financial security as a result of his own efforts, but even the contribution of working wives and children leaves many families in poverty.

The total incomes of families with full-time working heads are given in Table 4.2; included in these totals are the wages of the other family members. It is evident that the wages of poor workers are extremely limited. Especially

TABLE 4.2   Incomes of the Working Poor (total income of families whose head worked full time year round)

Total Income	Percent of Families
Under $2,000	36%
$2,000-2,999	19
$3,000-3,999	20
$4,000-4,999	15
$5,000-5,999	9
$6,000 or more	1
Total	100%
Number of families	1,068,000

Source: U.S. Bureau of the Census.

disheartening is the high concentration of working families with incomes of less than $2,000 per year.

The hard-working poor are not the only workers to command low wages. While the poor are slightly more visible than other low-wage workers, more than one-sixth of all full-time workers earn less than $2.00 an hour (see Table 4.3). Of these, over 2.5 million earn even less than $1.00 per hour! Low-wage workers abound and can be found in all occupational classes. What keeps these persons out of poverty is the fact that they have slightly smaller families or none at all, or keep more family members in the labor force for longer periods of time. Many, too, are dependents of workers who command more substantial incomes. Nonetheless, these workers are not very far removed from poverty; they and their families have incomes very close to our poverty standards. In the best of circumstances, they are referred to as the near-poor. In less favorable times they become part of the poverty population.

TABLE 4.3   Distribution of Low-wage Workers, 1969

Occupation	Number (in thousands) and Proportion of Full-time Workers Earning Less Than:		
	$1.00 per hr.	$1.50 per hr.	$2.00 per hr.
Professional and technical	198 (2.3%)	302 (3.5%)	467 (5.5%)
Managers, officials, and proprietors	303 (4.2)	455 (6.4)	675 (9.5)
Clerical workers	211 (2.4)	545 (6.2)	1630 (18.8)
Sales workers	121 (4.5)	290 (10.8)	570 (21.2)
Craftsmen and foremen	148 (1.8)	273 (3.3)	543 (6.7)
Operatives	219 (2.3)	727 (7.6)	1928 (20.3)
Private household workers	213 (59.9)	287 (80.8)	333 (93.7)
Other service workers	414 (10.4)	894 (22.6)	1610 (40.7)
Unskilled laborers	104 (5.8)	201 (11.2)	418 (23.3)
Farmers and farm managers	421 (29.8)	571 (40.4)	715 (50.6)
Farm laborers and foremen	156 (33.4)	238 (51.1)	314 (67.3)
All occupations	2,508 (4.7%)	4,783 (9.1%)	9,203 (17.5%)

Source: U.S. Bureau of the Census.

Poor Jobs

If there is any moral to be gleaned from the foregoing figures, perhaps it is this: a poor janitor who works hard stands a very good chance of becoming a hard-working, poor janitor. There seems to be little prospect of economic security for the poor as a result of their own efforts. Too many people earn too little. Elliot Liebow has summarized the prospects for the working poor:

. . . the man does not have any reasonable expectation that, however bad it is, his job will lead to better things. Menial jobs are not, by and large, the starting point of a track system which leads to even better jobs for those who are able and willing to do them. The busboy or dishwasher in a restaurant is not on a job track which, if negotiated skillfully, leads to chef or manager of the restaurant. The busboy or dish washer who works hard becomes, simply, a hard-working busboy or dishwasher. Neither hard work nor perseverance can conceivably carry the janitor to a sit-down job in the office building he cleans up.[1]

Not all the poor, of course, are janitors. Most middle-class persons, in fact, probably think of janitors as low-income workers, but not poor. More likely to come to mind—if it is acknowledged at all that the poor do, in fact, work—are bellboys, busboys, and nonunionized street cleaners, plus a small army of aged farmers and stooping sharecroppers. Once again, however, the preconception departs considerably from the reality of everyday poverty. The working poor are likely to be found in all broad occupational categories. Table 4.4 depicts the actual occupational distribution of the poor. While it is true that more than 70 percent of all farmers and farm workers are poor, these two occupations account for only one-fifth of the jobs held by the poor; as many poor work as operatives or service workers. Even white-collar jobs do not guarantee financial security, as more than 500,000 people depicted in the table testify.

TABLE 4.4 Occupations of the Poor (working heads-of-households)

Occupation	Number of Persons
Professional and technical	111,000
Managers, officials, and proprietors	199,000
Clerical workers	127,000
Sales workers	88,000
Craftsmen and foremen	311,000
Operatives	499,000
Private household workers	153,000
Other service workers	357,000
Unskilled laborers	285,000
Farmers and farm managers	349,000
Farm laborers and foremen	222,000
Total	2,701,000

Source: U.S. Bureau of Census.

It is, perhaps, just as easy to overstate the occupational status of the poor as it is to understate it. The occupational profile of Table 4.4 includes very broad employment categories and may lead to erroneous impressions. While there are 111,000 poor professional and technical workers, there are very few poor scientists, dentists, or even college professors among them. More likely to be poor within that occupational classification are hospital technicians,

[1] Elliot Liebow, *Tally's Corner: A Study of Negro Streetcorner Men* (Boston: Little, Brown and Company, 1967), p. 63.

recreation and social workers, and evangelist healers. Similarly, in other occupational categories, the poor tend to hold the least desirable, most marginal kinds of jobs. Thus, they are dishwashers, loggers, theater ushers, porters, tailors, shoe repairmen, and laundry workers. Accordingly, while it is true that the working poor are distributed throughout the labor market and in all industries, they will always be found in the lowest-ranking, least noticeable jobs. They constitute what might be called a phantom labor force.

The Significance of Secondary Workers

We have already drawn attention to the fact that poor families often send wives and other family members into the labor force to supplement the low wages of the family head. These secondary workers contribute a great deal to family incomes and are often able to help lift the family above the poverty standard. What must be emphasized is that these secondary workers are often the only available bridge between poverty and near-poverty. Poor families, however, are often prevented from sending secondary workers into the job market by the presence of young children in the household. Younger children tend to keep the mother out of the labor market, and younger families have fewer older children available for part-time work. Consequently, a major distinction between poor families and near-poor families is that the former are slightly younger and less likely to contain secondary workers. One implication of this distinction is that many of the near-poor passed through poverty in the natural course of family development. Later chapters will consider how and why they return to that status.

WHY ARE WAGES SO LOW?

While poverty among full-time workers is a seeming paradox, there is no shortage of available explanations for the low wages of the working poor. Predominant among these are that the poor are undereducated, inexperienced, underskilled, trained in the wrong occupations, and geographically handicapped. There exists abundant evidence to support each of these explanations, and we cannot deny their importance in holding down the wages of the poor. What we must also recognize, however, is that these explanations focus almost exclusively on the supply side of the labor market. They tell us what qualities an individual brings with him to the labor market but do not provide a complete explanation of why those particular qualities are paid so little. To understand the process by which wages are determined, we must also ask what the demand side of the labor market looks like.

In the most general terms, we say that a worker's wages are determined by the contribution he makes to output, that is, by his marginal product. But what is it that makes the output of a pipe fitter less valuable than the output of an advertising executive? Clearly, what most differentiates the incomes of these two people is not the physical output that each produces, but rather the value that society attaches to their products. If society were suddenly to become disenchanted with the wares of advertising executives and find increased value in fitted pipes, then the incomes of pipe fitters would exceed those of advertising executives, regardless of their respective physical outputs. By the same reasoning, if society were to attach more value to the kinds of output that the poor can and do produce, then we could expect the incomes of the working poor to rise.

The notion that the extent and structure of demand are significant determinants of the wages of the poor does not constitute a revolution in economic thinking. On the contrary, economists have long attributed to themselves the discovery that prices, and thus wages, are determined by the interaction of supply and demand. In the realm of policy formulation, however, the impact of the demand side of the market on the economic position of the poor is easily neglected. To do so is to ignore tremendous potential for eliminating poverty.

During the 1940s, there was a tendency for wage rates and incomes at the bottom of the occupational ladder to rise faster than those at the top, due to an upsurge in demand for unskilled, semiskilled, and operative kinds of labor needed for war production. The structure of demand since the 1940s, however, has primarily benefited workers with higher education and more technical expertise. Accordingly, we find the unskilled, semiskilled, and operative workers heavily represented among the poor. What must be acknowledged in this development is that the distribution of wages and incomes is partly a reflection of collective social decisions regarding the merits of particular kinds of output. Socio-political decisions to expand the educational system, to arm for peace, and to explore the moon have all had a profound impact on the structure of demand for labor. Had we decided instead to dredge more rivers, to build more houses, or to expand municipal services, the extent and nature of poverty might now be markedly different. Without attempting to predict those changes here, we may at least take note of the fact that the poor now suffer from some of society's past and current manpower utilization decisions and stand to benefit if and when society decides to place higher value on the available services of the poor.

SUMMARY

In Chapter 3, we observed that labor market forces have a substantial impact on the rate of employment for the poor. In particular, we observed that, in 1970, something like 1.5 million poor families suffered income losses as a direct or indirect consequence of unemployment. We noted further that this unemployment was beyond the control of the poor and largely determined by labor market forces. We may add to that analysis now by observing that the level and structure of demand also helps determine what incomes the poor will command when they do work. Relatively low levels of aggregate demand will restrain all wages, while particularized demand shortages may, and do, depress the wages of the working poor.

We suggested earlier that about 40 percent of all nonaged poor families were affected by unemployment. We have now counted another 1 million poor families whose heads work full time but whose wages are too low. Because these wages are themselves influenced by the same variables that determine unemployment rates, we may reasonably, and probably conservatively, conclude that labor market forces are responsible for substantially more than half of today's poverty among nonaged families.

APPENDIX: THE IMPACT OF UNIONS ON WAGES AND EMPLOYMENT

The extent and structure of aggregate demand are critical, though not the sole, determinants of wages and employment; also to be reckoned with are the forces of labor supply. One of the most obvious and controversial forces on the supply side of the market is labor unions. The issue that concerns us here is whether and to what extent unions have contributed to the low wages and subemployment of the poor. In everyday experience, it appears obvious that unions restrict the employment opportunities of the poor. Numerous cases are available to verify that one local union or another has turned down the job application of a poverty-stricken worker, especially where the potential worker is black. The excluded individual thereby loses one opportunity to escape poverty. To end union exclusionism, however, is not necessarily the solution. Imagine, for example, what would happen if *all* poor workers were suddenly to gain entrance to local unions: the market would be flooded with particular job skills; union wages would plummet; and union employment would cease to provide escape from poverty. Obviously, what works for one person, or even 5,000 people, will not work for the 2,702,000 poor heads-of-household in the labor market.

Another complication to the simple scenario of union exclusionism arises from the existence of alternate employment. Any individual rejected by the unions still has the option of seeking a nonunionized job. The question is whether, and to what extent, labor unions are able to affect the individual's prospects for alternate employment. When unions exclude workers from particular jobs, those workers are forced into nonunion employment. The effect of this movement is to reduce the supply of union workers while increasing the supply of nonunion workers. With no change in the demand for either type of labor, union wages will rise, while nonunion wages fall. If enough workers are shifted from union to nonunion work, nonunion wages may be depressed to the point where many workers are left poor.

FIGURE 4.2 The Impact of Unions

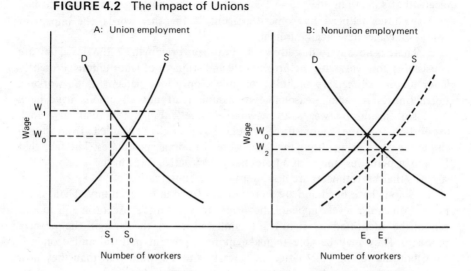

The sequence of events leading to a depression of nonunion wages is depicted in Figure 4.2. Suppose, in the first instance, that average wages in both union and nonunion employment are identical, at W_0. If the union is somehow able to raise wages to W_1, there will exist a surplus of workers anxious to obtain union employment. W_1 wage levels cannot be maintained, however, if all S_0 number of workers are employed, because there is not enough demand for labor at that higher wage. Accordingly, the union will have to exclude S_0-S_1 number of workers to uphold union wages. The excluded workers will have no choice but to enter nonunion employment.

The effect of union exclusion appears as an expansion in the supply of nonunion workers. There are now an additional S_0-S_1 workers ready to work at existing wages W_0. As a result, the nonunion supply curve shifts to the right. Average nonunion wages are depressed to W_2 in the process, since supply has expanded while the structure of demand is unchanged. The simple geometry of union exclusionism reinforces the presumption that unions have some impact on the wages and employment of the poor. By itself, however, the geometry does not tell us how significant that impact is. What we must determine empirically is how many persons have been forced into nonunion employment and what the net effect on wages has been.

In spite of widespread interest in union activities, no exacting estimates of these employment and wage effects have been made. Nevertheless, economist Milton Friedman has provided some notion as to the likely dimensions of such impact. He estimates that "something like 10 to 15 percent of the working population has had its wage rates raised by something like 10 to 15 percent. This means that something like 85 or 90 percent of the working population has had its wage rates reduced by some 4 percent."[2] In other words, the impact of unions on wages have been minimal.

There is no way to directly verify Professor Friedman's estimates. They are consistent, however, with the present size and strength of labor unions. Presently labor union membership includes roughly twenty-four percent of all workers. Furthermore, it seems reasonable to assume that not all unions have been successful in raising wages above market levels. Finally, a relatively small proportion of the labor force would have to be excluded from union employment to bring about the wage gains, Friedman postulates. The fact that Friedman perceives unions as a potentially destructive force in the economy also suggests that his estimates are not intentionally conservative.

Unions have been and are an important force in the economy. Their direct impact on wage levels appears, however, to be limited. Accordingly, unions cannot be identified as significant contributors to the size of the poverty problem. They may be able to make more important political and economic contributions to the elimination of poverty and discrimination than they now make; however, they cannot be blamed for the poverty that exists.

REFERENCES

AFL-CIO, "The Low-Paid Worker," in *Poverty in America,* Louis A. Ferman et al., eds. Ann Arbor: University of Michigan Press, 1969.

DOERINGER, PETER and MICHAEL PIORE, *Internal Labor Markets and Manpower Analysis.* Lexington, Mass.: D. C. Heath & Company, 1971, Ch. 8.

HARRISON, BENNETT, "Human Capital, Black Poverty, and 'Radical' Economics," *Industrial Relations,* October, 1971, pp. 277-86.

HIESTAND, DALE, *Economic Growth and Employment Opportunities for Minorities.* New York: Columbia University Press, 1964.

WILLIE, CHARLES A. and WALTER E. RIDDICK, "The Employed Poor: A Case Study", in *Poverty as a Public Issue,* Ben Seligman, ed. New York: The Free Press, 1965.

The Impact of Unions on Wages and Employment

FRIEDMAN, MILTON, *Capitalism and Freedom.* Chicago: University of Chicago Press, 1962.

GALLAWAY, LOWELL E., *Manpower Economics.* Homewood, Ill.: Richard D. Irwin, Inc., 1971.

[2] Milton Friedman, *Capitalism and Freedom* (Chicago: University of Chicago Press, 1962), p. 124.

B Demographic Forces

5 Age and Health

The apparent impact of labor market forces explains much existing poverty, but not all. Nor is the labor market explanation really satisfactory to most people. As previously noted, most nonpoor analysts are predisposed to attribute poverty to the character and traits of the individuals so afflicted. Accordingly, this chapter begins a detailed inquiry into the demographic characteristics of the poor and the potential that such characteristics possess for explaining poverty.

AGE

We have already counted among the poor 4,709,000 individuals over the age of sixty-five. Our purpose in reexamining the situation of the aged poor is not to remind ourselves how desperate they are but to investigate the link between their age and their economic status. What we seek to determine is whether there is something in the process of aging itself that leads to poverty.

The very size of the aged poor population creates a strong presumption that a causal link exists between age and poverty. Not only are 25 percent of the aged poor, but such individuals comprise one-fifth of the total poverty population. Moreover, the economic problems of the aged will be of increasing importance over time as the number of people living past the age of 65 continues to grow. The extension of life expectancies from 49 years in 1900 to 71 years in 1970 is reflected in the fact that the number of aged has increased by nearly 700 percent since the start of the century. And the aged population can be expected to continue to grow at a faster rate than the rest of the population as medical science advances.

These considerations have led Michael Harrington to observe that "the poverty of old age in America is rooted in a biological revolution."[1] We must take care, however, not to attribute to biology the economic ills of the aged. Medical advances are responsible only for the fact that so many more people live to old age. They do not explain why so many of these people live in poverty. To understand more fully the forces that lead to economic destitution, we begin by reviewing the sources of support that the aged command.

Sources of Economic Support

The most obvious constraint on the incomes of the aged is the fact that so few older individuals remain in the labor force. Only 50 percent of all aged couples have at least one member in the labor force, while a mere 16 percent of aged individuals, most of whom are women, work. Accordingly, earnings from employment account for less than one-third of the incomes of the aged and provide little income at that. The poor among the aged are even less likely to work (see Table 2.4), and this absence of employment income is a major determinant of their economic status.

Low labor force participation among the aged reflects a continuing trend in American society. At the beginning of the century, more than two-thirds of all men over the age of sixty-five were in the labor force; today, only a third of such men work. The reasons for this decline in labor force participation are many but surely do not include increased physical requirements of labor or diminished health status of the aged. More likely to have contributed to the decline are an increased desire for leisure, an abatement of the economic necessity to work, and a reduced demand for the skills of the aged.

There is considerable evidence that many of the aged are involuntarily out of the labor force due to forced retirements and prolonged unemployment. If an older worker is laid off for any reason, for example, plant shutdowns, production slowdowns, or forced retirement, he faces little opportunity of finding another job. He is likely to have developed highly specialized skills in an occupation that is on the decline. Moreover, because of his advanced age, other employers see little benefit in retraining him or redirecting his skills. Other employers also anticipate increased costs as a result of higher disability rates and imminent retirement. Simple economics thus militate against the aged job-seeker. Because his employment prospects are so unpromising, the aged job-seeker is likely to drop out of the labor force earlier than he wants to, thereby closing a prospective income source.

There are alternatives to employment income, of course. One of the commonest substitutes for employment income is income from savings, assets, and various retirement plans. If the aged are generously provided with these,

[1]Michael Harrington, *The Other America* (New York: The Macmillan Company, 1962), p. 102.

then the loss of employment income may not be serious. The question is, are the aged adequately provided with nonemployment retirement income?

Because the aged live longer today and retire earlier, they must accumulate greater savings than families once did. The unfortunate but simple economics of this relationship is that the longer one lives, the greater are the chances of destitution. Savings are depleted at the same time as one's employment capabilities and opportunities disappear. Hence, the aged of today must command considerable assets and savings if they are to experience a comfortable retirement. At present, the aged poor clearly do not possess such savings, and many of the nonpoor aged do not fare much better, either. A recent survey indicated that only one-fourth of *all* aged families possess savings large enough to support themselves for more than two years. Hence, many more aged persons will experience poverty shortly. Moreover, there is abundant evidence that the near-aged, that is, people fifty-five to sixty-five years old, have no greater savings. It appears, then, that the presently aged poor are only a small fraction of those who will follow.

Two more questions arise with regard to the savings of the aged: first, did the aged ever possess enough resources to save for old age; and second, did they save what resources they had? The distinction is important for policy purposes because many observers still believe it is necessary to distinguish the deserving poor from the undeserving poor, even among the aged. From this perspective, an impoverished older individual may simply be experiencing the consequences of an earlier decision to make merry while the sun was shining.

An examination of the previous experiences of the aged poor offers no evidence that they enjoyed an especially lascivious or spendthrift past. A 1962 study by the University of Michigan suggested that the aged poor had never earned enough income to provide for retirement or, for that matter, a comfortable living prior to retirement. Among those aged poor whose incomes were known, over 40 percent had never earned as much as $2,000 per year. Such statistics have led at least one observer to conclude of the aged poor that "the misery of their old age is simply the conclusion of a life of misery. They are the ones who have grown up, lived, and will die under conditions of poverty."[2] Many, and probably most, of the aged poor were always in or on the margins of poverty.

Some individuals do experience impoverishment for the first time, however, as they grow old. Just as few people think about dying, few ever plan to get old and retire. Despite the statistical expectation of extended retirement and diminished incomes, only a small number of people make provisions for old age. People's essential optimism is revealed in consumer surveys, such as the one that disclosed that families who have not had as much as $500 in the bank during the last five years confidently anticipate a comfortable retirement.

[2] Harrington, *Other America*, p. 105.

Confidence appears to fade with age, however: among younger families, only 9 percent foresee hard times after retirement; among middle-aged families, 16 percent sense trouble ahead. But when they reach old age, at least 25 percent of these individuals end up in poverty.

Aside from their own savings, aged persons may draw income either from private pension plans or social security, but these sources usually provide much less income than most persons anticipate. Pension plans are often a great disillusionment. Many workers who confidently subscribe to company pension plans find that they have no pension rights upon retirement. If a worker is laid off or disabled before working, say, twenty years, he may not be eligible for *any* pension payments. The same is often true if the company he works for goes bankrupt.[3] Presently, only 12 percent of all aged people receive private pensions, and these payments are primarily available only to those who had better jobs and higher incomes earlier.

Social security payments reach far more of the aged—nearly 90 percent of the aged now receive or are eligible for benefits—and constitute the single most important source of income for the elderly. But social security benefits are largely based on previous income, so those who are most impoverished as they reach old age are least likely to receive substantial social security aid. While a fuller discussion of the social security program is contained in Chapter 11, we may note here that it alone does not assure the economic security the aged require.

Their own families have long represented the most dependable source of social and economic security for many people, but continuing industrialization and urbanization have tended to disintegrate the extended family, leaving each core family unit to fend for itself. Despite whatever material and social benefits this development has yielded for others, it has deprived the aged of a source of support, immediate companionship, and, in many cases, a roof over their heads. Today, less than a third of the aged live with their relatives, and of those that do not, less than 5 percent receive any income support from their offspring. Accordingly, kinsmen rarely constitute a source of economic security for the aged and cannot be expected to provide an escape from poverty.

The income sources of the aged are summarized in Table 5.1. Related in the table are two distinct kinds of information. Column two depicts the proportion of aged households that receive any income at all from the sources discussed above. Thus, an aged couple that receives only $4.32 interest on their bank savings is included among those with asset income. If they receive social security payments too, then they are also included in that category. As the table shows, very few elderly persons receive any monetary assistance from relatives or friends.

---

[3] The U.S. Department of Labor estimates that from 30 to 50 percent of the 30 million workers covered by private pensions will never see a nickel in benefits. Some 30,000 workers lose out on pensions each year simply because their employers go broke.

TABLE 5.1   Income Sources of the Aged

Source of Income	Percent of Aged Households Receiving Such Income	Total Share of Income Provided by Source
Employment earnings	27%	29%
Private pensions	12	5
Social Security	86	34
Other public pensions	10	7
Veteran's benefits	10	3
Public assistance	12	4
Asset income	50	15
Personal contributions	3	1
Other sources	3	2
		100%

Source: Lenore Bixby, "Income of People Aged 65 and Older," Social Security Bulletin, April, 1970, Tables 2 and 3.

The last column of Table 5.1 depicts the relative importance of each income source; social security and employment earnings are clearly the most significant. It is interesting to note how the importance of asset income diminishes as we move from column two to column three: while 50 percent of the aged receive some asset income, that source accounts for only 15 percent of all income for the aged, implying that most asset holdings are quite small. If, in fact, a small minority of the aged have very large asset holdings, which include savings, bonds, stocks, and property, then the rest of the aged own virtually nothing.

Expenses of the Aged

The serious decline in the sources and amounts of income that the aged command creates enough momentum to impoverish a high proportion of these individuals. But dwindling incomes are not their only burden; the aged also confront very large, and often rising, expenses. The interaction of these two forces is a virtual guarantee that a still higher proportion of the aged will experience material want before they die.

Everyone knows that the aged are likely to experience high rates of sickness and disability. Often forgotten, however, is the tremendous financial burden that such disabilities impose. In 1969, for example, the average health bill for a person sixty-five or older was $692, including the expenses of hospital care, physician's services, and all drugs. This is a bill the average aged person cannot afford to pay. These health costs are equal to one-fourth of an aged individual's annual income and over 40 percent of his yearly income if he is old and poor.

Even these average expenses understate the burden of illness for those actually most sick. Hospitalization expenditures, for example, are incurred by only a portion of the poor, and these individuals pay all the costs, not just the "average" cost (which amounted to $335 in 1970). Furthermore, most likely to be sick or disabled are those who have endured impoverishment and hard labor the longest and are thus least able to afford the costs of sickness. Accordingly, many individuals who manage to fend off poverty during their working years are likely to succumb to financial impoverishment when illness strikes. For those who have always been poor, illness in old age represents one more burden and indignity.

Recent reforms in medical insurance—most notably Medicare—have done a great deal to reduce the threat of impoverishment among the aged due to illness. But even Medicare pays only one-half of all medical costs and provides the least security to those who need it most. For the poor and near-poor among the aged, health expenses remain a significant burden. Worse yet, the aged poor, who cannot afford preventive health care, are unable to fend off many avoidable illnesses. Doubly burdened with sickness and poverty, they are condemned to await death miserably, often in an unsympathetic and inadequate institution.

A second major financial burden for the aged results from taxes, particularly property taxes. For most of the aged, their homes represent the only significant asset they possess and embody a lifetime of savings. But because local property taxes continue to rise, many of the aged find themselves unable to maintain their investment. Property taxes alone may consume as much as 30 percent of the incomes of aged persons living just above the poverty line. As a result, the U.S. Senate Special Committee on Aging reports that hundreds of thousands of aged persons are being driven from their homes by mounting property taxes. Still more are being forced to liquidate other assets to pay their taxes. Thus, the only visible economic security of many of the aged may itself contribute to their impoverishment.

Home ownership often imposes another unforeseen cost. Many of the aged purchased their homes in central cities at a time when inner city locations seemed most attractive. As the years have passed, however, inner city neighborhoods have deteriorated. Younger families have sought the freshness and space of the suburbs, while racial segregation and hostility have contributed to a general depreciation of inner city property values. As a consequence, the aged are apt to find themselves socially and racially isolated in neighborhoods they once thought attractive. They cannot afford to sell, because the value of their homes has fallen, while suburban values have skyrocketed. Hence, they can only hold on until the burden of property taxes leads them to rented quarters or nursing homes.

Making Do

An aged person with diminishing income and mounting expenses has little hope for economic security. His chances have simply run out, and his past labors and thrift are able only to postpone impoverishment in most cases. The question arises, then, as to how the aged actually manage in the face of such imposing circumstances. The most succinct answer came forth in hearings before a committee of the U.S. Senate:

> "How do you manage?" I asked. A lady replied, "It's hard, Pat, oh, it's hard." "Well, what do you do?" "We don't do," someone replied, "That's how we manage!"

> "I don't" is a most accurate description of the older adult living in retirement. I don't entertain. I don't go out with friends. I don't eat in restaurants. I don't go to movies. I don't buy new clothes. I don't ride subways and buses. I don't buy cake. I don't eat a lot. I don't take care of my health like I should. I don't, I don't, I don't. [4]

For the aged, then, growing older means giving up one thing after another, until there is nothing more to forsake. When that time comes, they can only wait for death; sometime before that, they are unquestionably poor.

Assessing Causation

Poverty among the aged is not a natural product of biological development. Rather, it emerges from a diminuition of income sources, a lack of accumulated resources, and the imposition of extraordinary property and health expenses. Maintaining income sources or providing financial relief from taxation and illness will effectively prevent many aged individuals from falling into poverty. For others, however, poverty does not emerge in old age but is, instead, a continuing condition. The causes of poverty for these people must be sought elsewhere and earlier. Identifying and eliminating the causes of poverty for the nonaged will help to prevent later poverty among the aged.

HEALTH

One way to assure individuals greater prosperity and security in old age is to maintain their good health in younger years. Better health contributes to economic security in two important ways: by permitting persons to earn more income; and by reducing financial expenditures arising from health needs. All other things being equal, a person with good health is likely to accumulate greater financial reserves when he is young and to need them less when he is old.

It is not difficult to surmise the potential poor health has for undermining a family's economic security. A sick or disabled father not only fails to earn a full income; he also increases household expenses. To appreciate how expensive illness can be, we may observe recent income losses and health expenditures. In

---

[4] Special Committee on Aging, *Economics of Aging: Toward a Full Share in Abundance,* U.S. Senate, 91st Cong., 2d sess., 1970 (Washington, D.C.: Government Printing Office, 1970), p. 34.

1970, for example, illness and disability imposed an income loss in excess of $15 billion on American workers, and more than $70 billion was spent for health maintenance and care. This works out to an average income loss of $210 per worker and average health expenses of $324 per person. Even if the poor experienced only an average amount of illness and disability, their incomes would be severely depleted by poor health.

The relationship between health and income status is not simple enough, however, to permit the use of averages in ascertaining the cost of illness to the poor. Just as illness may tend to deplete a family's resources and leave it poor, so may poverty itself increase the likelihood of getting sick. Poor families suffer notoriously from chronic malnutrition and unsanitary environments, both of which effectively nurture ill health. As a consequence, they are apt to be ill or disabled more often than the nonpoor, and they are. Poor families have markedly higher disease and mortality rates and miss more than twice as many days of work due to illness than do the nonpoor.

Poverty and illness, then, interact in a reciprocal relationship. Illness contributes to poverty at the same time that poverty contributes to bad health. The circular nature of the relationship is depicted in Figure 5.1. To acknowledge that illness leads to poverty while poverty leads to poor health is not to suggest that the significance of each path of causation—from poverty to illness and back—is equally important. To acknowledge some circularity in the relationship is not equivalent to admitting equal causal significance in either direction. We may still inquire as to how many families or persons actually fall into poverty as a result of illness or disability; that is, we may still ask to what extent poverty is actually caused by ill health. Many persons were poor before they were sick, so we cannot claim that illness caused their poverty. At most, we may say that illness maintains their poverty or that it makes poverty more miserable.

The search for causal significance thus centers on the question of how many nonpoor persons sink into poverty as a result of illness. The answer, of course, depends on how far above the poverty line families begin and how much

FIGURE 5.1   Illness and Poverty

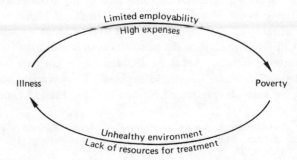

illness they contract. Also important is the extent to which families are protected by insurance from the impositions of work loss and medical expenses.

A family need not be far above the poverty line to have an adequate margin against the burdens of ill health. Our poverty line for a family of four is just under $4,000. Average yearly medical expenses for a family this size are around $1,000 per year. Hence, for the typical family, an income of $5,000 would easily prevent slippage into poverty as a result of illness. Moreover, as we have already suggested, the incidence of illness falls as income rises, further immunizing the nonpoor against poverty. Families with higher incomes also have more public and private health insurance, protection that currently pays two-thirds of all medical expenses. Consequently, for families with some margin of income above the poverty standard, only severe and protracted illnesses represent a real threat to economic security. Illness is still painful and may even lower standards of living for these families; it is unlikely, however, to lead to poverty.

Families on the margin of economic security are not so well fortified against the onslaught of illness. With an income of $4,000 to $5,000, a family has little financial reserve. Such families are likely to be ill more often and less likely to be protected by insurance. Consequently, they are prone to fall into poverty when illness strikes. Near-poor families do, in fact, move back and forth across the poverty line with great frequency. In part, this movement is due to the sporadic occurrence of illness. Economic security for these families is, at all times, vulnerable to any kind of setback, be it illness, increased unemployment, or other misfortune. We cannot say exactly how much poverty is caused by illness and disability, but it is safe to conclude that very few people fall into poverty from any significant height as a result of ill health.

The relationship between ill health and poverty is further illuminated by a look at the relationship between mental disability and economic status. The issue here is the same as before: does mental disability lead downward to the slums, or does slum life accentuate tendencies toward mental illness? The former question embodies a popular "drift" hypothesis. According to this thesis, failures from all walks of life drift into the slums, creating our present poor population. The available evidence, however, once again shatters the popular myth. One of the few detailed studies undertaken on this subject traced the socioeconomic histories of schizophrenic individuals. The results were unambiguous: 91 percent of such patients were in the same socioeconomic class as their parents. There was no evidence of substantial drift. Instead, the results suggest again that poverty is more likely to lead to ill health than result from it.

Before leaving the question of the causal relationship of ill health to poverty, we must at least take notice of one additional dimension to the problem. As noted earlier, a person in poverty is apt to be malnourished and highly susceptible to disease. What this implies is that a child born to a poverty-stricken mother is likely to be undernourished both before and after birth. Furthermore, the child is less likely to be cared for properly after birth, to be immunized against disease, or even to have his eyes and teeth examined. As a result, the child is likely to grow up prone to illness and poverty, and in the most insidious of cases, be impaired by organic brain damage. Under such circumstances, the identification of causation becomes a very difficult task. Seldom do we know enough about poor persons to be able to trace their disabilities to birth, much less before. Even if we could, we would still have to face up to the question of whether the child's poverty was caused by his disabilities, his mother's illness, and/or his mother's poverty. While we cannot yet resolve these issues, the questions themselves at least draw attention to some of the intergenerational handicaps that poverty may impose.

SUMMARY

Age and illness are highly visible correlates of poverty and, because of this, are often assumed to bear a causal relationship to economic impoverishment. The reasoning behind such an assumption is simple and appears eminently plausible. As reasonable as such a conclusion is, however, there are several reasons for attaching only limited causal importance to the impact of age and illness. Many of the aged poor, for example, were always poor, so that aging itself is of little significance for their economic status. Similarly, poor persons are more prone to illness, and illness for them represents no sudden loss of well-being. Even for those who are driven to poverty for the first time by age or illness, the loss of economic status is occasioned by a variety of forces, none of which is inseparable from the natural processes of aging and illness.

It is not possible to attach exact quantitative significance to the amount of poverty caused by age and illness. Given the data reviewed in this chapter, however, we may tentatively estimate that no more than 10 to 15 percent of the poor are impoverished as a result of age or illness. This assumes that only one-half of the aged poor experience poverty for the first time in old age and that only 5 to 10 percent of the poor have been destituted by the effects of ill health.

REFERENCES

BIXBY, LENORE E., "Income of People Aged 65 and Over: Overview from 1968 Survey of the Aged," *Social Security Bulletin*, 33, No. 4, April 1970.

CITIZEN'S BOARD OF INQUIRY INTO HUNGER AND MALNUTRITION IN THE UNITED STATES, *Hunger, U.S.A.* Washington, D.C.: New Community Press, 1968.

HARRINGTON, MICHAEL, *The Other America*. New York: The Macmillan Company, 1962, Ch. 6.

HENRY, LOUIS H., "Caring For Our Aged Poor," *The New Republic,* 164, May 22, 1971, pp. 17-22.

HURLEY, RODGER L., *Poverty and Mental Retardation: A Causal Relationship.* Trenton, N.J.: New Jersey Department of Institutions and Agencies, April 1968.

LAURIAT, PATIENCE, "Benefit Levels and Socio-Economic Characteristics: Findings from the 1968 Survey of the Aged," *Social Security Bulletin,* August, 1970.

MORGAN, JAMES N., MARTIN H. DAVID, WILBUR J. COHEN, and HARVEY E. BRAZER, *Income and Welfare in the United States.* McGraw-Hill Book Company, 1962.

OFFICE OF RESEARCH AND STATISTICS, SOCIAL SECURITY ADMINISTRATION, *Research Notes,* numbers: 1968, No. 11; 1969, No. 6; 1970, Nos. 23, 25, and 27.

ORNATI, OSCAR, *Poverty Amid Affluence.* New York: The Twentieth Century Fund, 1966, Ch. 10.

SELIGMAN, BEN B., *Permanent Poverty.* Chicago: Quadrangle Books, 1968, Ch. 4.

U.S. DEPARTMENT OF HEALTH, EDUCATION, AND WELFARE, *The Aged Population in the United States.* Washington, D.C.: Government Printing Office, 1967.

U.S. SENATE, SPECIAL COMMITTEE ON AGING, *Economics of Aging: Toward a Full Share in Abundance,* 91st Cong., 2d sess., 1970. Washington, D.C.: Government Printing Office, 1970.

6   Family Size and Status

There are two persistent accusations leveled against the poor: One is that the poor do not limit their family size; the other is that they do not maintain stable families. The implication in both cases is that the poor exhibit too little self-control and are thus responsible for much of their own poverty. The purposes of this chapter are to examine more closely the relationship between poverty and family size and status and to determine the extent of responsibility that the poor themselves must bear for their own deprivation.

The central questions of this chapter are much like those of Chapter 5. That is, we inquire whether either large family size or family instability preceded economic impoverishment. If not, then there exists a basic presumption that poverty was not caused by either phenomenon. Indeed, in such circumstances, we may be led to ask whether the sequence of causation is reversible, that is, whether poverty itself may lead to family instability or excessive procreation.

FAMILY SIZE

Large numbers of children constitute a sizeable drain on family resources. Not only are the physical needs of the family increased, but the mother is likely to be restricted to the home. If the mother chooses not to stay at home, she must pay someone else to tend the house while she works. Childbearing and rearing thus make it either physically impossible or economically unrewarding for many mothers to participate in the labor force. Confronted with more needs and fewer resources, many large families are unable to fend off poverty.

The sequence of events leading from family growth to poverty is simple and logical, but it is not the only sequence possible. Just as excessive procreation may lead to poverty, so might poverty lead to undesired family expansion. For example, if poor families do not know about birth control, poverty itself may inhibit family planning. Such a situation could exist where the poor tend to be less educated or where they have less access to medical consultation. Poverty could also contribute to excessive procreation where the techniques of birth control, although known, are too expensive for the poor. In such circumstances, the oft-repeated observation that poverty breeds poverty would take on very direct and special significance.

Before attempting to disentangle the possible causal relationships between poverty and family size, it is interesting to observe the present association between family income and size. Such an overview provides a few clues as to the direction of causation and, more importantly, outlines the potential importance of the causal relationship, whichever direction it takes.

Most people are surprised to learn that family size increases with income. Average family size rises from a low of 2.77 for families in the $1,500-2,000 income class to a high of 4.06 in the income class of $25,000-50,000. The surprise that accompanies this discovery emanates from the common observation that the poor have more children. This apparent contradiction can be explained easily, however. Although average income rises with average family size, it does not keep pace with increasing family needs. Moreover, the average income or family size for any population group tells us very little about the distribution of incomes or children within the group. Many large families, for example the Kennedys and Rockefellers, possess enormous wealth, while others command few resources. Accordingly, the high average income of large families masks the poverty of many.

Figure 6.1 depicts the incidence of poverty for different family sizes. The incidence clearly rises as the number of children increases, first slowly, and then

FIGURE 6.1 Incidence of Poverty by Family Size (Source: U.S. Bureau of the Census)

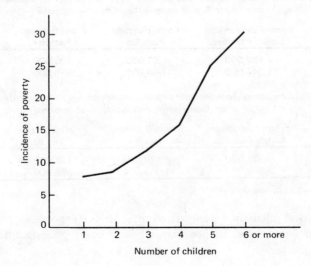

quite sharply after the fourth child. Clearly, there are a disproportionate number of families among the poor who have a large number of children. Nearly 30 percent of all poor families with children have at least four children; among nonpoor families, only 13 percent have that many children.

To grasp the implications of larger family sizes among the poor, we may ask how many larger poor families would move out of poverty if they had fewer family members. For example, we know from Table 1.4 that five-member families are considered poor if their 1970 incomes were under $4,680, but the same poverty standard for a family of four was $3,968. Hence, any family of five whose income was less than $4,680 but more than $3,968 would no longer be counted as poor if it could somehow eliminate one family member. Or, to put it slightly differently, we may say that such a family would not have fallen into poverty if it had bred one less child. By counting the total number of such families, we may estimate the potential of family planning as a means for reducing poverty.

The statistical exercise required to make such an estimate is summarized in Table 6.1. The exercise is carried out on two levels: the first calculation tells how many larger poor families (of five or more persons) would move out of poverty if they had one less member. Among poor five-person families, we look for all those whose current income could support four persons; among six-person families, incomes that will support five people, and so on. Based on these calculations, we observe that 410,000 families, a total of 2,523,000 individuals, would no longer be counted as poor if each poor family had one person less.

TABLE 6.1 The Potential Impact of Family Planning

A. *QUESTION: How many families and persons would no longer be counted as poor if each larger poor family were reduced by one person?*

ANSWER:	From 7-person and Larger Families	From 6-person Families	From 5-person Families	Total
Families	192,000	83,000	135,000	410,000
Persons	1,344,000	504,000	675,000	2,523,000

B. *QUESTION: How many families and persons would no longer be counted as poor if each larger poor family were reduced to four persons?*

ANSWER:	From 7-person or Larger Families	From 6-person Families	From 5-person Families	Total
Families	398,000	177,000	135,000	710,000
Persons	2,786,000	1,062,000	675,000	4,523,000

Source: U.S. Bureau of the Census.

The second calculation summarized in Table 6.1 imposes an even stricter constraint on family size. Rather than trim all larger poor families by one person, it reduces all such families to the standard four persons. Hence, six-person families statistically lose two members, and their poverty line falls from $5,260 to $3,968. This kind of standardization creates an astounding reduction in the size of the poverty population. On these assumptions, 710,000 families and 4,523,000 individuals—nearly one-fourth of all the nonaged poor—would no longer be counted as poor.

Our statistical exercise leads us to the conclusion that mild restraints on family size (one person less) would reduce the nonaged poverty population by some 13 percent, while severe limits on family size (maximum of four) would effect a 23 percent reduction in the number of poor. Such results underscore the potential importance of the causal link between family size and poverty. Before returning to a discussion of causality, however, it is necessary to subject our statistical results to some critical scrutiny.

First of all, our statistical exercise tacitly assumes that there is no positive relationship between family size and family income. Hence, the statistical elimination of one family member is presumed to have no effect on family income. But this is not necessarily true. Among families dependent on public assistance, for example, family income usually rises with additional children. Thus, if we were to eliminate one family member, we would also have to adjust the size of the welfare grant. One less child would mean less income and continued poverty. Accordingly, few, if any, welfare families—who constitute one-half of the population of poor families with children—can be included in our calculations.

Family income may also rise with family size for other reasons. The father of the family may be impelled to work overtime or at a second job as his family responsibilities expand; hence larger families may constitute a special kind of incentive to work. Larger families may also enable other family members to work; they may have a greater number of older children who can contribute directly to family income by working part time or who enable the mother to work by assuming child-care responsibilities. Hence, the statistical reduction carried out above may, in fact, diminish sources of family income.

Further consideration must also be given to those families and persons whom we suppose statistically to escape poverty by our calculations. Some family members are constrained by our arithmetic to disappear, and we can ignore them for the moment. Surviving family members, however, improve their economic status only marginally, and we must recognize that their statistical "escape" is, therefore, not very impressive. Almost all such families remain within a few hundred dollars of our poverty standards, even after they manage to leave the poverty population.

These qualifications to our earlier calculations reduce the impact of family size as a cause of poverty; unfortunately, there is not enough information about the poor to make a meaningful estimate of its true impact. We can observe, however, that even if we envision only limited birth control (one less child in each larger family) and consider the above qualifications important enough to reduce our estimates by at least half, then large family size still accounts for 7 percent of the nonaged poverty population. Under stricter family size controls, the reduction would amount to 12 percent.

Even when reduced by cautious skepticism, then, family size still appears to possess some potential for explaining the existence of poverty. Given the obvious association between these two phenomena, it would not seem necessary to pursue the subject of causation further, but the direction of causation is an important ingredient of policy decisions and must be examined. If the poor are mindlessly, even willfully, propagating beyond their financial means, policy intervention will be more difficult and less available; but if the poor are excluded from access to birth control, intervention is easier and more broadly acceptable. The former case comes closest to the position that excessive family size leads to poverty, while the latter case implies the reverse.

There is no evidence at all that presently large poor families ever enjoyed a more comfortable economic status. Larger families do have an effect on the dimensions of poverty to the extent that continued procreation may lengthen a family's stay in the poverty population rather than cause it to fall from nonpoverty to poverty. Large family size thus retards the flow of people moving out of poverty and contributes over time to an expansion of the poverty population. By itself, however, it creates very little new poverty.

Against this background, we must also ponder the accumulation of evidence suggesting that the poor continue to have little access to birth control information. Public schools, especially in low-income areas, are still reluctant to provide birth control information, while public welfare authorities are, in most cases, prohibited from providing it. As a consequence, poor families end up with more children than other families, not because they want them, but because they are unable to prevent them. One study by the National Academy of Sciences indicated that over one-third of the least-educated families had unwanted children, and a survey of welfare mothers in New York yielded similar findings. If, in fact, the poor do not want large families, the need for easy access to birth control information and contraceptive devices is clear.

We must conclude that excessive family size is not an important cause of poverty on the basis of our earlier observation that larger poor families were, by and large, once smaller poor families rather than smaller nonpoor families. Hence, if causation were to be specified here, we would have to surmise that lack of access to birth control is one of the ways in which poverty itself creates more poverty. Eliminating family size as a significant independent cause of poverty should not, therefore, divert attention away from the potential of greater family planning efforts to alleviate the conditions of the poor. The fact remains that greater availability of birth control would help reduce the number that are poor.

FAMILY STATUS

One-parent families, especially black ones, have long attracted the attention of social scientists, politicians, and the general public. They have been regarded with pity, with scorn, and even with a sense of fear. Single-parent, or broken, families do not fit easily into traditional American patterns and are often regarded as a threat to community morality, not to mention the whole institutional character of marriage. Recently, added concern over the existence of broken families has emerged from the observation that they tend to become financially dependent on the public purse. Within the confines of this chapter, there is hardly room for a thorough examination of the economics and sociology of one-parent families. Instead, the subject of family status, as of all other demographic characteristics, is treated with a focus on the existence of possible causal links to poverty.

In virtually all cases where only one parent resides in the family, that parent is the mother. Accordingly, the somewhat colorless census classification, female-headed families with children, refers to nearly all those families whose social and economic life has been ruptured by the loss of a parent. Broken families actually arise from two different contingencies: either a previously two-parent family is literally broken up by the death or separation (by divorce, legal separation, or desertion) of one parent; or the parents never formed a stable union, legal or otherwise. While the net effect in either case is to leave only one parent in the family, the economic and social ramifications of each situation may be quite distinct. A twenty-six year old widow, for example, may command more social support and economic resources than an unwed mother of the same age.

A one-parent family is severely handicapped in the effort to attain economic security. The loss of one potential breadwinner is a large and obvious constraint on economic stability. Potential family income is reduced by *more than half* with the departure of one parent. Where two parents exist in the family, one parent can devote full time to labor market activity, while the other is free to combine household and labor market activity. When only one parent resides in the family, such flexibility is diminished. The single parent is unable to devote all time to labor market activity, at least not without paying someone else to assume household responsibilities. Hence, the potential net income of a one-parent family is often closer to one-third rather than to one-half of a two-parent family's income. If women's employment opportunities in the labor market are further constricted by conventional sexual stereotypes, their potential income will be lower still. Accordingly, one-parent families bear an extraordinarily high risk of economic impoverishment.

While the potential of family breakup (or nonformation) for impoverishment is clear, the direction of causation is not necessarily so apparent. We need evidence that family breakup *leads to* poverty, and not the reverse, or at least that it effectively acts as an independent barrier to economic security.

Historically, there has seldom been any reluctance to "explain" the existence of one-parent families among blacks. As late as the 1920s, allegations of "animalism," "moral putridity," and "primitive sexualism" were often advanced as explanations for the great incidence of broken families among American blacks. The latent implication was always that blacks were responsible for their own destitution, because they were morally, physically, or culturally unable to stabilize family relationships. Such explanations for black family instability and poverty have never fared well under scholarly examination. Among others, E. Franklin Frazier, an outstanding expert on the Negro family, has shown that family patterns are comprehensible only in the context of existing social and economic forces. Moreover, the fact that there are many more poor white female-headed families than poor black female-headed families would tend to undermine purely racial explanations of the link between family status and poverty.

There is strong evidence against racial theories of causation between family status and poverty, but the theories persist because people want to believe them. In addition, the whole subject experienced a certain rejuvenation in 1965 when President Lyndon Johnson, speaking at Howard University, drew attention to the breakdown of Negro family structure as one of the most important causes of Negro poverty. While he did not seem to mean that black poverty could be explained on simple racial grounds, his words sparked instant misunderstanding and anger. James Farmer of CORE, for example, saw President Johnson's statement as a "massive academic cop-out for the white conscience" that would provide fuel for a new racism. Martin Luther King, Jr., saw in the President's words a danger that the poverty of blacks would be attributed to innate Negro weaknesses, and therein he feared yet another basis for racial neglect and oppression.

Behind President Johnson's Howard University speech lay a theoretical paper written by Daniel P. Moynihan, then an assistant secretary of labor. In what became known as the Moynihan Report, he had said:

> At the heart of the deterioration of the fabric of Negro society is the deterioration of the Negro family.
>
> It is the fundamental source of the weakness of the Negro community at the present time. . . .
>
> . . . Once or twice removed, it will be found to be the principal source of most of the aberrant, inadequate, or anti-social behavior that did not establish, but now serves to perpetuate the cycle of poverty and deprivation.[1]

[1] U.S. Department of Labor, *The Negro Family: The Case for National Action* (Washington, D.C.: Government Printing Office, 1965).

Because the Moynihan Report sparked such a controversy, and because it deals explicitly with the relationship between family status and poverty, we will use it as a case study.

To recapitulate, the central issue is whether family breakup independently causes poverty, or vice versa. For most commentators, the Moynihan Report seemed to confirm black family structure as a cause of poverty. Moynihan himself, however, had in mind a more complex relationship. In the recesses of the report, Moynihan suggested, as had Frazier earlier, that family structure itself was shaped by prevailing social and economic forces. Hence, one could not argue that family breakup had caused poverty; at most, black family structures only reflected economic forces and made escape from poverty more difficult. Poverty and social injustice were more likely to cause family breakup, not the reverse.

One particularly interesting bit of evidence collected by Moynihan concerns the relationship between unemployment rates and family structure: looking at the trend of unemployment rates and family structures, Moynihan found that the rates of separation and divorce followed economic events very closely. Thus, the rate of separations among black women shot up shortly after the economy faltered, while it sank when the economy prospered (see Figure 6.2). The conclusion seemed unavoidable that family stability was the result, not the cause, of economic events. As a family faced increased unemployment and deprivation, the father's position as breadwinner and family head became untenable; divorce, separation, or desertion often followed.

Further support for this position was found in illegitimacy statistics: in

FIGURE 6.2 Black Unemployment and Separation Rates (Source: U.S. Department of Labor, *The Negro Family* (the Moynihan Report), March 1965, p. 22)

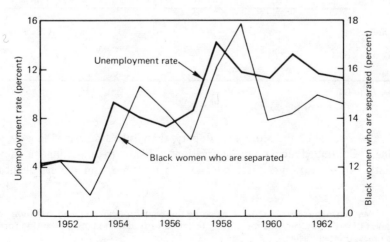

poor black neighborhoods, rates of illegitimacy were more than triple those of black neighborhoods with middle-class incomes. Again it appeared that family formation itself was significantly affected by economic circumstances. Those parents with little prospect for economic security foresaw little hope for family stability; hence, decided not to marry.

A. Philip Randolph, long a leader in labor and civil rights movements, found evidence similar to Moynihan's in World War II experience. During the exceptionally low unemployment years of the war, rates of divorce and illegitimacy among blacks took a sharp drop. Greater economic security thus manifested itself in greater family stability.

More recent information on families appears to further confirm Moynihan's observations and to extend his hypothesis to all families, black or white. Table 6.2 shows the pattern of marital status for men by income class. Among all men aged 25 to 64 who were ever married, 7 percent no longer have their wives present; they are divorced, separated, deserted, or widowed. The incidence of absent wives varies enormously by income class, however. Over one-fifth of married men in the lowest income class no longer live with their wives, while fewer than one out of twenty-five men in the highest income class are likely to be so positioned. This relationship conveys two important impressions: first, it appears to reconfirm the point that family stability is affected by economic conditions; and, it suggests that economic impoverishment preceded family dissolution so that restoration of the family would do little by itself to achieve economic security. A disproportionately high percentage of the departed fathers and husbands were, and are still, poor.

TABLE 6.2 Absence of the Wife, by Income Class (1969)

Income class	Percentage of Married Men* With Wife No Longer Present
Under $3,000	21.0
$3,000-5,999	10.3
$6,000-9,999	5.6
$10,000 and over	3.5
All classes	7.4

*Aged 25 to 64.
Source: U.S. Bureau of the Census.

The essence of the Moynihan Report, then, is best described in a dynamic setting.[2] Continued economic deprivation is likely to undermine a family's stability. At some point, the family unit is ruptured, and the female-headed

---

[2] Moynihan himself must bear much of the blame for not drawing attention to the dynamics of his thesis. He was too willing to let controversy and public attention focus on the passages quoted earlier.

family is left to fend for itself. No loss of economic status is necessarily implied by the departure of the father, especially where he was unemployed and/or the female-headed unit turned to public assistance. While at any point in time a high proportion of poor families will be female-headed, family breakup cannot be identified as a major cause of poverty. Family disunity may help sustain poverty, but in most cases it appears that poverty preceded, and itself helped to cause, family dissolution.

This conclusion does not necessitate a purely economic-deterministic view of family relations. Clearly, not all divorces and separations are occasioned by financial stress. Family dissolutions will continue to take place even after all families are assured economic security. The point is that a disproportionately high percentage of family breakups occurs among the poor due to economic stress and that relatively few broken poor families were decidedly nonpoor before family dissolution occurred.

SUMMARY

Large families and broken families are among the most salient characteristics of the poor. Over 40 percent of all the poor are in families with at least five members, while one-fourth of the poor are in broken families; many of the latter are also from large families. Accordingly, there exists a strong presumption that family size and status are important causes of poverty. However, the presumed causal significance of family size and status does not fare well upon closer examination. For most of the families in question, poverty prevailed before the family either grew larger or broke up. Moreover, economic insecurity itself may have contributed to the dissolution of the family or to excessive reproduction. Hence, stronger causality appears to flow from poverty to family size and status than in the opposite direction.

Some families do fall into poverty as a result of the burdens of additional children or an absent parent, but the number appears to be small. Family breakup and growth are more likely to extend and deepen a family's poverty than bring it about. Efforts to increase the economic opportunities of the poor should promote greater family stability and smaller family size. At the same time, direct efforts to make birth control available to the poor will do much to alleviate present poverty and retard its intergenerational transmission.

REFERENCES

On Family Size

LEVITAN, SAR A., "Programs in Aid of the Poor," in *Poverty in America*, L. Ferman, J. Kornbluh, and A. Haber, eds. Ann Arbor: University of Michigan Press, 1968.

MAY, EDGAR, *The Wasted Americans*. New York: Harper & Row, Publishers, 1964, Ch. 8.

PODELL, LAWRENCE, *Families on Welfare in New York City*. New York: City University of New York Press, 1968.

SHEPPARD, HAROLD L., *Effects of Family Planning on Poverty in the United States*. Upjohn Institute, 1967.

SHOSTAK, ARTHUR, "Birth Control and Poverty", in *New Perspectives on Poverty*, Arthur Shostak and William Gomberg, eds. Englewood Cliffs, N.J.: Prentice-Hall, Inc., 1965.

On Family Status

CARPER, LAURA, "The Negro Family and the Moynihan Report," in *Poverty: Views from the Left*, Jeremy Larner and Irving Howe, eds. New York: William Morrow & Co., Inc., 1968.

FERMAN, LOUIS ET. AL., eds., *Negroes and Jobs*, foreword by A. Philip Randolph and article by Harold Sheppard and Herbert Striner. Ann Arbor: The University of Michigan Press, 1968.

FRAZIER, E. FRANKLIN, *The Negro in the United States*. New York: The Macmillan Company, 1957, Chs. 13 and 24.

LIEBOW, ELLIOT, *Tally's Corner: A Study of Negro Streetcorner Men*. Boston: Little, Brown and Company, 1967.

RAINWATER, LEE and WM. L. YANCEY, *The Moynihan Report and the Politics of Controversy*. Cambridge, Mass.: The M.I.T. Press, 1967.

7 Culture and Race

The issues of culture and race are closely linked to the demographic characteristics of family size and status. Some people detect in the marital status of the poor a distinctly racial phenomenon. Other observers have argued that the poor have an overpowering desire to bear children and that this cultural trait maintains their poverty. These particular allegations are part of broader theories about the racial and cultural potential of the poor. The most familiar theories are that the poor lack initiative and aspirations and that the blacks among the poor are inherently less able. Both theories offer still more "explanations" for the persistence of poverty.

The theory of inherent racial inferiority has fallen into distinct disfavor in recent years. Nevertheless, it still influences thinking on the subjects of poverty and education and continues to appear, albeit in more subtle forms. The theory of cultural inferiority—more objective exponents speak of cultural "differences"—still commands broad acceptance and is examined first.

THE "CULTURE OF POVERTY"

In colonial America, poverty was regarded as the manifestation of vice and sin. Because everyone except Negro slaves was thought to enjoy the opportunity to acquire economic security by his own labor, those who did not attain such security were deemed to be morally flawed. Poverty thus became proof of moral bankruptcy, and the poor were treated accordingly. In Pennsylvania, paupers had the shoulders of their right sleeves adorned with the letter *P*, to warn off unsuspecting strangers. In other jurisdictions, the poor were sent packing, sometimes having first been chastened with a public whipping. As the puritanical Humane Society summarized the situation in 1809: . . . "by a just and inflexible law of Providence, misery is ordained to be the companion and punishment of vice."[1]

In more modern times, the theoretical conjunction of poverty and sin has not fared well. There now exists a general reluctance to ascribe the misery of the poor to the laws of Providence. Nevertheless, belief in the universality of economic opportunity remains firmly embedded in the American consciousness. Accordingly, there is need for a substitute explanation to account for the persistence of poverty in a land of abundance and opportunity. This, in part, explains the ascendency of cultural theories of poverty. To formulate a cultural theory of poverty causation is to assert that the poor lack sufficient desire and motivation to escape poverty. It is to allege that the goal of economic security is of lesser importance in the value matrix of the poor. By this hypothesis, the poor are impoverished because their "culture" prevents them from taking advantage of opportunities to escape poverty.

If the poor are culturally bound to poverty, then the task of eliminating poverty becomes infinitely more difficult and time-consuming. Public efforts must be directed toward changing attitudes and environments with programs like the Job Corps, rather than simply toward changing opportunities. Communication between poor and nonpoor groups will also be more difficult, with interclass tension and anxiety the likely results. Hence, the culture of poverty thesis cannot be dismissed lightly.

A completely satisfactory definition of *culture* is not easy to come by. Nevertheless, for the purposes of this inquiry, we may understand culture to refer to the norms, values, and aspirations of an individual or group. These components of culture are not observable, however. Only behavioral traits of individuals and groups are observable; from these we must infer underlying aspirations and values. This means that the assertion of distinct cultural attributes among the poor is largely founded on observations of distinct behavioral patterns. The assertion, however, is vulnerable to criticism, since not all behavioral differences reflect cultural differences. Even persons with identical norms and aspirations may behave differently in different situations. Our task is to determine how legitimate the inferential reasoning is that underlies the cultural hypothesis.

Consider the case of a welfare recipient who declines what appears to be a reasonable job offer. For many middle-class observers, such a rejection constitutes incontrovertible proof that the recipient lacks normal initiative, aspirations, and goals—clear evidence of a culture of poverty. Middle-class individuals, it is argued, would never reject an offer to improve their economic status, especially in the dire financial straits of the welfare recipient. The accusation can be challenged, however; it is possible that the rejection of

---

[1] Cited by Paul Jacobs in Jeremy Larner and Irving Howe, eds., *Poverty: Views from the Left* (New York: William Morrow & Company, Inc., 1968), p. 40.

employment opportunities reflects other circumstances not readily apparent to the nonpoor observer. The job offer itself may, of course, be inherently unattractive and provide no economic advancement, but the rejection may also be based on public welfare policy. If it is difficult and time-consuming to obtain public welfare assistance, then the individual who leaves the welfare rolls for employment incurs a distinct risk. If the job proves to be unsatisfactory or temporary, then he and his family are left without any financial support while he awaits a new job or more welfare. For families at the margin of impoverishment and confronting largely transitory kinds of jobs, such a risk may be unwarranted. Thus, the job rejection may proceed not from different values and aspirations but from tangible behavioral constraints.

The culture of poverty hypothesis, then, requires rather stringent evidence. It must be shown that the norms and aspirations—not necessarily or exclusively the behavior—of the poor are different and that these differences impede escape from poverty. It should also be shown whether and to what degree such differences would disappear under changing socioeconomic circumstances.

Oscar Lewis is the most familiar and forceful proponent of the culture of poverty thesis. His observations of lifestyles among the poor convinced him that the behavior patterns of the poor are different and that these differences reflect distinct values. Although his empirical research was confined largely to Mexico and Puerto Rico, he believed that these differences transcend national boundaries. He offered the following explanation for the perpetuation of poverty:

> Once [the culture of poverty] comes into existence it tends to perpetuate itself from generation to generation because of its effect on the children. By the time slum children are age six or seven they have usually absorbed the basic values and attitudes of their subculture and are not psychologically geared to take full advantage of changing conditions or increased opportunities which may occur in their lifetime.[2]

From Lewis's perspective, then, the poor are clearly prolonging their own impoverishment. As evidence, he claims to have identified no less than 70 behavioral traits, including little use of banks or museums and nonparticipation in labor unions, that distinguish the poor. Although he acknowledges that the poor may be aware of, and even profess, middle-class values, he regards their aberrant behavior as proof that they do not share those values.

Other sociologists and anthropologists have been quick to follow Lewis's lead. Another popular diagnosis of the poor, for example, focuses on their alleged self-indulgence. Out of Lewis's more general depiction of lower-class culture, other observers claim to perceive a pattern of nondeferred gratification: whereas the middle-class person supposedly feels the need and desire to save, postpone, and renounce certain immediate pleasures, the poor person is alleged

[2] Oscar Lewis, *La Vida* (New York: Random House, Inc., 1966), p. xiv.

to experience no such motivations. This alleged impulse following is presumed to be embedded in the personality dynamics of the poor individual, thus obstructing his self-improvement.

This pattern of self-indulgence is additionally presumed to have strong intergenerational effects. Self-indulgent parents have little interest in their children's futures, thus contributing to further poverty. As one observer has asserted:

> Where middle and upper class parents think in terms of a college education for their offspring, lower class parents' aspirations usually stop at a high school diploma, at the very best. Poor parents, with little education, are more likely to believe in luck than in education and to be contemptuous of "book learning". . . Indeed, among low-income families, both the low educational attainments of the head of the household and the quality of family life create a social environment that leads the poor to believe that "education is not for them."[3]

Not all sociologists, of course, share these views of lower-class culture. On the contrary, much recent sociological discussion has focused on some of the basic weaknesses in the culture of poverty thesis. It has been pointed out, for example, that the attribution of cultural differences based on the observation of behavioral differences incorporates many assumptions of questionable validity. Within the subject area of deferred gratification, the following conditions must be fulfilled before a valid inference about differential values can be made:

1. The satisfaction being deferred must be equally important to the poor and nonpoor;
2. There must exist equal opportunity to defer the satisfaction;
3. The poor and nonpoor must equally suffer from deferment; and
4. The probability of obtaining gratification at the end of the deferment period must be equal for both groups.

If any or all of these conditions are violated, then behavioral differences may be explained by situational differences; no reference to alleged cultural phenomena is necessary.

The case of educational attainment illustrates some of the above conditions. The children of the poor undeniably drop out of school earlier than other children, but does this behavioral difference reflect cultural orientations? Schools in lower-income areas are notoriously ill-equipped to transmit interest, enjoyment, or ability in the learning process. Hence, the third and fourth conditions in our list are violated: middle-class school experience is both more pleasant and more profitable. Furthermore, the low-income family cannot afford to support a child's education for as long as a middle-class family: thus, the second condition is violated also. Given these inequalities in opportunity, it

[3] Oscar Ornati, *Poverty Amid Affluence* (New York: The Twentieth Century Fund, 1966), p. 66.

might be equally valid to conclude that the poor value education more highly than the nonpoor because of the greater sacrifices they make to get as far as they do.

A similar array of qualifications to the "impulse following" hypothesis is encountered when saving behavior is considered. The poor save less money less often than the nonpoor. Does this reflect a present-time orientation (as contrasted with a future-time orientation)? Presumably not. The poor have very little to save in the first place. Whatever they do manage to put aside represents a real sacrifice in terms of present consumption. Hence, there is no foundation for inferring cultural inadequacies on the basis of observed differences in spending.

The central weakness of the culture of poverty proposition, then, is the assumption that behavioral differences between the poor and nonpoor reflect differences in goals and aspirations. In reality, the poor do not have an equal opportunity to fulfill, or even to pursue, their goals. Hence, there is a sharp divergence between the aspirations and the behavior of the poor that does not exist among middle-class groups. With more equal opportunities for achievement, there is a strong presumption that the entire foundation of the culture of poverty thesis would disintegrate. At the very least, we may say that the cultural thesis rests on a very uncertain foundation until that equality of opportunity is fully achieved.

If testimony of the poor themselves is valid, there is little reason to believe that behavioral patterns of the poor will remain the same under improved socioeconomic conditions. Welfare mothers, for example, express a strong desire to see their children attain better social and economic positions. Moreover, they perceive clearly—more so than many academic observers—the great divergence between their aspirations and their actual opportunities. One survey, for example, questioned welfare mothers about both their desires and their expectations for their children's employment. The responses, portrayed in Table 7.1, are illuminating. Seventy percent of the mothers have white-collar aspirations for their eldest child, yet only 46 percent have any expectation that

TABLE 7.1 Welfare Mothers' Desires and Expectations For Eldest Child's Occupational Status (in percentages)

Occupation	Desire	Expectation
Professional and managerial	48	27
Clerical	22	19
Craft	8	8
Police, army	2	6
Other paid work	6	14
Housewife	1	4
Don't know	13	23

Source: Lawrence Podell, *Families on Welfare in New York City* (New York: City University of New York, 1968), Tables 7-C and 7-D.

their children will attain this status. (Even fewer actually do.) Hence, the lower occupational status of poor children apparently does not reflect their parents' aspirations so much as it reflects the opportunities of the poor.

If their aspirations and values were really as different as some observers claim, then the poor should be satisfied with their standard of living and resistant to new opportunity. Many modern cultural theorists argue, in fact, that the poor are content and unable to progress. (Similar arguments were once employed in defense of slavery.) Such views are not consistent with reality. Not only have organized groups of the poor repeatedly expressed their discontent, but the poor have demonstrated a marked ability to move out of poverty when economic opportunities improved. (See Chapter 2 concerning the period 1963-1969.)

Even the most adamant exponents of the culture of poverty do not argue, of course, that all persons in poverty are psychodynamically attached to impoverishment. Oscar Lewis himself estimated that only 20 percent of the poor in America are culturally bound to poverty. Walter Miller, another advocate of the culture of poverty position, does not specify what proportion of the poor are so afflicted but warns that the proportion is rising. Nevertheless, the basis for these propositions is no stronger than that for the rest of the theory.

Among the 25 million people who were poor in 1970, there were, no doubt, some individuals whose aspirations were extraordinarily low. Many may even have succumbed to a fatalistic attitude regarding their condition and future prospects, thus diminishing their ability to exploit new opportunities. It cannot be assumed, however, that this fatalism emerged from a cultural orientation rather than an unpromising situation or that this apparent fatalism is totally impervious to changing circumstances. Yet it is on these assumptions that the culture of poverty theory rests. To the extent that some of the poor do believe their chances for advancement to be negligible, new opportunities will be grasped with hesitancy. The more the poor have experienced repeated failure and disappointment, the more skeptically they will respond to new policy initiatives. This does not imply cultural dissonance; it may very well be a rational response based on prior experience.

RACE

Poor blacks are apt to appear particularly constrained by "cultural" patterns. They have been extended more new promises more often than any other group among the poor. Some promises of improved opportunity were well-intentioned, others were not; most remain unfulfilled. Many poor blacks respond accordingly—with cynicism and hesitancy—when still further promises and programs are offered. Unfortunately, whites tend to regard this absence of unbridled enthusiasm as additional evidence that blacks lack aspiration. But a distinctive cultural pattern is not the only explanation offered to explain black poverty by those who view previous policy initiatives and present opportunities to be ample, even generous. In addition to the culture allegation, many whites continue to regard the inferior socioeconomic position of blacks as a natural consequence of racial disabilities. In this section, the nature and basis of such racially based perspectives are examined.

In 1970, median family income among black Americans was $6,279, while among white Americans the median was $10,236. As we have already seen, nearly one out of every three blacks was poor, while only one out of ten whites was so disadvantaged. Hence, there is no question about whether a link exists between race and poverty; instead, we are concerned with the causal nature of the established link. Furthermore, in discussing the causal association between race and poverty, we need not worry about the circular kinds of relationships that attracted our attention earlier. Whereas poverty may lead to ill health, broken families, or more children, there is no prospect of poverty changing people's skin color. Accordingly, both the existence of a link and the direction of causality are known: being black does lead to poverty.

The causal path leading from race to poverty may be explained in two ways. It can be argued that inherent racial disabilities limit income-earning abilities. This, of course is the racial argument that has arisen before. Another possible explanation for the established path emanates from the alleged existence of discrimination. By this argument, blacks are more apt to be poor, not because of differential physical, mental, or cultural capacities, but because they are treated differently by society. Whites have no difficulty in choosing between the alternative explanations of black status: the president's National Advisory Commission on Civil Disorders discovered that white Americans favor the racial explanation three to one. Accordingly, we postpone a discussion of the discrimination argument until Chapters 9 and 10.

The thesis of racial inferiority is not new. Aristotle, for example, used it to explain the superiority of the Greeks over the European barbarians. Still later, the barbarians, who by then had produced Shakespeare, Kant, and Newton, used this argument to explain their superiority over the Greeks. Later still, English intellectuals were predicting that America would never achieve greatness because its colonies were heavily populated by the rejected and inferior classes of Europe.

Despite the somewhat dismal record of racial theories, they remain popular. Among those who adhere to a primarily racial explanation of black socioeconomic status in America is Dr. William Shockley. Dr. Shockley is an inventor of the transistor and a recipient of the Nobel Prize in physics. As he explained to the National Academy of Sciences in 1969: "The major deficit in Negro intellectual performance must be primarily of hereditary origin and thus relatively irremediable by practical improvements in the environment." In other words, blacks are poor because they are not smart enough, and they are not smart enough due to racial heredity.

Professor Shockley is a rather extreme adherent to the racial inferiority thesis, but he is not alone in his beliefs about innate racial differences. Such beliefs are a common component of racial prejudice and linger on in the minds of many. They even acquire a certain plausibility for most people because of the demonstrated link between genetic characteristics and achievement: nearly everyone accepts the notion that smarter people do better and get further. Such a notion leads easily to the position that blacks fare poorly because they are not as smart as whites.

The significance of genetic characteristics for *individual* attainment is rarely challenged. It has been demonstrated that inherited abilities do influence achievements, regardless of environmental circumstances. Identical twins, for example, have exactly the same genetic characteristics, including intelligence. A study by English sociologists determined that even when they are separated and reared in different environments, identical twins attain very similar socio-economic statuses. Such observations confirm the significance of inherited abilities. To demonstrate that genetic abilities are important does not deny the existence of environmental influences, however. In the studies of English twins, varying environments were shown to have some effect on achievement. Those effects would be still stronger where environmental differences were greater. The Osage Indians in America provide a dramatic illustration: not only achievements, but even measured IQ, increased substantially after the tribe discovered oil!

A broader understanding of human achievement recognizes that both genetic and environmental factors influence the attainments of individuals and puts the issue of racial differences in an entirely different setting. Because blacks and whites in America live in distinct areas and under different conditions, racial abilities alone cannot explain disparities in economic status. To the extent that differences in racial abilities exist at all, we are led to inquire what *proportion* of observed status disparities can be attributed to them. In logical order, then, we must focus on three separate questions:

1. Do genetic differences exist between whites and blacks?
2. If so, how large are any such differences?
3. What is the relative significance of any such differences for observed socioeconomic status?

Very little interest attaches to the question of physical differences between whites and blacks, at least as far as socioeconomic status is involved. Instead, the issue of genetic differences focuses on the relative mental abilities of the two races. The first question, then, really asks whether or not whites are innately more intelligent than blacks.

IQ Scores and Intelligence

The most commonly accepted measure of one's intelligence is his score on an IQ test. The IQ score indicates how well an individual has performed on a standardized test relative to others of the same age. An IQ score of 100 indicates that one has performed up to average, while higher or lower scores indicate above or below average performance. There are a variety of such tests available, but all incorporate exercises of perceptual, verbal, arithmetical, and reasoning abilities.

Since the nineteenth century, there have been literally hundreds of research studies directed towards measuring the relative IQs of blacks and whites. All of them have demonstrated that blacks, on average, score lower on intelligence tests than whites. The average difference between whites and blacks amounts to 15 to 20 IQ points, indicating that the typical black has an IQ of 80 to 85. These figures are now widely accepted; what is still debated is how they should be interpreted.

Basically, an IQ test measures various kinds of performance abilities, such as perception, memory, and verbal knowledge. Accordingly, it is subject to the influences of both genetic intelligence and environmental experience. A child who has never seen a giraffe or a waterfall, for example, has difficulty identifying them in an IQ examination, whatever his native intelligence may be. Because IQ scores incorporate both environmental and genetic experiences, there is no easy method for isolating genetic factors. All we can say with assurance is that IQ differences reflect genetic differences when administered to children who have shared very similar environmental experiences. Clearly, black and white children do not satisfy this condition.

The nature of IQ-score determinants suggests that black and white IQ scores could be brought into harmony by appropriate environmental changes. In fact, studies that have attempted to control for such differences by testing black and white children from similar backgrounds have narrowed the average IQ score difference to as little as five points. Other research has demonstrated that the IQ test performances of blacks and whites move further apart the longer they are maintained in unequal situations—ghetto schools, for example. Accordingly, we may conclude that there is nothing natural or unchangeable in any observed racial pattern of IQ scores.

Further evidence of environmental impact on IQ scores is provided by the variation in these scores for individuals and groups. We have already noted the effect of oil discoveries for the Osage Indians. For the country as a whole, IQ scores have been rising consistently over the last 50 years. This suggests either that we are breeding selectively or that IQ scores are subject to environmental improvement (and perhaps even familiarity with testing procedures). More to our point, it has also been observed that black children moving from rural to urban areas raise their IQ scores significantly, reflecting an improved environment. Still other studies have shown that intensive teaching and supportive environments can materially improve the IQ scores of any group, even mentally retarded children! And finally, it has been demonstrated that improving the diets of poor expectant mothers results in higher IQ scores for their children.

Resolving the Issues

These observations about the nature of IQ scores allow us to answer the three questions listed before. First of all, we may note that there is no basis for concluding that there exist genetic differences in intelligence between blacks and whites. This conclusion emerges from the fact that we do not really know what intelligence is and from the observation that the test scores we use to measure intelligence are themselves subject to environmental influence. We could just as easily assert that blacks are more intelligent than whites as the reverse. In the absence of any evidence to the contrary, it seems most reasonable to conclude that there are no such genetic differences between the two racial groups.

Even if one were to adhere adamantly to the position that IQ scores accurately reflect intelligence, there would still be little basis for attributing the inferior economic status of blacks to genetic deficiencies. At most, such an argument would have to rely on the average IQ score difference of five to ten points obtained in controlled tests. It would be extremely difficult, if not outright comic, to suggest that this difference could account for an existing income disparity of nearly $4,000 a year. One would then be arguing that a 5 or 10 percent difference in intelligence could account for a 40 percent disparity in income. Hence, even the unfounded assertion that genetic differences do exist between blacks and whites leads to the conclusion that such differences are of relatively minor significance for observed socioeconomic status.

Other Weaknesses of the Racial Doctrine

The foregoing observations demonstrate the essential weaknesses in the doctrine of racial inferiority. The evidence presented has been rather technical, but there are even simpler inconsistencies in the doctrine that discredit racial theories of black poverty. To begin with, blacks do not fare equally well or poorly in all regions of the country. For the nation as a whole, black incomes in 1970 were 61 percent as large as white incomes. In the South, however, they were only 52 percent as large, while in the West, they were 80 percent. Hence, to argue that genetic disabilities account for status disparities would require one to argue that western blacks are genetically better equipped than southern blacks.

A similar problem arises with the rise in black status over time. In the last ten years, black incomes have risen considerably relative to white incomes. A theory of racial determination would be compelled to explain this development on the basis of improving genetic abilities among blacks or declining genetic potential among whites.

Finally, and most damaging to the doctrine of racial superiority, is the concept of *race* itself. There is not, and never has been, a clear understanding of what the term race means, or for that matter, of how many races exist. As an English zoologist has noted, "geneticists believe anthropologists know what a race is, ethnologists assume their racial classifications are backed up by genetics, and politicians believe that their prejudices have the sanction of both genetics and anthropology."[4] In the resultant confusion, anywhere from three to thirty separate races have been identified at various times. In the American context, the term is used interchangeably to refer to religious, national, or ethnic groups. In the context of the immediate discussion, the term refers basically to skin color. Given the history of miscegenation in America, no one could conceivably argue that there exist distinctive pure white and black genetic characteristics: it is estimated that over 90 percent of American blacks have some white ancestry. Hence, American blacks hardly comprise a suitable test for racial theories of inherent differences.

Interestingly enough, adherents to the racial doctrine have attempted to employ this phenomenon of miscegenation to their advantage. They argue that the success of mulattos is due to the presence of "white" genes, which improve their intellectual endowments, and that such success proves the thesis of racial superiority. The argument is also used to explain rising black status over time. The evidence presented, however, is exceedingly weak. Mulattos apparently did fare relatively better than "pure" blacks during and shortly after the slave era, but children of mixed parentage were often favored by their white father-masters. Thus, they received greater opportunity and support. Other research has shown that more successful blacks today do not differ in patterns of white ancestry. Moreover, the highest black IQ score yet reported, 200, was attained by a child who had no traceable white heritage whatsoever. Hence, whatever the other virtues and liabilities of miscegenation may be, its effects on genetic abilities appear to be negligible.

SUMMARY

Theories of poverty causation based on cultural or racial phenomena have long commanded a certain acceptability. In part, they are based on prejudices of the nonpoor against the poor and, in part, on the confidence with which the nonpoor perceive economic opportunity to exist for all. Since the earliest days of colonization, it has been asserted that anyone with enough stamina and initiative could succeed in America. Accordingly, those who did not succeed have been regarded variously as immoral, culturally apart, or racially inferior. This chapter has considered the latter two allegations and examined the direct evidence on which they are based.

The argument that the poor do not possess aspiration and initiative enough to raise themselves out of poverty rests on misconceptions rather than factual evidence. Divergent behavioral patterns, in themselves, do not prove the

[4] Anthony Smith, *The Body* (New York: Walker and Company, 1968), p. 14.

existence of divergent aspirations and goals; instead, they may well represent rational responses to continuing inopportune circumstances. Hence, the sometimes different behavior of the poor, in the areas of saving, education, and job acquisition, for example, may reflect great aspirations equally as well as it does few aspirations. Direct research on the goals and ambitions of the poor suggests that they share middle-class goals and await improved opportunities to pursue them.

Allegations about racial disabilities suffer equally from misconception and prejudice. There is no basis for concluding that differences in intelligence exist between whites and blacks. Not only do we not yet know what intelligence is, but the instruments we assume to measure it yield ambiguous results. Moreover, even the most extreme assumptions about the meaning and reliability of observed IQ scores would still lead to the conclusion that genetic factors are of negligible significance in explaining the existing economic disparities between whites and blacks.

REFERENCES

On Culture

FERMAN, LOUIS, JOYCE L. KORNBLUH, and ALAN HABER, eds., *Poverty in America.* Ann Arbor: University of Michigan Press, 1968.

LARNER, JEREMY and IRVING HOWE, *Poverty: Views from the Left,* William Morrow & Co., Inc., 1968.

LIEBOW, ELLIOT, *Tally's Corner: A Study of Negro Streetcorner Men.* Boston: Little, Brown and Company, 1967.

MAY, EDGAR, *The Wasted Americans.* New York: Harper & Row, Publishers, 1964, Ch. 1.

MOYNIHAN, DANIEL P., ed., *On Understanding Poverty.* New York: Basic Books, Inc., 1969.

ORNATI, OSCAR, *Poverty Amid Affluence.* New York: The Twentieth Century Fund, 1966, Ch. 8.

WINTER, J. ALAN, ed., *The Poor: A Culture of Poverty or a Poverty of Culture.* Grand Rapids, Mich.: Wm. B. Eerdmans Publishing Co., 1971.

On Race

CARTWRIGHT, WALTER J. and THOMAS R. BURTIS, "Race and Intelligence: Changing Opinions in Social Science," *Social Science Quarterly,* December, 1968, pp. 603-18.

HARVARD EDUCATIONAL REVIEW, Winter, Spring, and Summer issues, 1969.

HUNT, MORTON, "The Intelligent Man's Guide to Intelligence," *Playboy,* November, 1970, p. 94 passim.

HURLEY, RODGER, *Poverty & Mental Retardation: A Causal Relationship.* Trenton, N.J.: New Jersey Department of Institutions and Agencies, April, 1968, Ch. 1.

INSTITUTE FOR SOCIAL RESEARCH, *Racial Attitudes in Fifteen American Cities.* Ann Arbor: University of Michigan Press, 1968.

MYRDAL, GUNNAR, *An American Dilemma.* New York: Harper & Row, Publishers, 1962, Chs. 4-6.

SMITH, ANTHONY, *The Body.* New York: Walker and Company, 1968, Ch. 2.

8 Education and Ability

The empirical relationship between education and ability on the one hand and economic status on the other are essential components of American folklore. In fact, the observations that "to get ahead, get an education" and "you can't keep a good man down" have acquired the aura of ideological convictions. Everyone has heard of Horatio Alger, and no one doubts that doctors get rich. Conditioned by these examples and mindful of their own security, Americans react accordingly. Middle-class parents begin preparing their children for college soon after birth, and the children themselves learn to regard success as the reward to virtue, ability, and good grades in school. By the same token, those who do not succeed are regarded as less virtuous, less able, or less diligent in the pursuit of education. From this perspective, lack of ability or education emerges as an important cause of poverty. The distribution of poverty even acquires a democratic flavor, since it is also presumed that the development of abilities and education is largely a matter of individual choice.

The conviction that education and ability lead to material success is not easily challenged, and few persons even pause to reflect on the nature and reliability of the underlying associations. With educated people moving ahead all around them, how many individuals can take the time and effort to question the pace of events? Nevertheless, the implied importance of education for the existence of poverty demands that such an inquiry be made. Our discussion focuses on two issues: (1) does educational achievement determine *who* is poor; and (2) does the level of educational achievement determine *how many* people are poor. The same questions are asked of the relationship between ability and poverty.

EDUCATION AND INCOME

The conviction that more education leads to higher income finds extensive support in statistical data. The simple correlation between educational attainment and income is very strong and consistent: more years of education *do* lead to higher income. In 1970, for example, men with no more than eight years of schooling had an average income of only $5,200; high school dropouts commanded an average of $7,600; high school graduates had incomes of $9,200; and college graduates had average incomes above $14,400. Hence, there is an impressive foundation to the belief that education pays.

The relationship between education and income is equally effective in separating the poor from the nonpoor. The typical nonpoor family head has a high school diploma, while the average poor family head has completed fewer than nine years of school. This disparity in educational attainment is reflected in the incidence of poverty. As Table 8.1 confirms, the likelihood of impoverishment declines rapidly as a person scales the educational ladder. Only one out of fifty college graduates was in poverty in 1970, while more than one out of ten high school dropouts were so misfortuned.

TABLE 8.1 Incidence of Poverty, by Education of Head of Family, 1970

Education	Number in Poverty	Incidence of Poverty
Elementary school	2,426,000	19.2%
High school dropout	940,000	11.7
High school graduate	889,000	5.8
College dropout	241,000	4.5
College graduate	137,000	2.0

Source: U. S. Bureau of the Census.

Higher educational attainment contributes to income in several ways: it increases a person's productivity by expanding his knowledge and skills, and prospective employers tend to regard it as indicative of commendable diligence. Diplomas, regardless of their content, are likely to provide access to more jobs. Educational institutions may also serve as job placement services, providing employers and students with ready access to each other. The combination of these factors suggests that the person who stays in school longer will be treated and will perform differently in the labor market. Educational attainment affects every facet of labor market success. A person's participation in the labor force, his occupation, the frequency of his employment, the number of hours he works, and the wage rate he receives, are all affected by the schooling he has achieved. In conjunction, these factors determine an individual's income.

A person with little education is least likely to get and hold a job. If he does obtain a job, he is first to be laid off by his employer as production schedules change. With fewer skills and credentials, his ability to acquire other jobs will be restricted. Consequently, he is apt to be unemployed far more often and for longer periods than those with greater educational attainments. In 1970-71, male high school dropouts experienced a 8.0 unemployment rate,

TABLE 8.2   Education and the Labor Market*

	High School Dropouts	High School Graduates	College Graduates
Unemployment rates	8.0%	5.0%	2.0%
Labor force participation	83.5	90.1	89.8
Full-time workers	76.9	83.9	89.2
Occupational status	Blue collar	Clerical	Professional
Average Incomes	$7,600	$9,200	$14,400

*For all males 16 years or older and out of school, 1970.
Source: U.S. Department of Labor.

while high school and college graduates confronted unemployment rates of 5.0 and 2.0, respectively.

As was noted in Chapter 3, long and repeated spells of unemployment may induce a person to leave the labor force altogether. Frustrated by lack of employment opportunities, he may give up the job search, relying instead on public or private financial assistance. Few men can, however, resign themselves to nonparticipation, in part because available social and financial supports are extremely limited. Nevertheless, the impact of educational attainment is discernible in the relevant statistics. Whereas 90 percent of all male high school and college graduates participate in the labor force, only 83 percent of high school dropouts do so.

Getting and holding a job does not guarantee financial success, of course. At least as important are the nature of the job one obtains, how many hours he works, and what wage he is paid. On all these fronts, the less educated individual fares poorly. High school dropouts are disproportionately concentrated in the blue-collar occupations as unskilled laborers, operatives, service workers, and craftsmen. By contrast, high school graduates are most heavily concentrated in the lower white-collar occupations, at the clerical and sales levels, for example, and in the higher blue-collar positions. College graduates crowd the professional and managerial classes and are virtually nonexistent in the lowest job categories.

The cumulative impact of these labor market phenomena is to differentiate sharply the incomes of the lesser- and greater-educated. As we have already noted, the income differences amount to thousands of dollars a year. Over a lifetime, this disparity reaches tremendous proportions. During their careers, high school graduates can anticipate earning $50,000 more than high school dropouts, while college graduates will earn $150,000 more than high school graduates before they retire.

Education and the Distribution of Poverty

The weight of accumulated evidence on the association between income and education reinforces the belief that inadequate education is a major cause of poverty. It appears obvious, at this point, that the least educated will receive the least income. Before fully accepting this interpretation, however, several additional issues must be considered.

Even if, on average, better educated individuals earn more money, it does not follow that *all* persons with more schooling will have higher incomes, for the simple reason that education is not the *only* determinant of income. Inherent ability, inherited wealth, geographical location, discrimination, economic conditions, and simple luck will all influence a person's income opportunities. Hence, we want to determine how consistent the relationship is between education and income and how much poverty can be explained by education alone.

The relationship between education and income is far from perfect. Indeed, the labor market rewards the educational attainments of some people much more handsomely than the attainments of others. Consider Figure 8.1, for

FIGURE 8.1 Mean Incomes of Males Twenty-five Years of Age and Over, by Educational Attainment, by Race—1969 (Source: U.S. Bureau of the Census)

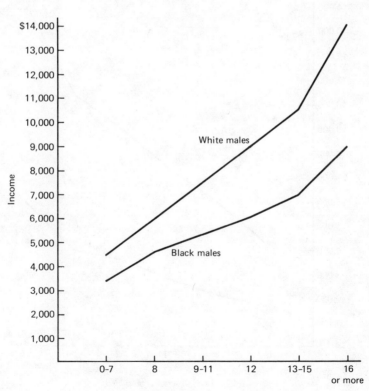

example: each step up the educational ladder clearly improves the incomes of both blacks and whites. Even more striking, however, is the gross disparity shown on the graphs that exists between white and black males. A black college graduate, for example, earns on average no more ($9,030) than a white high school graduate ($9,032); while a white high school dropout earns considerably more ($7,539) than a black high school graduate (6,122). Whatever benefits education provides, they are clearly not equally accessible to all. Hence, if lack of education is regarded as an explanation for poverty, it must be recognized at the outset that that explanation is not complete.

The same kind of disparity can be observed between men and women (see figure 8.2). Women college graduates earn only slightly more ($5,984) than men who complete just eight years of school ($5,809). Moreover, the average male high school dropout commands an income ($7,279), not only higher than nearly all groups of women, but on a par with the incomes of women who have

FIGURE 8.2 Mean Incomes, by Educational Attainment, by Sex (Source: U.S. Bureau of the Census)

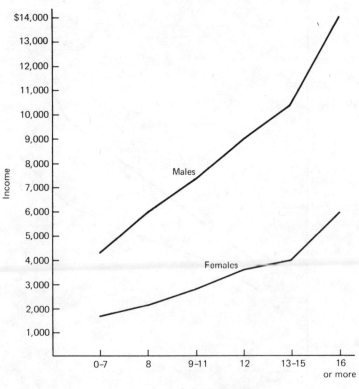

Years of school completed

attended graduate school. Again, it is obvious that the rewards for educational achievement, while perhaps large, are not distributed evenly.

It is not difficult to find explanations for the income disparities that exist between races and sexes. Some of these are discussed more thoroughly in Chapters 9 and 10. For present purposes, we may confine ourselves to the simple observation that more education, in itself, is no guarantee of escaping poverty. Keeping some poor persons in school longer may not effectively raise their incomes. Even in situations where racial or sexual discrimination is not present, the link between education and income is not perfect. There are over a million white high school dropouts, for example, who earn more money than one out of three college graduates. Most surprising is the fact that there are more families in poverty headed by white male high school graduates than white high school dropouts.

Education as a Sorting Device

The full significance of education for the distribution and extent of poverty can be understood only in the framework of the entire labor market. As we have seen, observing the relationship of average incomes to average educational attainments can lead to erroneous impressions about the importance of education. Within the context of any labor market situation there exists a certain quantity of job vacancies and so many prospective employees. When the number of vacancies falls far short of the number of job-seekers, the economy is in a depressed state, and unemployment rates are high. This implies that employers will be able to choose among many applicants in filling any job vacancy. How will the employer proceed? That is, on what basis should he or will he make his selection?

In some cases, the process of selection is comparatively simple. If the job is highly technical, it may be easy to identify the most competent applicants on the basis of tests or prior accomplishments. Or, if the employer or his community are prejudiced, blacks, women, or other groups may be eliminated from further consideration. These persons will gain access to employment only after most others have been hired.

The process of elimination is not always this simple, however. In areas of high unemployment, there are likely to remain a large number of otherwise acceptable applicants. At this juncture, other employment criteria must be utilized. One such criterion—the most important one—is educational attainment. The employer has several reasons for separating the more educated from the less educated in the application process. First, it is assumed that more schooling usually results in greater ability. Then, too, the employer may feel that perseverance in school merits greater opportunity. And finally, educational minimums constitute a cheap and easy means for holding down the time and cost of interviewing.

The effect of these considerations is to transform educational credentials such as a high school diploma into admission tickets for job interviews, especially in times of high unemployment. The recession of 1971 amply illustrated how selective employers can become; consider this help-wanted ad from the Austin, Texas *American*:

> TOPLESS DANCERS. Must have two years college. Prefer English major, languages or humanities.[1]

From the standpoint of this employer, all prospective go-go girls are in competition for available jobs, and educational attainments separate the finalists from the rejects. Other employers are likely to react similarly when jobs are scarce. Hence, even though a high school dropout, for example, could easily perform the responsibilities of, say, a sales clerk, he is not given the opportunity if high school graduates are also available. As a consequence, he remains unemployed and poor.

The implications of this selection process for the relationship of education to poverty are profound. Quite obviously, the distribution of education will have a significant impact on the distribution of poverty. As a rule, those with the least education will end up in poverty. This will be especially true among otherwise similar labor market, racial, and sexual groups. But what about the extent of poverty? Will education have a similar influence in determining how many persons are poor?

Consider again the case of the high school dropout seeking the job of sales clerk. If he had a high school diploma, his competitive position would undoubtedly be stronger, but would his graduation, by itself, contribute to an increase in the number of such jobs available? Clearly not. His graduation may enable him to compete successfully for the available job, but his success will leave someone else unemployed. If there is only one job and four applicants, no amount of educational improvement or redistribution will succeed in leaving fewer than three persons unemployed. Education may influence who gets the available jobs, but the demand for labor will determine how many jobs there are.

Confusion about the causal significance of education comes from the failure to distinguish between individual and group needs, or, as an economist would say, between micro and macro phenomena. Observing that individual incomes are related to educational attainments leads easily to the supposition that raising the educational attainments of all the poor will eliminate poverty. Yet, bestowing a high school diploma, or even a Ph.D., on all the poor will do little to alter the number or kinds of jobs available. A few more vacancies might be filled, but the greatest impact would be to alter the composition of the poor and to raise their educational attainments. By itself, such an effort would do little to reduce the extent of poverty.

The situation with respect to education is very much like the one regarding

[1] Cited in *Playboy*, December 1971, p. 26.

labor unions (see appendix to Chapter 4). On a microeconomic scale, it is surely true that labor union membership would provide escape from poverty for many individuals. To infer from that observation, however, that *all* poor persons could gain economic security via union membership is to indulge in a fallacy of composition. Such a mass expansion of union labor supply would only serve to give union labels to the poor; union wages would plummet. Likewise with education: it may provide an escape for some of the poor, but it will not enable a mass exodus from poverty.

The Content of Education

The foregoing discussion has said nothing about the content of education. Instead, the term has been used to refer to schooling in general. Accordingly, some of the most vital and controversial issues relevant to the education-income nexus have been neglected. Among the more salient of those issues are the questions of how much vocational content should be offered in school curricula and who should provide it. Training in specific skills might be especially valuable to those who are not going to pursue higher education. Greater earning potential could be generated by simply restructuring educational curricula rather than extending them.

Of even greater importance for policy consideration is the question of access to education. Because educational attainments significantly determine who will be poor in any given economic situation, we must also determine who receives the necessary credentials and why. Some consideration of these issues is taken up in Chapters 9 and 10. For the present, we may note that neither the issue of educational content nor of access materially alters the above conclusions. Regardless of what is taught or who it is taught to, education, of itself, can do very little to alter the number of jobs available at any given moment.

ABILITY AND INCOME

Ability, like education, is presumed to be an important determinant of income. In fact, it is generally deemed desirable for the distribution of incomes to reflect the distribution of productive abilities. We are accustomed to thinking that greater ability merits richer rewards and, indeed, that material success manifests ability. It is, of course, possible to question the idea that income *should* reflect ability. Why, for example, should a man who inherits the capacity to learn to steer rockets through space command a higher income than the man who is born with the capacity to learn to drive buses? Are justice and equity any better served when rewards are distributed according to inherited genes rather than according to inherited dollars?

In Chapter 7, we encountered some of the difficulties that engulf discussions of individual ability. The term *ability*, as it is commonly employed, incorporates elements of both innate capacity and developed performance. Accordingly, there is a certain vagueness in the question of whether the income distribution reflects ability distribution. If we mean to refer to innate abilities, then we really have no means for answering the question, because we do not know precisely what innate abilities are or how to measure them. However, if we look only at developed performance, we must recognize that we are departing from the pattern of innate abilities, since all individuals do not share equal opportunity to develop their capacities. Hence, an income distribution based on performance abilities may not meet our standards of equity.

Another problem with the measurement of performance ability is the fact that no single, all-inclusive performance criterion exists. The ability to sing or to run is distributed differently from the ability to solve complex mathematical problems. There are literally hundreds, if not thousands, of varied abilities, all distributed uniquely among the population. It is an impossible task to determine whether incomes accurately reflect even performance ability. At most, one could assert that the distribution of incomes reflects the distribution of abilities valued highly in the marketplace. But even that cautious assertion masks a tautology, since one could then proclaim that *any* income distribution reflects the same thing. Thus, there is no means for determining whether a given income distribution departs from the distribution of abilities. In the face of this impasse, we are accustomed to proceed in reverse. That is, we gauge the distribution of abilities by inference from the distribution of incomes: people with more money are *assumed* to be more able. In this way the income distribution becomes a justification unto itself.

In view of these considerations, it is apparent that we have little basis for assessing objectively the fairness or appropriateness of any existing income distribution. At most, we may simply observe how well the distribution reflects certain specific kinds of attainments or characteristics. We must then resort to our own values to determine how appropriate these criteria are and how equitably they are reflected in incomes. The inherent subjectivity of this approach does not render it impracticable, but it does make consensus difficult.

Two kinds of abilities continue to attract the most attention in discussions of income distributions—measured IQ and educational attainment. IQ is of interest both because it gauges highly valued performance abilities, such as perception and problem solving, and because, despite admonitions to the contrary, it is assumed to reflect innate capacities. Educational attainment is of interest for much the same reasons. Accordingly, we may ask how well the existing income distribution reflects these criteria. Figure 8.3 provides the answer to this question.

The educational, IQ, and income distributions are all depicted in Figure 8.3. One can see, for example, that slightly less than 30 percent of the male population completed just 12 years of school; that somewhat under 10 percent

FIGURE 8.3 Distribution of Income, Education, and IQ for Males Twenty-five Years of Age and Over, 1965 (Source: Lester C. Thurow, *Poverty and Discrimination.* Washington, D.C.: The Brookings Institution, 1969, p. 68)

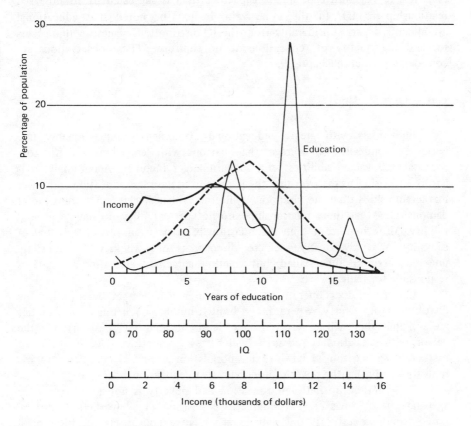

had an income of about $2,000; and that approximately 15 percent had exactly average IQ. One striking impression obtained from the graphs in Figure 8.3 is that the shape of the income distribution is very different from those of the educational and IQ distributions. There is a relatively high concentration of persons in the lower end of the income scale, say under $5,000, while relatively few people are in the lower educational or IQ categories. One way of expressing this disparity is to say that incomes are distributed much less equally than are IQs or educational attainments. Or, one could say that the distribution of poverty is not well explained by the distributions of either IQ or educational achievement.

Some interesting implications follow from Figure 8.3 and our previous discussions of ability and education. We have already suggested that high IQ scores are not equally accessible to all individuals of similar genetic capacity. Black children, for example, have less of an opportunity to develop their capacities into performing abilities. This implies that the income distribution is even less representative of innate capacities than is suggested by its observed relationship to IQ. In the same vein, it may be noted that educational attainments depart considerably from the IQ distribution, suggesting that access to, and the quality of, education are not uniform. These observations are considered further in Chapter 9.

SUMMARY

Individuals with greater educational attainments unquestionably fare better economically, on average, than persons with less education. So, too, persons with valued abilities tend to earn larger incomes. Accordingly, it is hardly surprising to discover that the poor tend to have less education and fewer marketable skills than the nonpoor. While the evidence reviewed in this chapter demonstrates that these relationships are not perfect, they do have a general validity. More important than the question of association, however, is that of causality. What we really seek to discover is not whether the poor are undereducated or underskilled, but whether a lack of education or skills is responsible for their poverty.

Education does operate as a powerful mechanism in determining the distribution of poverty. Where only a limited number of income opportunities are available, they will be reserved on a "least-educated last" basis. That is, the person with educational credentials will have a competitive edge in the labor market, at least within racial or sexual population groups. Hence, there is some basis for attributing the poverty of individuals to educational deficiency.

The relationship between education and poverty is not so simple on an aggregate basis, however. The competitive position of all workers cannot be raised simultaneously; if one individual's relative educational position rises, someone else's falls. Hence, education cannot be a cause of aggregate poverty unless direct links from educational attainments to social productivity to wages can be demonstrated. Such links are plausible but not apparent. Moreover, the close links between education and income are susceptible to another interpretation: in a large and institutionalized labor market, educational credentials provide a convenient and acceptable way of determining relative positions—even if education contributes in no way to job performance. If credentials are widely used for this purpose, general educational improvements will contribute little to reductions in poverty. Lack of education would be a cause of poverty only on an individual, not an aggregate, basis.

The relationship of ability to poverty is also more complex than commonly assumed. Because we lack standard definitions and measurements of ability, there is no firm basis for declaring that the poor are less able. At most, such an observation means only that the poor make less money. Even when confined to measures of performance, such as IQ, we find that the relationship of ability to income is oblique. The distribution of incomes diverges considerably from educational or IQ distributions and even further from the distribution of innate talents.

REFERENCES

BATCHELDER, ALAN B., *The Economics of Poverty*, 2nd ed. New York: John Wiley & Sons, Inc., 1971, Chs. 4 and 5.

BERG, IVAR, *Education and Jobs: The Great Training Robbery*. New York: Frederick A. Praeger, Inc., 1970.

COMMITTEE FOR ECONOMIC DEVELOPMENT, *Raising Low Incomes through Improved Education*. New York: Committee for Economic Development, 1965.

HERRNSTEIN, RICHARD, "I.Q.," *The Atlantic Monthly*, September 1971, pp. 43-64.

LYDALL, HAROLD, *The Structure of Earnings*. New York: Oxford University Press, Inc., Clarendon Press, 1968, Ch. 4.

THUROW, LESTER C., *Poverty and Discrimination*. Washington, D.C.: The Brookings Institution, 1969.

9 Discrimination in Education

Among demographic characteristics, education appears to have a major impact in determining the distribution, if not necessarily the extent, of poverty. Accordingly, any forces that affect the acquisition of educational attainments indirectly determine who will be poor. If access is not equally available to all, then we may not only predict who will be poor, but we may also identify barriers to access as causes of individual poverty.

Barriers to the utilization of an individual's abilities and attainments operate in a similar fashion. To achieve nonpoverty status, an individual must be able to employ his abilities in the labor market. Acquisition of acceptable characteristics alone, then, is no guarantee of escape from poverty. If there exist forces that prevent or limit access to the labor market, then the rewards to demographic achievements are never realized.

Barriers to either the acquisition or utilization of one's demographic characteristics, or, in economic terms, one's human capital, are the subject of this and the following chapter. The discussion in this chapter begins with a consideration of the meaning and nature of "discrimination" and ends with an examination of discriminatory barriers in the educational system. Chapter 10 focuses on discrimination in the labor market.

DISCRIMINATION

The terms *discrimination, prejudice,* and *racism* are widely used in American society today. Seldom do they fail to evoke emotional, often heated, responses. While most people do not always understand what is meant by these concepts, they stand forever ready to deny or proclaim the significance of each. A striking illustration of just how volatile these words can be was provided by the report of the National Advisory Commission on Civil Disorders (the "Riot Commission") in early 1968. In searching for an explanation of the urban strife that was becoming characteristic of American cities, the commission concluded that white racism was a principal source of injustice and unrest. In the reaction that followed, heated exchange took precedence over reasoned debate. Very few white Americans, the President included, were ready to accept the commission's sweeping indictment. White Americans generally felt neither significantly prejudiced nor sufficiently involved in the ghetto to be responsible for the conditions therein.

Much of the misunderstanding revolving around the commission's report is traceable to the oftentimes vague meaning of the term *racism*. For many people, it conveys an impression of aggressively hostile attitudes and behavior, exemplified by their memories of Police Chief "Bull" Conner in Selma, Alabama, or Lester Maddox brandishing an axe handle in Georgia. Relatively few Americans identify easily with such characterizations. Racism, however, may have other meanings. In fact, as used by the commission, the concept transcends the attitudes and behavior of individuals. Instead, the commission's indictment refers to entire patterns of racial interaction and the institutional character of much discrimination.

To approach an understanding of the nature of racism, we may begin by distinguishing between attitudes and actions. People often think differently than they act. As a result, they may adopt patterns of behavior that are injurious to others without consciously wishing to inflict injury. Or, conversely, they may harbor hostile feelings towards particular individuals or groups but refrain from acting them out due to personal, moral, or legal inhibitions. The term *prejudice* refers to the unfavorable feelings and attitudes that people harbor against others, especially other population groups. These are to be distinguished from unfavorable actions or behavior, which fall under the heading of discrimination. Hence, prejudiced individuals may or may not discriminate, and discrimination does not necessarily imply the existence of prejudice.

While the prejudices of people are often the origin of discriminatory behavior and may be appropriate targets for public policy, they are relevant to our discussion only in so far as they find expression in behavior. Accordingly, we focus on the nature of discrimination. We may note here, however, that the broader term, racism, encompasses the concepts of both prejudice and discrimination.

The concept of discrimination need not convey notions of injustice or injury. In general, it refers only to the differential treatment of persons. Thus, we discriminate when we assign the tallest boys to the basketball team or when we cheer for the local football team, but we hardly think of these phenomena as being related in any meaningful way to, say, the exclusion of blacks from higher status jobs or classrooms. Clearly, a concept of discrimination that is so general as to encompass both kinds of situations is too anemic to be of practical use. But how, then, are we to identify the kind of discriminatory treatment that we regard as the proper concern of public policy?

We can move closer to a relevant concept of discrimination by recognizing the criteria on which differential treatment is based. Assigning taller boys to a basketball team, for example, serves a very specific and productive function. Hence, the criterion of selection is directly relevant to the task at hand. The same cannot be said for the selection of a less qualified white competing with a more qualified black. Here the basis of selection, color, is irrelevant to the task at hand, and the resultant choice is actually counterproductive. Hence, we could refine our concept of discrimination by incorporating the relevancy of selection criteria. That kind of discrimination based on irrelevant or nonproductive criteria we may identify as injurious to the public welfare.

Unfortunately, even this refinement of the concept of discrimination does not provide a completely workable definition. There remain many choices we would consider socially injurious that are still not identifiable by the criterion of relevancy. The choice of one's neighbors is an example: the only obviously relevant criterion in choosing neighbors is one's own desires and satisfaction. Thus, the choice of a white neighbor over a black one conforms to the standard of relevancy. Nevertheless, we have come to regard racial discrimination in housing as a socially pernicious practice. On what grounds do we distinguish this kind of individual choice from others? Are there fundamental differences between the situation where a homeowner chooses a white neighbor and, say, the situation where you choose to listen to a rock singer rather than an opera singer? Both situations reflect the free expression of individual choice.

There are few objective grounds for distinguishing between the choice of neighbors and the choice of singers. In both situations, someone is harmed by the selection decision: the opera singer loses potential income and the black home-seeker loses a potential residence. Our distinction between the two situations rests instead on more subjective grounds. Racial discrimination in housing is singled out for special attention because it violates our subjective notions of social justice. Against a combined background of religious, moral, and historical considerations, we have collectively determined that racial discrimination is a particularly deleterious form of individual choice. It is on the basis of this subjective determination that racial discrimination has become a pressing public concern.

An important factor in our subjective judgment about the nature of racial discrimination is our perception of its effects. Where all whites discriminate against all blacks, the expression of free choice becomes especially pernicious. The black home-seeker is denied not one potential home, but all potential homes in white areas. Free choice for whites thus implies restricted choice for blacks and, hence, violates a basic dimension of freedom. Other choices that are less uniform or pervasive are not equally worthy of public concern. Racial discrimination itself would cease to be a public concern were it the practice of only a relatively few and scattered whites.

Costs and Benefits of Discrimination

While it is obvious that blacks suffer real and intangible losses from the practice of racial discrimination, it is not so apparent whether or how the white community gains. Psychologically, of course, many whites will feel better off for having subordinated someone else. And if white individuals actually feel uncomfortable around blacks, on the job, in school, or at home, we may conclude that they are even happier as a result of discrimination.[1] But our immediate concern here is with the economic costs and benefits that may accrue to the white community.

Many whites do reap tangible benefits from the practice of discrimination. Where blacks are discriminated against in the labor market, for example, black workers will receive lower wages than white workers who possess equal qualifications. As a result, two groups of whites gain: white workers who are immunized against competition from blacks obtain higher wages than otherwise; and those employers (laundries and hotels, for example) who actually hire black workers benefit by getting higher quality labor than they are, in fact, paying for. In the educational field, white children gain from discrimination by monopolizing better facilities and teachers. White children of lesser ability are also released from the necessity of competing with more able black children in the quest for admissions.

Not all whites gain directly, however, from racial discrimination; some, in fact, actually lose. White workers who cannot escape menial occupations suffer from increased competition from blacks. The wages of white laundry and hotel workers, for example, will be held down by the large number of blacks excluded from other occupations. Some employers, too, will suffer losses. In a segregated community, employers will often incur higher labor costs through the use of lesser-qualified whites. In the field of education, many whites will suffer from racial discrimination. Not all whites can flee the inner city; those left behind will be trapped in increasingly inferior educational systems, unable to enjoy the white monopolies held in the suburbs.

On an individual basis, then, some whites gain and some lose as a direct result of discrimination, making it difficult to calculate the net microeconomic gain or loss to the white community. No such ambiguity attaches to the indirect losses that are incurred on an aggregate, or macroeconomic, level, however. Where discrimination against blacks is pervasive, society as a whole loses potential human capital. Black abilities and creativity remain underdeveloped and underemployed. Hence, total output of goods and services is less than it

---

[1] The perception of psychological benefits may, of course, rest on prejudices, in which case the nature of benefits could be altered by illuminating and reducing racial stereotypes.

would be in the absence of discrimination. Estimates of the size of this loss run as high as $20 billion a year. In addition, much of the output we do produce is directed to relatively unattractive uses such as the surveillance of homes, streets, jails, and welfare caseloads. Thus, whatever direct gains or losses individual whites incur are overwhelmed by the very large indirect losses to the economy as a whole.

Proving Discrimination

Given the potential socioeconomic cost of discrimination, it is clearly in society's interest to recognize its existence and eliminate it. The identification of discrimination is not always easy, however. Consider a situation where a white worker and a black worker both apply for the same job: the white applicant is accepted, and the black applicant claims that he was unfairly discriminated against. What grounds do we have for accepting the charge of discrimination, as opposed to, say, the charge that the black applicant is simply a poor loser?

The easiest cases of discrimination to prove are those that involve blatant discrepancies in treatment. In our example, if the black applicant was required to take special tests or possessed identifiably superior qualifications, the issue is readily resolved. The same simplicity exists where black children are confined to dilapidated schools or a prospective black home buyer is turned down after offering to pay the full retail value of a house.

But the practice of discrimination is not always so apparent. Indeed, with the public eye focused on discrimination, those who engage in discriminatory practices are likely to develop great subtlety, and, accordingly, evidence of discriminatory treatment may have to rest on the observation of end results. If a company has four thousand employees, none of whom is black, there exists a strong presumption that its hiring procedures are not impartial. So it is with the schools: if blacks and whites go into the educational system comparatively equal but come out with gross disparities in ability, we may conclude that they were treated differently somewhere along the line. Evidence of discriminatory treatment may be gathered by direct observation of treatment or by inference from results. Both types of evidence will be considered in our discussion of the educational and labor market systems.

RACIAL DISCRIMINATION IN EDUCATION

There is an exceedingly strong presumption that racial discrimination exists within the educational system. While this assertion will surprise very few readers today, it is worthwhile to review the evidence on which it is based. Blacks and whites go into the educational system comparatively equal but come out of the system very different. In fact, the longer whites and blacks remain in the system, the further their respective abilities diverge. In northeastern metropolitan areas of the country, for example, black pupils in the sixth grade are about one and one-half years behind white pupils in verbal abilities. By ninth grade, however, they have slipped almost two and one-half years behind, and by the time they reach twelfth grade, the black pupils are well over three years behind. In the South, verbal achievement disparities grow even faster and larger, as do mathematical achievement disparities in all geographical areas of the United States.

Strong as these grounds are for believing that the education provided whites and blacks is not equal, they tend to *understate* disparities in black and white educations. The ability comparisons of black and white high school seniors, for example, necessarily exclude those students who dropped out of school before reaching the twelfth grade. Yet, the decision to quit school may itself reflect inferior educational opportunities and recognition of widening achievement disparities. Seen in this light, black dropout rates are especially disturbing. While only 20 percent of white students fail to complete high school, 40 percent of all black students fail to do so. Indeed, black educational attainments are so low that one out of four black males, as opposed to one out of twenty whites, fails even the Armed Forces Qualification Test.

Segregation in the Schools

The indirect evidence suggesting discriminatory treatment in the educational system is highly suggestive. In fact, the observed disparities in achievement between white and black students are so great that direct evidence of discrepancies in educational opportunity should be easy to find. Segregation of facilities provides one such example. Where separate schools are maintained for whites and blacks, the documentation of inequalities is simple.

Before looking at the extent of continuing racial segregation in American schools, we need to establish some perspective on the meaning of segregation. When most people refer to *integrated* schools, they are encompassing all schools serving both whites and blacks. Such a definition is deceptive, however. Consider the case of a city with only two high schools: School A has 2,000 students, only one of whom is black; School B, on the other hand, is all black. By the usual criterion of biracial enrollment, School A would be regarded as integrated, yet the racial isolation common in both schools is surely of greater significance than School A's dubious claim to biracial enrollment.

A more meaningful concept of integration must refer to the proportion of students that attend school with children of another race. From this perspective, we are able to identify the completeness of integration. Complete integration, of course, would be a situation where all black students attended school with white children, and vice versa. By this stricter definition of integration, the distinction between School A and School B disappears. For the city as a whole, we may say that only 0.1 percent of the black population attends school with whites. This is far more descriptive than saying that 50 percent of the city schools are integrated.

This broader concept of integration has tremendous significance for our perceptions of educational desegregation. Ten years after the Supreme Court's historic order to desegregate, the state of Florida boasted that nearly a third of its schools were integrated. Closer scrutiny revealed, however, that only 2.65 percent of Florida's black pupils were attending school with whites. Progress was even slower in other southern states.

Table 9.1 summarizes the extent of school integration across the country in 1970. One half of all black pupils in elementary and secondary grades were still attending schools in 1970 that were almost exclusively black. While there were significant regional variations, the basic segregation of educational facilities prevailed everywhere. Whether he lives in the North or the South, in the city or on a farm, a black child is very unlikely to attend a truly integrated school. Racial isolation in the schools is still the hallmark of American educational systems.

TABLE 9.1   School Integration, 1970

	Percent of Black Students in Schools Where Enrollment Is:		
	80-100% Black	*50-79% Black*	*Less Than 50% Black*
U.S. Total	49.4%	17.5%	33.1%
North and West	57.6	14.9	27.5
South	39.4	21.5	39.1
Border States	60.6	9.6	29.8

Source: U.S. Department of Health, Education, and Welfare, Office of the Secretary, News Release of June 18, 1971, Table 2.

One additional note of caution about the concept of integration is necessary. The concept of integration we have offered goes no further than the outer walls of the school, but even an ostensibly integrated school may be severely segrated within. Students may be assigned rooms, teachers, and facilities within the school on an explicitly racial basis. An extreme illustration of such internal segregation was encountered in Milwaukee. Like most other cities, Milwaukee was prodded by the courts to integrate its schools. In part, integration was achieved by busing black pupils to previously white schools. The substance of educational opportunity was little changed, however. The bused-in black pupils were maintained in separate classrooms and bused back and forth to their old schools for lunch. Black students who lived close to the white schools were even required to proceed to the more distant black schools for bus transportation to the receiving schools!

Not all internal school segregation is as explicit and extreme as the case in Milwaukee. A more popular and subtle form of segregation is embodied in the so-called *tracking* systems, under which the more able students are separated from the rest and provided special opportunities to advance, while the least able students are held back for intensive remedial work. What makes the system so racially discriminatory is the fact that black pupils have received inferior education prior to integration, so that using IQ tests or other achievement examinations to allocate pupils serves to perpetuate racial separation. A still subtler form of segregation within the classroom may prevail where teachers regard black pupils as innately or culturally incapable of attaining success.

Equality of Facilities

The statistics of Table 9.1, together with our observations on the nature of integration, provide a sobering view of our efforts to provide equal opportunity "with all deliberate speed." In light of that background, we may argue that blacks and whites still attend school separately. How equal, then, are their separate opportunities?

A comparison of educational opportunities at the local level is easily made: visit any black school and any white school in the same city. You can readily detect enough qualitative differences in their educational environments to make a judgment about the relative attractiveness of the black school. These local observations of school quality cannot be expanded across the country, however. It would be too expensive and time-consuming to visit all the school districts across the nation in order to assess the average quality of black and white schools. Even if we had enough time and money, our judgments would depend on the perspectives and standards of many different observers. And, finally, any conclusions we reached would be limited to such statements as "white schools are better (or very much better)," with no clear indication of how great existing inequalities are. Accordingly, we are compelled to seek more objective, easily quantified measures of school quality.

In the most comprehensive survey of educational facilities ever undertaken, the U.S. Office of Education employed 67 separate measures of school quality. These measures ranged from the number of books in the school library to the education of the teacher's mother. They represented a concerted effort to capture and measure every dimension of the educational environment that might distinguish white schools from black schools. What the Office of Education discovered is that black and white schools differ on a multitude of separate measures but that such individual differences were relatively small. The only clear pattern to emerge from their mountain of statistics was that black schools tended to be most deficient in those primarily academic facilities, such as science labs, textbooks, and debate clubs.

In assessing these results, the Office of Education recognized many limitations in their approach. They reported that:

The school environment of a child consists of many things, ranging from the desk he sits at to the child who sits next to him, and including the teacher who stands in front of his class. Any statistical survey gives only the most meager evidence of these environments, for two reasons. First, the reduction of the various aspects of the environment to quantitative measures must inherently miss many elements, tangible and more subtle, that are relevant to the child. The measures must be comparable from school to school; yet the elements which are experienced as most important by the child will likely differ from one school to another, and may well differ among children in the same school.

Second, the child experiences his environment as a whole, while the statistical measures necessarily fragment it. Having a teacher without a college degree may indicate an element of disadvantage; but in the concrete situation, a schoolchild may be taught by a teacher who is not only without a college degree, but who has grown up and received his schooling in the local community, who has never been out of the State, who has a 10th-grade vocabulary, and who shares the local community's attitudes.

For both these reasons, the statistical examination of difference in school environments for minority and majority children will give an impression of lesser differences than actually exist.[2]

We are left, then, with a very incomplete assessment of the school facilities available to whites and blacks. All we can say with certainty is that both everyday observation and the survey of the Office of Education lead one to conclude that there exist tangible differences in black and white educational facilities. We have no summary measure, however, of how large those differences are or how important they may be.

Inherent Inequalities

The Supreme Court provided a way out of this statistical ambiguity when it determined in 1954 that segregated facilities were *inherently* unequal. The Court declared that "to separate them [black children] from others of similar age and qualifications solely because of their race generates a feeling of inferiority as to their status in the community that may affect their hearts and minds in a way unlikely ever to be undone."[3] The Court thus relegated the issue of tangible facilities to one of distinctly secondary importance. Even ostensibly "equal" schools for blacks and whites could never generate equal educational opportunity.

There were several specific considerations that led the Supreme Court justices to their landmark decision. They recognized that black pupils in

---

[2] U.S. Office of Education, *Equality of Educational Opportunity* (The Coleman Report) (Washington, D.C.: Government Printing Office, 1966), p. 37.

[3] Brown V. Board of Education.

segregated schools would have low self-esteem derived from the knowledge that they were surrounded by failures and in schools regarded as inferior. Moreover, they would acquire a personal sense of futility knowing that, regardless of their individual attainments, they would always be identified by the community as members of a group viewed as less able, less successful, and less acceptable. Hence, the individual black child would see little reason to develop his individual talents. Community views would affect the attitudes of teachers, also. Aware of, and probably sharing, the white community's low regard for blacks, teachers attached to black schools would tend to accept and transmit low expectations. They would not teach as much, or as well, to children deemed less teachable.

Impressive evidence in support of the Court's judgment was assembled by the U.S. Commission on Civil Rights in 1967. The commission discovered that black pupils of similar backgrounds performed quite differently in varying racial situations. In particular, it found that black educational achievements increased substantially where schools were more thoroughly integrated. In addition to the fact that white schools were generally better, it was observed that black pupils benefited from integration by believing their opportunities had improved and by seeing others succeeding around them. Discrimination, then, and more especially school segregation, were seen to be major determinants of black achievements and status.

CLASS DISCRIMINATION IN EDUCATION

While blacks do suffer from serious and pervasive discrimination in the educational system, there is no reason to believe that they alone are singled out for substandard treatment. On the contrary, we have learned that other minority groups, among them Mexican-Americans, Puerto Ricans, and American Indians, confront barriers at least as formidable as do blacks. Accordingly, nearly everything we have said about racial discrimination against blacks applies with equal force to all minority group members. But even to include other minority groups in our discussion does not completely cover the subject of discrimination. As we are just beginning to perceive, racism has its counterpart in what has become known as *classism*. Poor individuals as a group, irrespective of their ethnic origins, are provided substandard facilities and opportunities in America.

We have already noted that many whites lose out as a result of racial discrimination in education, namely those who are not able to escape predominantly black neighborhoods and schools. But even where blacks are not present, poor whites may be confined to separate and substandard schools. Neighborhoods are even more likely to be homogeneous by income classes than by race; that is, poor families will be located in distinct areas of any city. Moreover, because school expenditures and decisions are determined by administrative bodies composed largely of the nonpoor, schools in low-income neighborhoods are likely to receive less than equal facilities. At present, this inequity finds most profound expression in the fact that poor children are much less likely than nonpoor children to receive free or subsidized school food programs, exemplifying the point that class discrimination in education involves a pattern of segregated and substandard schools for the poor.

The analogy of class discrimination to racial discrimination goes beyond differences in school facilities. Like blacks, poor white children tend to be surrounded by families that have failed to achieve material success. Poor white children see few demonstrations of personal aspiration and talent leading to higher socioeconomic status. Furthermore, they are aware that society regards material success as a mark of personal worth and thus see themselves and their families as stigmatized by the larger community. They know, too, that their schools are inferior and that completion of their studies will leave them ill-prepared to compete in the labor market. As a consequence, they are likely to internalize a sense of futility and inferiority.

The cumulative impact of class discrimination is apparent in the educational attainments of lower-class children. Poor children drop out of high school at over twice the rate of nonpoor children. Even more startling is the fact that a substantial number of poor children leave the educational system even before they enter high school. And those relatively few lower-income children who do manage to make it through until high school graduation cannot depend on their abilities to get them into college. College admissions are still reserved for those who can support themselves or forego several years of employment income.

It is generally assumed by the nonpoor that poor children do not attain higher educational status because they are uniformly less able, but there are some very obvious weaknesses in this assumption. For example, a very talented poor youngster has no control over his family's finances. Hence, if the family cannot afford either to forego his earnings or even to supply him with school clothes and lunches, he will not be able to take advantage of even a "free" high school education. Furthermore, there are no scholarship or loan programs for high school students. Hence, we may anticipate that many talented poor children will never complete high school. Even for those who do attain high school diplomas, college admission will be barred by similar financial obstacles and by a legacy of inferior schooling.

It is not easy to determine how many bright, poor children are denied higher education because of their poverty. IQ tests remain our only standardized measure of ability, and those tests create problems for poor whites similar to those for blacks. Because their schools are substandard, poor whites fall increasingly far behind the nonpoor in educational performance. Hence, they demonstrate decreasing IQs over time, and it is difficult to discern how many originally bright children existed among the poor. And yet, even on the restrictive criterion of IQ tests, we can identify a large number of poor and able high school graduates who never attained a college degree.

As Table 9.2 reveals, the socioeconomic status of one's family has tremendous impact on a child's chances for college graduation. For any demonstrated level of twelfth-grade IQ, children from higher status families are far more likely to reach college graduation. What is especially noteworthy here is the comparatively small proportion (20%) of very able poor students who graduate from college. Children of lesser ability but more prosperous families take the places of the more gifted among the poor. Educational opportunity is distributed neither equally nor even on the basis of demonstrated ability.

TABLE 9.2 College Graduation Rates, by Socioeconomic Status and IQ

Socioeconomic Status	IQ Score		
	Low	*Middle*	*High*
Low	0.3%	8.9%	20.1%
Middle	3.0	11.8	40.0
High	10.5	29.9	64.0

Source: Adapted from William Sewell and V. Shah, "Status, Intelligence and the Attainment of High Education," *Sociology of Education,* Winter 1967, Table 4.

Class discrimination in education, then, is a strong force in the educational system and helps to determine the distribution of poverty. Whatever aggregate level of poverty exists, we may confidently predict that the children of the poor will be heavily overrepresented in the poverty statistics. It is also possible that class discrimination has become a stronger force in American society than racial discrimination. The U.S. Commission on Civil Rights, for example, found that schools were severely segregated by socioeconomic class and that the social class composition of schools is a stronger determinant of achievement than race. Moreover, there is mounting evidence that middle-class whites, if forced to choose, would prefer as neighbors middle-class blacks to poor whites. Poor persons, of whatever color, are least accepted by the larger society. All of this will be of little comfort to poor blacks, of course, who are likely to be the subject of both racial and class discrimination.

SUMMARY

Discrimination against members of particular racial or socioeconomic groups violates commonly accepted standards of social justice. Where discrimination is pervasive, the freedom of minority groups is severely restricted, as are their opportunities for achievement. Such limitations harm not only those discriminated against, but also the larger community. Talents go undeveloped, potential output is irrevocably lost, and markets are unnecessarily restricted.

In the American educational system, racial discrimination has resulted in a pattern of segregated and inferior schools for blacks. Half of all black students continue to attend virtually all-black elementary and secondary schools. The inferiority of the education these children receive derives not only from disparities in school facilities but, more importantly, from a sense of isolation and subjugation imposed by the white community. The consequences of this discrimination are manifest in the low educational attainments of black youth. Even that minority of black youth that manages to attain a high school diploma remains more than three years behind white students in educational achievement (measured ability).

As serious and pervasive as discrimination against blacks is, it is not the only kind of discrimination practiced in the educational system. In addition to other minority groups who suffer from racial discrimination, many whites are also inequitably treated in American schools. Poor children, in particular, are maintained in schools segregated largely by socioeconomic class and provided with substandard facilities. They and their families are also stigmatized by the larger community for failure to attain material success. As a result, children of poor families drop out of school at alarming rates and generally lag behind nonpoor children in demonstrated achievement. Even those relatively few poor children who do demonstrate high levels of achievement are denied higher levels of education. Class discrimination, then, is directly analogous to discrimination against racial or minority groups.

Because educational attainments are a prime determinant of the distribution of poverty, those discriminated against in the schools are most likely to be among the poor. For whatever level of aggregate poverty exists, the children of yesterday's poor and blacks will be grossly overrepresented in the poverty statistics. Children of poor black families will be the most disadvantaged, since they are subject to both racial and class discrimination.

REFERENCES

On the Nature of Discrimination

DOLLARD, JOHN, *Caste and Class in a Southern Town.* Garden City, N.Y.: Doubleday & Company, Inc., 1957.

DOWNS, ANTHONY, *Urban Problems and Prospects.* Chicago: Markham Publishing Co., 1970, Ch. 3.

FRIEDMAN, MILTON, *Capitalism and Freedom.* Chicago: University of Chicago Press, 1962, Ch. 7.

Report of the National Advisory Commission on Civil Disorders, New York and Washington, D.C.: Bantam Books, Inc., and Government Printing Office, 1968.

On Discrimination in Education

BROOM, LEONARD and NORVAL D. GLENN, *Transformation of the Negro American*. New York: Harper & Row, Publishers, 1965, Ch. 5.

NATIONAL ASSOCIATION OF INTERGROUP RELATIONS OFFICIALS, *Public School Segregation and Integration in the North*. Washington, D.C., November 1963.

SEXTON, PATRICIA, *Education and Income*. New York: The Viking Press, Inc., 1961.

U.S. COMMISSION ON CIVIL RIGHTS, *Racial Isolation in the Public Schools*. Washington, D.C.: Government Printing Office, 1967.

U.S. OFFICE OF EDUCATION, *Equality of Educational Opportunity* (the Coleman Report). Washington, D.C.: Government Printing Office, 1966.

10 Discrimination in the Labor Market

In 1927, a clothing manufacturer in New York City advertised for help with the following wage offer: "White Workers $24; Colored Workers $20."[1] His offer embodied one of the most flagrant forms of racial discrimination in the labor market; namely, the payment of unequal wages for equal work. Few employers are so blatant today, and certainly no one advertises his discriminatory practices in print anymore. Nevertheless, it is still believed that blacks do not receive equal treatment in the labor markets.

If black workers are discriminated against in the labor market, they are being denied full use of their productive abilities. As a consequence, their incomes will be depressed, and they will be heavily represented in the ranks of the poor. Hence, racial discrimination in the labor market tends to affect both the distribution and extent of poverty. In this chapter, we examine the consequences, forms, and practices of discrimination in the labor market. As in the preceeding chapter, we begin with a discussion of discrimination against blacks and then consider the phenomenon of class discrimination.

RACIAL DISCRIMINATION IN THE LABOR MARKET

We know that there are tremendous disparities between the incomes of blacks and whites. In Chapter 2, we noted that nearly one out of three blacks is poor compared to only one out of ten whites, and in Chapter 7, we observed that median black family incomes are nearly $4,000 less than white incomes. Moreover, we have observed that racial or cultural theories cannot explain these inequalities. Thus, there are strong grounds for assuming that blacks continue to be the subject of discrimination, despite the lack of advertising to that effect.

However, it would be mistaken to conclude that all existing income

[1] Cited by Orley Ashenfelter, "Changes in Labor Market Discrimination Over Time," *Journal of Human Resources,* Fall, 1970, pp. 403-30.

inequalities can be explained by discriminatory practices in the labor market. We know, for instance, that blacks enter the labor market much less prepared than whites as a result of racial discrimination in the schools. Accordingly, a labor market that rewarded all individuals only on the basis of demonstrated achievement would still provide less income for blacks than whites. A very high proportion of blacks also continue to live in the South, where employment levels and wages are generally lower. Hence, income disparities alone do not prove the existence of racial discrimination in the labor market; they simply create a presumption that discrimination will be discovered if sought.

Even if we find that income disparities continue to exist after we have accounted for educational and geographical differences, we cannot conclusively assert that discriminatory practices are rampant in the labor market. If discrimination against blacks ceased altogether, black workers would still be handicapped by past labor market discrimination. They would be less skilled and experienced and lower on seniority ladders, for example. As in the area of education, blacks would remain disadvantaged by past discrimination, even if present discrimination were eliminated.

The observed income disparities between whites and blacks, then, are primarily the result of three forces: nonmarket discrimination, past labor market discrimination, and present labor market discrimination. What we seek to identify in this chapter is that portion of existing income disparities attributable solely to continuing racial discrimination in the labor market.

Disparities in Earnings

White families have accumulated vast amounts of wealth over time in the form of property, savings accounts, bond holdings, and stock ownership. Stockholders' equity alone now amounts to over $300 billion, while another $800 billion is tied up in savings, cash, and government bonds. Black families have comparatively little access to this store of wealth, as they have been denied the opportunity to earn and accumulate money in the past. Thus, there are disparities in wealth between blacks and whites that tend to overwhelm differences in income.

For the most part, these differences in wealth do not reflect current labor market discrimination. They do, however, tend to distort comparisons of current white and black incomes. Current income includes money derived from accumulated wealth, especially money received in the form of dividends, interest, and capital gains. Accordingly, *total* income differences between blacks and whites are much larger than differences in *earnings*, that is, income derived from labor market activity. To assess the impact of racial discrimination in the labor market, then, we need to focus on racial disparities in earnings alone.

In 1970, the average earnings of white male workers was $7,928. For black workers, the average was only $4,844, a mere 60 percent of white earnings. In absolute terms, there was an earnings disparity of over $3,000. How much of this difference was due to discrimination in the labor market? To isolate the impact of racial discrimination on this disparity, we need to identify the influence of other earnings determinants. Education, skills, age, and geographic location are all important factors in addition to race. Only as we control for these other factors can we perceive the independent influence of race.

We have already noted the tremendous importance of educational attainments for income. Therefore, we must control for the influence on earnings of the nonmarket discrimination suffered by blacks in schools. This may be done by observing the comparative earnings of blacks and whites with equal educations. If there is no racial discrimination in the labor market, blacks and whites with equal education should command approximately equal incomes. When this adjustment is actually made, however, the gap in earnings between whites and blacks is only partially closed; black workers generally earn only 70 percent as much as whites with equivalent years of schooling (see Figure 8.1, page 101). While this is an improvement over the unadjusted ratio of 60 percent, it is still far from equality.

Years of schooling, of course, do not have the same educational significance for blacks and whites, as we have observed. Hence, a complete adjustment for nonmarket discrimination would have to control for the significant differences in the quality of education received by each group. We must recognize that a typical black worker with twelve years of schooling comes to the job with as little educational preparation as the typical white worker with only nine years of schooling. When this additional control for nonmarket discrimination is imposed, observed labor market disparities shrink further. Black workers of equivalent educational backgrounds, including both quantity and quality of schooling, earn incomes nearly 80 percent as large as their white counterparts.

It appears, then, that approximately one-half of the earnings disparity between whites and blacks can be attributed to prior (nonmarket) discrimination in the schools. This means that no more than half of the observable earnings disparity can be attributed to present labor market discrimination. Indeed, the combined influence of other factors, including skills, age, and region, reduce the disparity further. Informed students of discrimination now estimate that only about one-fourth of existing earnings disparities are directly attributable to discriminatory labor market practices. We may say, then, that roughly one-half of the $3,000 earnings disparity is due to nonmarket discrimination (education, residence); one-fourth due to past market discrimination (work skills and experience); and one-fourth to current labor market discrimination.

While nonmarket discrimination appears to overwhelm other types of discrimination, some caution is necessary in interpreting these conclusions. First of all, an annual earnings loss of $750 is a substantial setback to black workers.

Racial discrimination in the labor market is, thus, a large and important racial barrier, even if outsized by discrimination in education. Furthermore, it cannot be assumed that these proportions are fixed. If, in fact, the quality and quantity of schooling for blacks increases, we have no assurance that black educational attainments will continue to be rewarded at the same rate. As more educated black workers emerge, racial discrimination in the labor market may intensify. Much potential discrimination in the labor market is now averted due to the fact that so few blacks are able to compete directly with whites. As black educational attainments—and thus labor market competition—increase, the situation may be altered dramatically. Accordingly, we have no firm basis for predicting a linear diminution of earnings disparities as educational opportunities become more equal. These calculations illustrate where the locus of discrimination is now; they cannot predict where it will be in the future.

Components of Earnings Disparities

While the image is provocative, it is mistaken to picture a thief called Discrimination openly robbing black workers of $3,000, even though the effect may be the same. Instead, we must realize that the consequent income loss emerges from several dimensions of the labor market process. Black workers are not robbed of their earnings outright. Very little of the discrimination that takes place in the labor market is of the sort exemplified by the New York garment manufacturer who paid different wages to white and black workers. Aside from being illegal, the visibility of such practices makes them especially vulnerable to public scrutiny and civil rights action. In addition, such overtly inequitable treatment violates the consciences of most employers. Rather, blacks are hired less often, for fewer hours, for less desirable jobs, and at lower wages (see Figure 10.1). It is the sum total of these different forces that leaves the black worker poorer. A more thorough understanding of discrimination is attained by considering the relative importance of each of these forces.

FIGURE 10.1   Components of Earnings Disparities

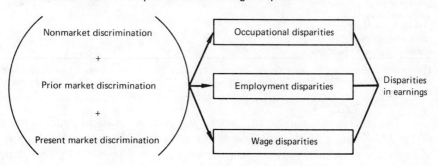

Because black workers are less educated, less experienced, and less attractive to most employers than available white workers, they are least likely to be hired. In any given job situation white workers will be hired first and laid off last. Hence, the frequency of employment and the number of hours worked will differ for blacks and whites as the combined result of nonmarket and market racial discrimination. Indeed, a significant part of the observed earnings disparity derives not from the decision to pay blacks lower wages but from the decision to employ them less often. Black unemployment rates are generally twice as high as white unemployment rates, while employed blacks are less likely than whites to work full time.

Of still greater significance to the observed earnings disparity is the decision to employ blacks at different kinds of jobs. Once again, all forms of discrimination take their toll. Blacks are denied entrance to many occupations because they lack necessary educational attainments or credentials. They also often lack required work skills and experience. And finally, there are many jobs which whites regard as inappropriate for blacks and from which they are, therefore, excluded. Garbage collection and bus driving are regarded as acceptable black occupations; retail salesmanship, management, or even teaching are not regarded by whites as equally appropriate. And only in the most dire of circumstances could most whites imagine trusting themselves to the services of a black doctor or lawyer. Accordingly, blacks are largely excluded from the more pleasant and remunerative occupations. Table 10.1 indicates the general nature of existing occupational patterns.

TABLE 10.1 Occupational Status of Blacks and Whites, by Sex (1970)

	Male		Female	
	Black	White	Black	White
Professional, technical, and managerial	13%	29%	13%	20%
Clerical and sales	9	13	23	44
Craftsmen and foremen	14	21	1	1
Operatives	28	19	18	14
Service workers, excluding household workers	13	6	26	15
Private household workers	-	-	18	3
Nonfarm laborers	18	6	1	-
Farmers and farm workers	6	5	2	2

Source: U.S. Bureau of Labor Statistics and U.S. Bureau of the Census, *The Social and Economic Status of Negroes in the United States, 1970* (Washington, D.C.: Government Printing Office, 1971).

The professional-managerial, clerical, and craft occupations embrace most of the better-paid and pleasant jobs in the economy. Nearly two-thirds of all white workers are in those positions now, but only one out of three black workers has gained access to these occupations. The situation is further aggravated by the fact that black workers who do gain access to the better occupations end up in the lowest and least desirable jobs *within* each occupational group. Within the professional, technical, and managerial class, for example, white workers tend to be lawyers, doctors, engineers, and social scientists. Black workers, on the other hand, are more likely to be funeral directors, welfare workers, and teachers in segregated schools. The same situation exists in the other occupational categories, sometimes in even more extreme form. For example, among clerical workers are grouped both white insurance adjusters and black postal clerks, among salesworkers both stock-brokers and black newsboys. In other words, the tremendous disparities evident in black and white occupational distributions reveal only a relatively small proportion of the job barriers that actually confront black workers.

At the bottom of the occupational ladder, the respective concentrations of blacks and whites are, of course, reversed. As Table 10.1 reveals, two-thirds of all black workers are concentrated in the lower occupational categories, and, again, the disparities in actual jobs are great. Black women are maids in private homes or maids in hotels and office buildings. Black men are bootblacks, elevator operators, porters, and janitors. The better service and blue-collar jobs, including firemen, policemen, bartenders, and teamsters, are largely reserved for whites. The fact that blacks work less often and for fewer hours is of relatively little significance in comparison with this uneven distribution of occupational opportunites.

Who Discriminates?

It is not easy to visualize so much discrimination taking place in the labor market. It is even more difficult to picture those persons or groups who actually engage in discrimination. Very few of us can readily identify anyone as an outright racist. The whole notion of purposeful maltreatment simply runs counter to the way we are accustomed to viewing ourselves or the marketplace. Nevertheless, a list of discriminators would encompass a catalogue of all labor market participants. Employers, unions, employees, employment agencies, and training programs are all implicated in the charge of labor market discrimination. To understand how so many individuals and groups are implicated, we must return to the nature of discrimination.

Much discrimination in the market is not intended. As we saw previously, even persons free of prejudice or animosity may engage in discriminatory patterns of behavior. While such unintentional practices make fewer headlines, their impact on black employment opportunities is no less important. Traditional company recruitment practices provide a simple illustration. Most companies, large or small, rely heavily on existing employees for new recruits. If new jobs open up, present employees usually are able to locate friends or relatives who want the new positions, and a word-of-mouth recruitment system is remarkably efficient. Present employees know the company, the jobs, and the applicants; therefore, they are in a position to match jobs and people accurately. Word-of-mouth recruitment is also inexpensive; no outside agencies need be contacted, and advertisement costs are kept to a minimum. Large companies are so impressed with this recruitment system that they offer bonuses to employees who bring in new workers.

Although efficient, word-of-mouth recruitment practices tend to exclude black workers from better jobs. Would-be black applicants do not have a network of friends already in better employment positions. Accordingly, they are seldom aware of developing opportunities and are rarely brought to the attention of recruitment personnel. Even in the absence of willful discrimination, they are effectively cut off from new jobs.

Recruitment outside the firm does not always yield much better results. Companies are generally unfamiliar with the people and skills available in black residential areas, especially ghetto areas. They do not know who, how, or where to recruit. As a result, they tend to rely on traditional sources and agencies of recruitment more readily accessible to whites. Would-be black applicants also experience a certain hesitancy in approaching unfamiliar companies or employment agencies. Knowing that prejudice exists and having possibly confronted explicit discrimination themselves, black job-seekers are often reluctant to risk embarrassment or harassment. They rely, instead, on familiar sources and companies that have established reputations in the community for fair treatment. Recent converts to equal employment opportunity thus have difficulty in communicating their new intentions.

While these institutionalized patterns of behavior constitute a barrier to truly equal employment opportunity, we cannot ignore the impact of overt discrimination. Not all discriminatory practices are innocent. Some persons and groups willfully exclude black workers from employment opportunities. Here we can only review the most obvious and widespread examples.

The Unions

Labor unions are a popular target for attack from many fronts, and the subject of racial discrimination provides no exception. It is widely believed that unions constitute the greatest barrier between black workers and improving employment opportunities. Labor unions are large, highly visible, and often contain outspoken racist members. They also tend to control access to the better-paid jobs for which black job-seekers are presently most qualified. High-status employment areas of lesser union strength, among them clerical, technical, and professional work, tend to require higher educational credentials. Hence, unions are in a position to provide the fastest route to improved economic status.

The past history of labor unions is not very encouraging. While the American Federation of Labor (the AFL) was founded on the principles of racial and worker solidarity, its practices quickly departed from that goal. As early as 1895, nine years after its inception, the AFL compromised on the issue of racial equality by admitting deliberately discriminatory unions. By 1899, the AFL was even admitting unions whose constitutions explicitly forbade black membership, thereby foresaking even the pretense of racial equality. This development was particularly damaging to black workers, because the AFL was strongest in those areas where black employment skills were concentrated, namely the crafts, such as carpentry, blacksmithing, and mechanical arts. Indeed at the time of the Civil War, black workers dominated craft employment in the South, outnumbering white craftsmen five to one. As the craft union movement grew, however, blacks lost their foothold in the job market. Black craftsmen were forced out of their jobs and denied access to new ones. Apprenticeship programs were also closed, thereby eliminating future opportunities for employment.

While racial prejudices were clearly at the root of much union discrimination, there is abundant evidence that economic motivations were dominant. The nascent unions knew that their strength and welfare depended on their ability to control job entry. Any potential craftsman was viewed as a direct economic threat. The AFL unions not only sought to eliminate existing and potential competition from blacks but also worked vigorously to restrain all immigration from abroad. The Chinese were viewed as "people of vice and sexual immorality who were incompatible with our moral concepts."[2] Japanese and Koreans were no less undesirable. Even European immigrants were viewed as a threat to economic security and organizational strength. Hence, it is probably fair to conclude that the AFL was egalitarian in its discriminatory practices; that is, it discriminated against all potential competition with little regard to race, creed, or color! Where racial arguments were employed, their primary purpose was to camouflage narrower economic interests. Nevertheless, black workers were most abused, since they were the largest and closest competition.

The Congress of Industrial Organizations (the CIO) emerged in 1935 in a changed economic climate and with a different constituency. Whereas the AFL had focused on craft labor, the CIO directed its attentions to the mass of workers on assembly lines and in less skilled jobs. These jobs generally required less training and experience and were concentrated more in the North. Not only were blacks significantly represented in these jobs, but they also constituted an enormous threat to future union strength. If excluded from the industrial unions, black workers could be used by employers as strikebreakers to undercut union power. The same possibility did not exist in craft unions, because specific skills were required for available jobs. Hence, the CIO had a powerful economic

---

[2] Cited by Herbert Hill in Arthur M. Ross and Herbert Hill, eds., *Employment, Race, and Poverty* (New York: Harcourt Brace Jovanovich, Inc., 1967), p. 389.

incentive to lower racial barriers to union entry. This, combined with the egalitarian outlook of its leaders, especially John L. Lewis, led the CIO to establish nondiscriminatory membership policies.

The AFL-CIO merger in 1955 did not revolutionize union practices. While the new union was founded on stronger antidiscrimination principles, it did little to alter the actual practices of local affiliates, especially the older AFL locals. Local unions retain a broad range of autonomy, and the national leadership has little power or incentive to discipline them on the subject of racial equality. Consequently, black workers continue to be excluded from many unions and relegated to inferior jobs or separate seniority lines when admitted. Experienced black workers are oftentimes required to undergo long and low-paid apprenticeship courses as a condition for union entry, while inexperienced black workers find that they cannot enter apprenticeship programs at all.

Employers

Like unions, business management tends to reflect the interests and attitudes of its members. Some employers, of course, harbor racial prejudices and stereotyped views of black workers. Even more prevalent, however, is a general reluctance to engage in actions that are controversial or outside of primary business pursuits. Employers are hesitant to challenge traditional practices in hiring or to confront what they regard as the community's racial attitudes. Hence, employers will often ignore potential black workers, not as a result of their own prejudice, but because they fear that such hiring will trigger the prejudices of white employees or existing customers. Employers have very little incentive to stir up racial troubles or even to determine whether such troubles would actually emerge. Profits, politics, recreation, and even the community chest command more attention and commitment. As a result, only the most cautious antidiscriminatory actions are undertaken, and then usually only as a result of economic or social pressures, such as boycotts or legal action.

Another barrier to more affirmative action on the part of business management arises from the nature of collective bargaining. Where management does, in fact, decide to hire black workers on a more equal basis, the unions are likely to demand reciprocal concessions. Unions tend to view management's initiatives as an encroachment on their own prerogatives. Changed hiring practices are interpreted as a concession to the desires of management, so the union seeks compensation in other areas, chiefly wages or working conditions. Thus, the cost to management of affirmative action escalates, and management is even less likely to press for the elimination of discriminatory employment patterns.

Just how cautiously management may proceed in the area of race relations has been amply demonstrated in Birmingham, Alabama. While managers in several steel companies there did make some progress in formal hiring and promotion practices, they were reluctant to tamper with the vestiges of Jim Crow. White and Colored signs were removed from drinking fountains and bathhouses, but twin facilities were maintained. Naturally, no workers took it upon themselves to integrate the newly desegregated facilites.

CLASS DISCRIMINATION IN THE LABOR MARKET

There is little need to draw attention at this point to the discrimination suffered by other minority groups. As in the field of education, nearly every form of racial discrimination in the labor market applies to Mexican Americans, Puerto Ricans, and Indians, as well as blacks. To detail the discrimination against them would be to repeat most of the foregoing discussion verbatim. Instead, the reader can make his own substitutions. The process of substitution is not so easy for the phenomenon of class discrimination, however. The phenomenon itself is not sufficiently familiar to most people, while the analogy to racial discrimination is not as complete. Accordingly, some brief consideration of how the labor market is stacked against the poor concludes this chapter.

Poor whites do not suffer the indignities of Jim Crow facilities or even explicitly separate hiring and promotion lines, but they are, nevertheless, at a disadvantage in the employment process. Employers, like the larger society, tend to have low estimates of the capabilities of job applicants who are poorly dressed or from poverty neighborhoods. There is an underlying conviction that poverty reflects personal inadequacy, and, as a result, poor applicants are viewed differently than others and must exhibit exceptional talents to obtain competitive jobs. If their talents are only equal to, say, middle-class applicants, then prejudice is likely to deny employment to the poor. Prejudices are reinforced, of course, by the use of academic achievement tests that often have little or no relation to the content of the available job.

These discriminatory practices are often institutionalized in the recruitment procedures of companies. As we noted earlier, corporations tend not to recruit in poverty areas. They know virtually nothing about available talent in poor neighborhoods and expend little effort to increase their knowledge. As a consequence, poor job seekers and company recruiters seldom make contact. The same kind of isolation results from the word-of-mouth recruitment practices previously mentioned. Like blacks generally, poor whites tend to have comparatively few friends or acquaintances employed at higher status jobs. They thus have little knowledge of or access to good jobs that are opening up. What jobs they hear of are those they have always encountered; dirty, low-paid, and menial.

Class discrimination in the labor market, then, means that poor job-seekers have less chance to obtain employment than nonpoor job seekers of equal ability. Racial discrimination has the same effect for blacks. In both cases, discrimination takes place as a result of individual prejudices and institutionalized practices. The poor, like blacks, have many personal characteristics and backgrounds unfamiliar to middle-class employers, employment agencies, and even unions. Conduct, speech, and dress are among those factors that create communication barriers. Employers tend to see these differences as indicators of ability rather than as the result of socioeconomic environment. It is assumed that the poor will not be as able or dependable on the job. Hence, workers are not sought from poorer areas and, when they come forth, are unfavorably considered.

SUMMARY

Minority racial groups and the poor generally start out in the labor market at a distinct competitive disadvantage, largely as a result of discrimination in the educational system; but their handicaps do not end there. In the labor market itself, minority groups and the poor do not even have an equal opportunity to make the best of their meager beginnings. Prejudice and institutional employment practices combine to handicap them still further.

Racial and class discrimination in the labor market takes many forms: some employers and unions willfully exclude blacks; others, perhaps less prejudiced, rely on recruitment procedures that have the same effect, both for blacks and the poor. Doubts about the capabilities of individuals who are black or poor also limit employment and promotional possibilities. Notions of what kind of work is "proper" for blacks and fear of employee or community disapproval restrains even unprejudiced, but profit-maximizing, employers from providing equal opportunity. The cumulative impact of these practices is evident: members of minority or poor populations end up working less often, for fewer hours, at less attractive jobs—and, ultimately, with less income.

REFERENCES

BERGMANN, BARBARA R., "The Effect on White Incomes of Discrimination in Employment," *Journal of Political Economy,* March 1971.

BROOM, LEONARD, and NORVAL GLENN, *Transformation of the American Negro.* New York: Harper & Row, Publishers, 1965, Ch. 6.

FERMAN, LOUIS, JOYCE KORNBLUH, and J. A. MILLER, *Negroes and Jobs.* Ann Arbor: University of Michigan Press, 1968.

HIESTAND, DALE L., *Discrimination in Employment.* Ann Arbor, Mich.: Institute of Labor and Industrial Relations, 1970.

JACOBSON, JULIUS, ed., *The Negro and the American Labor Movement.* Garden City, N.Y.: Doubleday & Company, Inc., Anchor Books, 1968.

RONY, VERNA, "Bogalusa: The Economics of Tragedy," in *Poverty: Views from the Left,* Jeremy Larner and Irving Howe, eds. New York: William Morrow & Co., Inc., 1968.

ROSS, ARTHUR M. and HERBERT HILL, eds., *Employment, Race, and Poverty*, New York: Harcourt Brace Jovanovich, Inc., 1967.

SCHILLER, BRADLEY, "Opportunity Stratification," in *Stratification and Poverty*, S. M. Lipset and S. M. Miller, eds., forthcoming.

U.S. BUREAU OF THE CENSUS, "Labor Union Membership in 1966," *Current Population Reports*, Series P-20, No. 216, March 1971.

III Public Programs and Policies

Introduction

The preceding eight chapters have focused on the potential causes of poverty in America. A variety of factors has been examined to determine what causal significance each might possess. The purpose of these detailed inquiries was twofold: to increase our understanding of poverty; and to establish a substantive basis for meaningful discussion of poverty policies. Part III focuses attention on those policies. References to our findings on causation are made throughout Part III, while Chapter 14 provides a summary of causal links and policy directions.

There are three basic approaches to reducing poverty: (1) provision of income; (2) provision of jobs; and (3) elimination of barriers between existing jobs and individuals. All three approaches are followed in current antipoverty efforts to some extent, but each approach does not command equal attention or support, nor do they have equal impact on the distribution and extent of poverty. What we seek to determine in Part III is how much emphasis is currently accorded each approach, what kinds of programs are implemented, and the potential effectiveness of each.

There are, of course, literally hundreds of distinct programs and policies that impinge in some way on the poor. Rarely does a session of Congress go by when less than a dozen new programs or amendments to existing ones are proposed. To discuss all of these programs would consume thousands of pages, but, fortunately, such an exhaustive review is not necessary. Many antipoverty programs are very similar in structure and scope and need not be examined individually. Instead, we may review the major features of some representative programs to acquire a perspective on the direction and magnitude of public efforts.

11   Income Maintenance Policies

Income transfer programs are often proposed as the most compelling and obvious solution to poverty. Simply give the poor enough money, it is argued, and poverty will disappear. Among others, economist Milton Friedman and urbanologist Irving Kristol have wondered aloud whether our public commitment to end poverty is sincere in light of our failure to provide the obvious remedy. The apparent simplicity of income transfer solutions to poverty is deceptive, however. We could, of course, provide enough money to close the poverty gap, which is the difference between what the poor now have and what they need to maintain minimum standards of living. In 1970, that gap was only $11 billion, or just 1 percent of the nation's total output. Public provision of this scope, however, might create significant problems. Persons just above the poverty line would have an economic incentive to abandon other sources of support and join the ranks of the poor. In so doing, they would gain much more leisure at little cost. Similarly, persons already counted as poor would have an incentive to substitute public transfers for whatever employment income they already possessed. Accordingly, we must recognize that both the size of the poverty population and its financial needs may be sensitive to public income transfer policies.

These basic problems of income transfer have led to a proliferation of income maintenance programs. Some programs provide income for persons on the basis of need alone, while others provide transfers on the basis of previous contributions. When you pay Social Security taxes, for example, you are providing income transfers for the elderly while establishing your right to receive such transfers in old age. Other programs demand no such contributions. To receive benefits from state general assistance programs, you need only be poor and unable to obtain employment or other support. In this case, money is transferred from the taxpaying public directly to those in need. We begin our discussion of income maintenance policies with a consideration of transfers based on need.

139

Income maintenance programs that provide income on the basis of need come in many forms and with a variety of names. Among the more familiar are public assistance, welfare, negative income taxation, and guaranteed incomes. Despite the apparent diversity, however, all these programs have basic similarities. Program differences tend to focus on the mechanisms for providing income and the conditions under which income is provided.

Previous experience with need-based income maintenance programs in America has been confined to what we know as welfare or public assistance. While such programs do provide income to persons in need, need is not the only condition for eligibility. The decision on whether and how much public assistance to provide any individual also depends on how deserving that individual is thought to be by the taxpaying public. This secondary condition for eligibility is distinctive to welfare programs and the focus of much controversy.

It is not easy to construct a definition of *deservedness*. To begin with, it is not in the interest of taxpayers to provide a clear statement of those conditions that determine deservedness and, thus, eligibility for welfare. By employing vague measures of deservedness, taxpayers retain autonomous control over welfare disbursements. When other public or private needs appear more urgent, society may curtail welfare outlays by arbitrarily reevaluating the deservedness of the poor. Were society to subscribe to clear, objective standards of eligibility, fluctuations in public concern and support for the poor would be difficult to justify. As it now stands, taxpayers can always claim that they are providing sufficiently for the "deserving" poor.

While an exact definition of deservedness is beyond reach, a close approximation is provided by the concept of employability. The potentially employable poor are traditionally viewed with more suspicion and distrust than those who are obviously unemployable; hence, potential employability is often used to justify public neglect. Of course, even the concept of employability is shrouded in ambiguities. A widowed mother with small children is regarded as less employable, and thus more deserving, than a deserted mother with children, regardless of their respective skills or job prospects.

Society's views of deservedness are manifested in the existing patchwork of public assistance programs. While there were over 25 million poor people in 1970, only 14 million of them received welfare payments in December of that year. Even these individuals were not receiving identical income support. Instead, they were categorized into five different public assistance programs, each with its own eligibility criteria and benefit levels, as summarized in Table 11.1.

Four of the programs listed in Table 11.1 are directed to specific population groups. Old Age Assistance provides income transfers only for the aged poor, Aid to the Blind for the blind poor, and so forth. The fifth program,

TABLE 11.1   Public Assistance Programs, December 1970

Program	Current Recipients	Payment per Recipient	Total Annual Payments (in millions)
Old Age Assistance (OAS)	2,081,000	$ 77.60/month	$1,938
Aid to the Blind (AB)	81,000	104.34	101
Aid to the Permanently and Totally Disabled (APTD)	933,000	96.55	1,038
Aid to Families with Dependent Children (AFDC)	9,657,000	49.50	5,735
General Assistance (GA)	1,062,000	57.75	736
Total	13,814,000		$9,548

Source: U.S. Department of Health, Education and Welfare.

General Assistance, aids those of the poor who do not fit one of the other categories. The distribution of public assistance dollars among these programs varies greatly. By far the largest share of assistance in 1970 was directed to the Aid to Families with Dependent Children (AFDC) program. However, AFDC recipients received less money on average than other welfare recipients, in conformity with society's concept of employability. Blind, disabled, and aged poor are clearly handicapped in the labor market; hence, society feels a greater obligation for their support. Mothers of young children are not so clearly unemployable, however, and public assistance is rendered to them with comparative reluctance and in smaller amounts.

The AFDC Program

The largest and most controversial public assistance program is the Aid to Families with Dependent Children (AFDC) program. It is the program people automatically associate with the name *welfare*. By studying it, we may learn much about the effectiveness of public assistance for eliminating poverty.

The controversial nature of the AFDC program stems largely from the assumed employability of those who receive its benefits. Not only are the adults who benefit from AFDC relatively young, but their marital status is suspect. Public distrust of the program is heightened by the observation that large numbers of blacks, families headed by women, and illegitimate children participate in the program. Even more distressing to taxpayers is the observation that the program's growth appears to be impervious to advances in the economy. Accordingly, discussion of the AFDC program usually begins against a background of public mistrust.

While the AFDC program is directed at poor families with young children, its coverage of this population is far from complete. Of the nearly 17 million individuals we have already counted in such families (Figure 2.1), fewer than 10 million were receiving assistance at the end of 1970 (Table 11.1). Thus, being poor in a family with children is not sufficient qualification for receiving AFDC support; a further distinction is made between the deserving and the undeserving poor. In this case, the deserving are those whose fathers or husbands are dead, deserted, or otherwise absent from the home. The presence of a male adult in the home is taken as prima facie evidence that the family is capable of its own support. AFDC payments are reserved for fatherless homes, regardless of whatever needs poor male-headed families may have.[1]

Even among those poor families fortunate enough to receive AFDC payments, there are tremendous disparities in the amount of support provided. The typical AFDC family, a mother and three children, received in 1970 an average of $2,200 per year in welfare payments. However, poor families of four in New Jersey or New York received $3,500 a year in welfare payments, while the same family in Mississippi received only $550 a year. Payment and qualifying levels in various states are described in Table 11.2.

TABLE 11.2 AFDC Payments and Asset Limitations in Selected States, 1969

State	Average Monthly Payments Per Family	Asset Limitations
California	$192.90	$600 + $5,000 home
Illinois	240.95	Enough to last one month
Maryland	162.60	$300 + home
Mississippi	46.40	$800 + $2,500 home
New Jersey	252.75	Liquidation in 6 months
New York	292.20	"Trust funds of an infant up to $1,000, more if personal injury award"
Rhode Island	230.00	No cash
Texas	118.05	$3,000 + "used home"

Source: U.S. Department of Health, Education and Welfare, and U. S. Senate, Committee on Finance, *Hearings on H.R. 16311,* April-May 1970, p. 166.

Disparities in support reflect far more than differences in the cost of living. In essence, they reflect the ability and willingness of taxpayers in each state to provide for the needy. At present, federal, state, and country governments must contribute to the financing of AFDC. If the county or state cannot or will not provide adequate funds, the federal contribution is also diminished. Welfare payments in Mississippi, for example, are low, both because there is little public or private money in the state and because white Mississippians do not want to spend what little there is in providing for the poor, many of whom are black.

[1] An exception to this rule is the AFDC-UP program, which provides benefits to poor families with unemployed fathers, but the program is too small and restrictive to merit attention here. At the end of 1970, only 796,000 persons were receiving AFDC-UP benefits.

Very few taxpayers actually derive special satisfaction from knowing that they are providing generously for the poor. Indeed, society tends to maintain payment levels as low as possible. The 1970 national average payment of $2,200 a year was itself less than 60 percent of the poverty budget, which means not only that public assistance is reserved for those in dire need but also that those we do assist remain in need. While public assistance does alleviate some hardship, it fails to lift recipients completely out of poverty.

In the minds of most hard-working taxpayers, welfare conjures up visions of the easy life—a beer on a hot afternoon, color television at night. Even President Nixon has referred to welfare as a "free ride." It is clear from actual welfare experience, however, that very few welfare families are even tolerably comfortable, much less riding high. A budget of $2,200 for four persons does not spread far, no matter how thinly it is spread. Recall how little food, shelter, and clothing is provided by the much larger poverty budget. It would be a strange individual who forsook any but the poorest paying and most loathsome job for such a "free ride."

Table 11.3 shows the monthly budget of an AFDC recipient in California, one of the more generous states. In computing the needs of an AFDC mother, the state legislature individually scrutinized each potential expense. The procedure is identical to the one we used earlier to construct hypothetical poverty lines. These figures, however, are real; they represent the maximum standard of living for an AFDC mother in 1970. Note that she was allowed no more than $62.60 for rent, no telephone, and only $3.50 per month for recreation and education! Her actual standard of living was lower yet, as much smaller allowances were provided for her children. In less generous states, of course, the situation was far worse.

In light of the pittance available to AFDC recipients, it seems most

TABLE 11.3 Maximum Monthly Budget for AFDC Mother in California, 1969

Consumption Items	Amount Allowed
Food	$26.50
Clothing	10.85
Personal and incidental	2.40
Recreation and education	3.50
Community participation	-
Telephone service	-
Transportation	1.00
Household operations	6.00
Intermittent needs	1.75
Rent and utilities (maximum)	62.60
Total	$114.60

Source: President's Commission on Income Maintenance Programs, *Poverty Amid Plenty* (Washington: Government Printing Office, 1969), p. 117.

unlikely that wage earners, even low paid ones, would rush to the welfare rolls. To guard against this remote possibility, however, stringent property limitations have been established for those who seek public assistance. You cannot turn to welfare, at least not for long, just because you run out of money. To enter and remain on the welfare rolls, you must also dispose of nearly all property. In most states, a welfare family may possess no more than $1,000 in personal property, although there is sometimes an additional asset allowance if the family owns a house. Very few Cadillacs are maintained at that price. In the state of Maryland, a family may own only $300 of property. A sampling of other states' asset limitations is contained in Table 11.2.

A discussion of welfare programs must begin, then, from the observation that financial dependence on public assistance is not comfortable. Families turn to public assistance only after they are impoverished and no other support is available. When on welfare, families will be maintained below levels society otherwise deems to be minimally adequate.

Given the nature of public assistance, it is not surprising to learn that welfare recipients are generally dissatisfied with the welfare system. As it turns out, however, no one else is particularly happy with it, either. Liberal critics of the program are dissatisfied with AFDC's coverage, its benefits, and the humiliation associated with the receipt of public assistance. Taxpayers generally are unhappy with the spiraling costs of the program and continue to view recipients with disfavor and suspicion. And finally, all critics unite in pointing out that the welfare system tends to undermine the motivation to work. Until quite recently, a family on welfare had very little financial incentive to seek employment, not because welfare represented the "good life," but because welfare regulations prohibited a family from improving its standard of living by working. How this situation came about can be explained by the AFDC budgeting process.

When a family applies for welfare, it is obliged to report any income at its disposal. A woman with small children, for example, might earn $50 a month by babysitting and ironing for neighbors. Up until quite recently, welfare authorities subtracted any such income from the family's needs—as determined by those same welfare authorities—and provided the difference. Suppose the welfare authorities concluded that Mrs. Jones and her three children needed $200 a month: they paid her only $150, knowing that Mrs. Jones herself could provide the rest. While this procedure perhaps distributed welfare funds equitably among recipients, it destroyed all initiative for self-improvement.

Imagine that Mrs. Jones was offered regular part-time employment, as a nurse's aide, for example, at $1.25 an hour for 20 hours a week. Now Mrs. Jones may be reluctant to leave her small children in the care of others, but she could certainly use the money. Consequently, she is inclined to accept the job, especially if transportation problems (she has no car) and child care arrangements can be worked out. But what will happen to her actual income if she takes this step toward self-improvement? Absolutely nothing. The welfare authorities simply note that she is earning $100 a month rather than $50, they reckon that she is better providing for her own needs and reduce her welfare payment to $100. Her family's income remains at $200 whether or not Mrs. Jones finds employment and regardless of how hard she strives for self-improvement.

Recent Welfare Reforms

The glaring failure of the AFDC program to reinforce work incentives has prompted some improvements in the welfare system. In 1967, Congress amended the program to provide slightly greater work incentives through more flexible budgets, expanded child care services, and new training programs. Unfortunately, those efforts were weakened by a widespread distrust of AFDC recipients and by the reluctance of the states to adopt congressional improvements. More recently, still broader modifications have been proposed in an environment of marginally improved public understanding.

In August, 1969, President Nixon proposed a major reform of the AFDC program. His proposal, called the Family Assistance Program, or FAP, was designed to eliminate most of the major defects in the welfare system. In particular, it sought to eliminate or reduce three acknowledged weaknesses in the existing AFDC program. First, FAP was intended to provide financial support to all families with children. The presence of fathers and husbands in the household would no longer be a barrier to public assistance. Second, the Nixon administration proposed to establish uniform federal minimum payments to all needy families, regardless of location. Thus, poor families in Mississippi would not be totally dependent on the income and good will of their neighbors. Finally, FAP was designed to provide meaningful incentives to find and secure employment.

The work incentive provisions of the Family Assistance proposal are especially interesting because they touch on the primary concern of all taxpayers and their congressmen: the public fervently seeks to curtail the growth in welfare costs. To achieve this aim, welfare recipients must be given the opportunity and incentive to provide for themselves. Recognizing this need, the Nixon administration incorporated provisions in the FAP plan that would allow recipients to retain some part of what they earn. Figure 11.1 illustrates how the system works.

Take the case of Mrs. Jones again. Under the FAP proposal, she and her children would receive a minimum welfare payment of at least $2,400 per year; her state may increase that minimum if it so chooses. If she does not work at all, she will be at point A. But suppose she decides to accept the job as nurse's aide. That job pays $1.25 an hour and offers 1000 hours of work a year (20 hours per week). Under the old AFDC system, she would move to point E, working more

FIGURE 11.1 Work Incentive Provisions under FAP

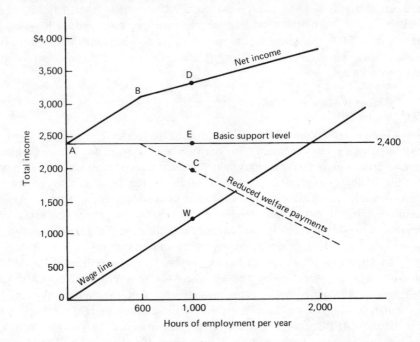

but with no change in total income. Under FAP, however, she moves to point D and increases her well-being by working. Instead of automatically deducting from her welfare payments every dollar she earns, the welfare authorities allow Mrs. Jones to utilize part of her earnings. They disregard completely the first $720 (or $60 per month) she earns, allowing Mrs. Jones to move from point A to point B. Only as she earns in excess of $720 does the welfare department begin to reduce the size of her welfare check. Beyond that point, her net income rises more slowly than her wage earnings. But the welfare authorities reduce her welfare check by only sixty-seven cents for each dollar she earns. Thus, Mrs. Jones has a continuing incentive to work.

The total income of Mrs. Jones and her family at point D is easily computed. If she works all year (1000 hours) at her new job, she receives the following amount: her wages ($1,250 at point W) plus a welfare check reduced by two thirds of her wages in excess of $720 [$2,400 − 2/3 ($1,250 − $720)]. In this case, she receives a welfare check in the amount of $2,047 (point C). Her total income at point D is thus $1,250 from working plus $2,047 from welfare, or $3,297. By her own modest efforts, then, she has managed to increase her family's economic status substantially.

The payment provisions of the FAP proposal, then, contain a significant incentive to work. Coupled with the extension of welfare to male-headed poor families and increased federal financing, FAP is an attractive substitute for AFDC. Unfortunately, these potential benefits of welfare reform have been undermined to some extent by continuing public distrust of recipients. Congressional debates have led to the incorporation into FAP legislation of potentially regressive conditions of eligibility and income maintenance. The Ninety-first Congress, for example, threatened welfare recipients with a ceiling and even a cutback on welfare benefit levels. Reporting and termination provisions suggested further that it would be difficult to get on welfare and all too easy to get off, regardless of need. These and similarly punitive conditions illustrate again the widespread conviction that recipients seek a "free ride." Final resolution of these issues still awaits congressional action.

The Impact on Poverty

Regardless of what form the welfare system finally takes, its impact on poverty can be assessed. Two questions stand out: (1) How much does the welfare system reduce existing poverty; and (2) how much does it contribute to the prevention of future poverty? Present and proposed welfare programs fare poorly on both counts.

We have already seen that the level of AFDC payments is so low that it effectively perpetuates poverty. No one receiving AFDC escapes the rigors of impoverishment. Life is rendered a little bit less difficult, to be sure, but no welfare family knows freedom from want. Accordingly, we may say that the AFDC program provides necessary assistance, but it fails to diminish the count of those who are poor.

The proposed Family Assistance Program does a better job of reducing present poverty. By allowing families to achieve a higher standard of living through a combination of employment and welfare, it provides an escape from absolute impoverishment. Under the FAP work incentive provisions, a family would receive assistance until it reached an income of $4,320.[2] At that level, they would be just above the figure society has defined as minimally necessary. While one or two hundred dollars above the poverty line is not a great distance, it is still a long way from the average of $2,200 a year received under AFDC. Hence, a modified welfare program would help to marginally reduce the number of persons we count as poor.

Higher welfare benefits are not, however, what society has in mind when it talks of eliminating poverty. Taxpayers seek not only to alleviate the plight of

---

[2] When a family earns $4,320, it loses all welfare assistance. Recall that FAP payments are reduced by sixty-seven cents for each dollar earned beyond $720. Hence, when it earns $4,320, the family loses 2/3($4,320-$720) or $2,400 in welfare assistance.

the poor but to eliminate the *need* for welfare. If the elimination of poverty is achieved only by greater transfer payments, there is no prospect of diminishing welfare rolls and costs; income transfers will have to be continued into perpetuity. Meaningful reduction of both poverty and welfare costs necessitates that welfare families be given greater opportunity to provide for themselves. To what extent does the welfare system yield this kind of long-run benefit?

The greater financial resources provided to families under AFDC or FAP most certainly do have some long-term effect. At the extreme, the payments at least enable families to avert starvation and function normally. In some cases, they even provide enough money for children to stay in school, properly fed and clothed, and for parents to seek a job. Adequate financial assistance may even help hold a family together. All this doubtlessly contributes to personal and economic development. Higher standards of living also raise morale, aspirations, and initiative. As Senator Fred Harris of Oklahoma pointed out during congressional deliberations on welfare reform: "If you provide an adequate level of income, people are in fact encouraged to work, and initiative and incentive are increased, while incomes below what is necessary for decent health, housing, and living standards destroy initiative and make it difficult for succeeding generations to break the welfare cycle."[3]

As important as these many contributions to personal and economic well-being are, however, they must still be evaluated within a more general economic context. Greater nutrition, stability, and initiative are necessary but not sufficient conditions for economic independence. To achieve independence, one must also have access to a meaningful job, yet welfare systems themselves do nothing to alter the number or types of jobs available. They were neither intended nor designed to expand employment opportunities. In essence, welfare programs strive only to provide income maintenance for families until other economic opportunities emerge.

The inherent limitations to welfare programs render them relatively ineffective as long-term solutions to poverty. They cannot be abolished because to do so would be to totally ignore the plight of the poor. And even in the best of economic and racial situations, many individuals will be temporarily or permanently incapable of self-support. Yet we must not confuse welfare reform with expansion of opportunity, nor should we indulge in the fiction that more generous assistance today will eliminate the need for assistance tomorrow. We must expand and improve the welfare system to provide for those in need. But to reduce the number of people who need assistance, we must expand opportunities for financial independence.

---

[3] Senate Committee on Finance, *Hearings on H.R. 16311* (Washington, D.C.: Government Printing Office, 1970), p. 158.

NEGATIVE INCOME TAXES

The existing system of public assistance is designed to aid only certain selected categories of the poor. For the most part, existing programs are predicated on the assumption that those capable of work need never resort to welfare; hence, the programs focus on the aged, the disabled, the blind, and mothers with dependent children. One consequence of this categorical approach, as the President's Commission on Income Maintenance Programs has noted, has been the exclusion from public assistance of many who are unquestionably in need of help. The proposed Family Assistance Program bridges most of this gap, but not all. FAP would provide assistance only to poor families with children. Single individuals or couples without children would remain unassisted even under the proposed expansion of the welfare system. To many observers, this exclusion seems inequitable and unnecessary. They propose to replace the sundry programs of public assistance with a single comprehensive system of negative income taxes.

The essence of a negative income tax (NIT) system is very simple. Like FAP, it provides an income floor. It also allows individuals to rise above this floor through identical work incentive provisions: for every dollar a person earns, he loses less than a dollar of income assistance. The amount lost or deducted is analogous to a tax on earnings. However, whereas normally taxes are deducted directly from earnings, negative income taxes represent reductions in income assistance. Hence, the name *negative income taxes.*

While the mechanics of the FAP and negative income tax programs are identical, there are important distinctions between the two approaches. One distinction we have already mentioned, namely, the more complete coverage of negative income tax programs; they are designed to reach all those in need.

The universality of negative income taxes (NIT) implies another advantage. The current patchwork of public assistance programs necessitates a case by case determination of eligibility, need, and grant levels. Not only is such a determination expensive and frustratingly slow; it often leads to administrative abuse. Welfare authorities have demonstrated a special concern for the morals of recipients and have even conducted midnight raids on the homes of AFDC mothers. Moral fitness requirements have been established by state legislatures and welfare authorities to supplement more objective income criteria of eligibility. Under a negative income tax program, case by case determinations would be unnecessary and administrative abuse unlikely.

Another consequence of present administrative arrangements is that welfare regulations are confusing and vary by state. Recipients have little access to information regarding the rules that govern them or the benefits to which they are entitled. Generally, they are compelled to rely on program personnel, such as caseworkers, for this information. In some jurisdictions the information is provided; in others it is systematically withheld. The net result is to render the recipient totally dependent on the capability and benevolence of local authorities.

NIT programs would overcome most of these deficiencies by standardizing eligibility criteria and by making assistance available as a matter of right. Every poor family would receive identical aid, based on the number of family members. Access to financial assistance would be as simple and direct as income taxes now are, and similar verification procedures would be utilized to certify eligibility. Local authorities would have no discretionary control over the behavior of recipients, whose identity would be confidential.

While NIT proposals do have many attractions, they are not without their faults. Like the proposed FAP, they suffer from competition among the goals of income provision, work encouragement, and administrative efficiency. If we really want to protect people from the indignities of poverty, we should establish a high income floor. If we also desire to encourage employment and self-improvement, we must impose low negative tax rates; that is, we must allow a recipient to keep a large share of his earnings above the minimum. And if we desire to hold program costs down to some reasonable level, we must limit the coverage of the program to those in need. All of these objectives are worthwhile, just as the means for achieving them are clear, but they are mutually exclusive. We cannot move in all directions at once.

The internal conflicts of NIT or FAP proposals can be illustrated easily. Figure 11.2 depicts again the mechanics of this kind of income transfer program. Let us suppose that we are determined to assure everyone a decent income. We begin by establishing an income floor of $4,000 for a family of four. Every family is guaranteed that amount regardless of whether or not any family member works. To encourage work, however, we also permit families to continue receiving assistance after they find employment. Thus, we set a negative tax rate of 50 percent, thereby gradually diminishing income transfers.[4] Thus, two of our goals are fulfilled: namely, income provision and work encouragement. But what about the third goal, cost minimization? Under our NIT plan, a family would continue to receive some assistance until its earnings reached $8,000. Accordingly, our NIT benefits would be received by many whom we do not consider poor. The size of the program would be enormous—over 100 million people!—and its cost unacceptable.

There is no way to resolve this conflict within the context of a single program. High income guarantees, low negative tax rates, and low breakeven incomes cannot coexist. The nature of their relationship is:

$$\text{breakeven level of income } = \frac{\text{income floor}}{\text{negative tax rate}}$$

[4] Note that no earnings exclusion is included here. Under FAP, a recipient could earn $720 without a consequent reduction in assistance. The earnings exclusion under FAP accounted for the kink in the net income line of Figure 11.1.

FIGURE 11.2   The Mechanics of a Negative Income Tax Program

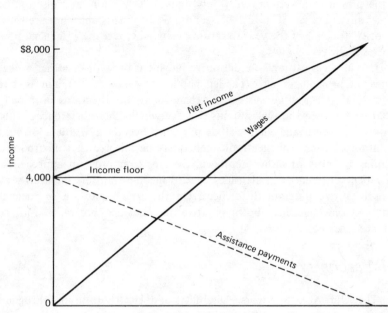

As the income floor rises, so do costs and coverage. If a lower breakeven level of income is desired, either a high income floor or low tax rates must be sacrificed. Accordingly, fulfillment of any two objectives necessitates sacrificing the third. The choice of how far to pursue each objective will ultimately have to be made in the political arena.

There are other criticisms of negative income tax programs. It is argued that a single, comprehensive income transfer program would not be flexible enough to meet the needs of various population groups. Aged poor, for example, require no work incentive provisions. Hence, a program tailored to their needs would differ from a program directed to the young. From this perspective, the present categorical approach to public assistance is both more flexible and more efficient.

Present welfare programs also provide various social services to the poor. Homemaking, day care, medical assistance, and employment training are just a few of the services now included in various public assistance programs. Many argue that it would be inefficient to divorce these services from the mechanics of income transfer. Presently, determination of need for income assistance and for social services can be performed simultaneously.

Finally, it is contended that a negative income tax program would not materially reduce administrative costs. Families would still need assistance on short notice and at frequent intervals. Hence, an NIT program could not operate like the present tax system, with only annual declarations and disbursements. Families at the margin of subsistence cannot wait for assistance, nor are they in a position at the end of the year to return overpayments if their financial position improves slightly.

It is not easy to make a definitive judgment in favor of either a negative income tax program or an expanded public assistance system, nor is it really necessary. If the welfare system is expanded in the directions proposed, the similarities between the two systems will overwhelm their differences. This will be especially true if and when welfare payments become available upon a simple declaration of need. Further refinements may be selected that incorporate the remaining benefits of either approach. Debates over program approaches will then reflect differences in attitudes toward income transfers themselves rather than substantive program differences. On the larger question of meaningful antipoverty mechanisms, both negative income tax programs and public assistance score equally low.

SOCIAL SECURITY

The Old Age, Survivors, Disability and Health Insurance Program—or Social Security—is a very different kind of income maintenance program. Social security benefits are not reserved for those in need. Instead, they are distributed primarily to those who have made prior contributions to the program's funds. Thus, the program is neither intended nor operated as an antipoverty mechanism. The majority of the 26 million individuals who receive social security payments have never experienced poverty, yet they receive more than $30 billion in annual payments, triple the size of annual public assistance payments.

The financing of social security is carried out by the imposition of special taxes on employment income. In 1971, social security taxes were 5.2 percent on the first $7,800 of wages. Thus, a person earning $7,800 or more contributed $405.60 to the social security program. His employer contributed an identical amount. These contributions are not reserved for those who currently pay taxes. Rather, they are used to provide benefits to those individuals over sixty-five who no longer work but once made contributions to the program. Later generations are expected to provide the funds for present workers when they retire.

Social security finances are a unique combination of insurance and income redistribution principles. To some extent, the amount of any person's eventual benefit is conditioned by the size of his earlier payments. A person who earned $7,800 or more in 1971 paid more social security taxes, that is, higher premiums, than people earning less. Accordingly, he is entitled to greater benefits when he retires. In 1971, the maximum monthly social security benefit was $295.40 per person, while the minimum payment was only $70.40.

Were social security benefits distributed solely according to previous contributions, the program's ability to alleviate poverty would be negligible. People who received high benefits after retirement would be those who had higher incomes while working. Those who are poor while in the labor force are unable to pay high premiums and would receive only meager benefits in old age. Thus, conditioning retirement benefits on the basis of previous ability to pay would have the effect of perpetuating impoverishment.

Fortunately, the social security program does not operate exclusively on insurance principles. Some redistribution of income is built into social security financing. Persons who earn little and thus pay very low social security taxes receive proportionately larger benefits than individuals who pay high premiums. Thus, workers near the bottom of the income distribution receive more retirement benefits for every dollar of taxes they pay than workers near the top of the income distribution. Nevertheless, minimum benefits for a retired couple remain 40 percent below the poverty line, and many aged individuals must rely on public welfare (Old Age Assistance) or do without. Still others receive no retirement benefits because they or their spouses were never employed in occupations subject to social security taxation.

Even people who managed to avert poverty while working are subject to impoverishment after retirement. This contingency applies especially to those who were at the margins of poverty while young and lose their primary source of income when old. For them, social security payments may represent the difference between poverty and nonpoverty in old age. In 1970, nearly four million aged persons fell into this category. They would have been poor were it not for the fact that social security benefits supplemented their modest pensions and savings.

The impact of the social security program testifies to its potential effectiveness as an antipoverty mechanism. The program has done a remarkable job of reducing the number of aged poor and of alleviating the condition of those who remain poor. Moreover, the program has remained popular with the public, despite its enormous size. Accordingly, efforts to enhance the program's antipoverty impact stand a good chance of success. In fact, increases in social security benefit levels are enacted by Congress regularly, as are new social security tax rates and ceilings. In 1972, minimum monthly benefits are expected to rise from $70.40 to $100, while the taxable wage ceiling will rise from $7,800 to $9,000. The higher benefit levels will sharply curtail existing poverty among the aged.

Across-the-board increases in social security benefits extend to the aged nonpoor as well as the poor. To offer greater aid to the poor among the aged requires more selective measures. To aid the aged poor while keeping program size down, minimum benefit levels must rise more than others. While this may be desirable, it runs the threat of undermining public support for the program. Congress walks a thin line when it seeks to aid the aged poor while maintaining broad public support. Nevertheless, the program reforms of 1971-1972 indicate that further enhancement of the program's antipoverty capability is feasible.

SUMMARY

There is no coherent *system* of income maintenance in the United States. Instead, we rely on a variety of diverse income transfer programs, designed and implemented independently of each other. Despite these patchwork origins, however, current public assistance and social security programs do provide much aid for the poor. Social Security eliminates poverty for millions of individuals, while Social Security and public assistance together relieve the hardships of impoverishment for still more persons.

Analysis of income maintenance programs may proceed from two distinct perspectives. We may inquire first how efficiently and equitably current programs now perform their intended transfer functions. However, it is also necessary to ask how appropriate *any* kind of income maintenance system is as a long-run solution to poverty.

While current income maintenance programs do provide much assistance, they do so with much inequity and little efficiency. Public assistance programs are particularly inequitable in their disregard of the needs of poor families with working fathers. These *working poor* are excluded from assistance due to a misplaced concern for work motivation and a general desire to contain public expenditures. Also maltreated are those who are eligible for categorical assistance programs but reside in impoverished or unsympathetic states. Even after receiving assistance, they remain pitifully below acceptable standards of living.

To a large extent, the proposed reform of public assistance (the Family Assistance Program) promises to correct these deficiencies. A negative income tax plan would move slightly further in the same direction with more universality and less implied control over behavior. Even these programs, however, would have to contend with the competing objectives of income provision, work encouragement, and cost minimization.

The social security program is the largest and most popular income transfer program, yet its ability to eliminate, rather than perpetuate, poverty depends on its ability to depart from insurance principles. The small departures that have been made in the past have yielded significant benefits for the aged poor. Still further increases in minimum social security benefits could virtually eliminate poverty among the aged.

Existing and foreseen income maintenance programs do have the potential, then, of alleviating poverty. They are not a solution to the poverty problem, however. They fail to provide more than a marginal impetus to financial independence. They can meet the need for income support, but they cannot eliminate the need itself. If relied on exclusively, public assistance programs would perpetuate poverty and the need for extensive public assistance expenditures. This is not consistent with the needs of the poor, the objectives of the taxpaying public, or the requirements of a viable economy. Income maintenance policies must be complemented by policies that provide opportunities for economic independence.

REFERENCES

BIXBY, LENORE, "Income of People Aged 65 and Over," *Social Security Bulletin,* April 1970.

COMMITTEE FOR ECONOMIC DEVELOPMENT, *Improving the Public Welfare System.* New York: Committee for Economic Development, 1970.

FRIEDMAN, MILTON, *Capitalism and Freedom.* Chicago: University of Chicago Press, 1962, Chs. 10-12.

GREEN, CHRISTOPHER, "The Negative Income Tax," in *Poverty in America,* Louis A. Ferman et al., eds. Ann Arbor: University of Michigan Press, 1968.

LAMPMAN, ROBERT J., "Transfer Approaches to Distribution Policy," *American Economic Review,* May 1970.

NATIONAL WELFARE RIGHTS ORGANIZATION, *Six Myths About Welfare.* Washington, D.C.: National Welfare Rights Organization, 1971.

PECHMAN, JOSEPH, HENRY AARON, and MICHAEL TAUSSIG, *Social Security: Perspectives for Reform.* Washington, D.C.: The Brookings Institution, 1968.

PRESIDENT'S COMMISSION ON INCOME MAINTENANCE PROGRAMS, *Poverty Amid Plenty.* Washington, D.C.: Government Printing Office, 1969.

SCHULTZE, CHARLES L., ET AL., *Setting National Priorities: The 1972 Budget.* Washington, D.C.: The Brookings Institution, 1971, Chs. 8, 10.

STEINER, GILBERT S., *The State of Welfare.* Washinton, D.C.: The Brookings Institution, 1971.

WILCOX, CLAIR, *Toward Social Welfare.* Homewood, Ill.: Richard D. Irwin, Inc., 1969, Chs. 14, 15.

12 Employment Policies

If meaningful and long-term solutions to the problem of poverty are to be implemented, public policy will have to venture beyond income maintenance. Simply providing money to the poor, particularly in meager amounts, has little potential for stimulating financial independence. The only possible lasting solution to the problem of poverty is to assure that decent jobs are available to all who seek them. Under such circumstances, the occurrence of poverty and the need for income maintenance will be at a minimum.

The government has several alternatives at its disposal when it seeks to expand employment opportunities. At the most general level, it may seek to increase the demand for labor by stimulating aggregate demand. A variety of fiscal and monetary measures are available to implement such a decision. On the other hand, government policy may concentrate on the supply of labor. Rather than stimulate new demand, government policy may focus on training unemployed workers for jobs already available. Or the government might take still more direct action by creating jobs itself. Public employment programs might even combine the features of labor demand and worker training through a judicious selection of employment opportunities.

To some extent, each of these policy alternatives has been implemented, but they have received markedly different degrees of attention. In the 1930s, a heavy emphasis was put on public employment. After World War II, the government placed primary reliance on aggregate economic policies to provide the necessary job opportunities. Only in the late 1950s and early 1960s did an awareness emerge that other approaches were also necessary to provide a requisite number of jobs; at that time, most of our current training programs were introduced. We are now rediscovering that public employment programs may also have a place in our job provision efforts. This chapter deals with the nature, history, and potential of each of these alternatives for eliminating poverty.

AGGREGATE DEMAND POLICIES

It is comforting to believe that the United States could have averted the Great Depression were we as knowledgeable in 1930 as we are now about the workings of the economy. In fact, some recent economic advisors to the president have suggested as much. The implication is that economists can now manage the economy to a degree formerly unheard of. Present-day arguments between economists concentrate, not on the issue of whether the level of demand can be affected, but on how much exactitude can be achieved by such policies. Today we speak of *fine-tuning* the economy rather than just affecting it.

The claims of modern economists inspire hope for the plight of the poor. If we can truly stimulate aggregate demand to any specifications, we can provide enough jobs for the unemployed, the underemployed, and the discouraged poor. Anyone who has even skimmed through an introductory economics textbook can provide an outline for action. Fiscal policies can expand demand through increased government expenditures, consumer tax cuts, or enlarged investment and depreciation allowances. Monetary policy may provide a stimulus to demand by making access to credit easier and cheaper. Together, such policies could move millions of persons out of poverty. The question remains as to why this has not yet been done. Either our claims to precision are exaggerated or we lack the necessary resolve.

Our resolve to expand aggregate employment opportunities visibly weakens when other objectives appear to conflict. As stated in the appendix to Chapter 3, the goal of full employment is readily sacrificed whenever inflation threatens. Our abandonment of full employment stems from a lack of committment to the elimination of poverty and from an incomplete understanding of the relationship between price stability and employment expansion. We simply do not take our claims to economic prowess seriously enough. We continue to believe that full employment is incompatible with price stability, despite claims to the contrary.

In the late 1950s, the goal of full employment was formulated as the attainment of less than 5 percent unemployment. When Walter Heller, President Kennedy's economic advisor, publicly aspired to reach a full employment of 4 percent, he was chided for recklessness. As unemployment sank below even 4 percent in the mid-1960s, some began to wonder whether we had not previously underestimated our abilities and unnecessarily relegated millions of individuals to poverty. The public never became wholly convinced, however. When the rate of inflation did spurt at the end of the sixties, it was concluded immediately that the rise in prices was due to our efforts to create full employment. The observation that these efforts had succeeded for five or six years inspired precious few second thoughts.

But lack of resolution has not been the only obstacle to more effective aggregate demand policies. In the general euphoria of our discovery that we could manipulate aggregate demand, we have neglected some simple truths. The way in which aggregate demand is stimulated will have significant impact on the economy. A large reduction in interest rates, for example, will stimulate the housing and lumber industries, where interest charges are a major component of total cost. Investment credit allowances, on the other hand, will benefit manufacturers of steel, airplanes, and heavy machinery, with little impact on housing production. Indeed, every fiscal or monetary action will affect the distribution of output, as well as its volume. There really is no such thing as a neutral aggregate demand policy.

Because each aggregate demand action affects the economy differently, particular demand policies will have different impacts on employment and price levels. Some actions will provide more jobs for the poor, with little effect on prices, while others will do just the reverse. This requires that policymakers not only decide to expand the demand for labor but that they strive to do so at minimum social cost. Fiscal and monetary actions must be designed for maximum impact on the poor, with minimum disruption and misallocation elsewhere.

Unfortunately, the public's general apathy toward questions of race and poverty has permitted policymakers to ignore these requirements. Instead, policymakers tend to attribute failures to the inherent unattainability of full employment rather than to their own errors of policy design and implementation. The early years of the Nixon administration provide a clear illustration of such escapism.

However, even truly enlightened full employment policies will not provide decent jobs for all who need them. As unemployment levels drop it becomes increasingly difficult—and socially expensive—to reach those who still need employment. Accordingly, expansionary fiscal and monetary policies alone cannot wholly eliminate poverty among those who are presently or potentially in the labor force. But it is even more important to emphasize that without determined full employment policies all other efforts to eliminate poverty are rendered impotent. In 1970 and 1971, for example, more money was spent on welfare, training, education, and other antipoverty efforts than in any other recent years. Nevertheless, the number of people in poverty grew because unemployment levels were allowed to rise. The demand for labor, especially labor provided by the poor, must be kept at high levels if the poor are to gain financial independence. All other efforts are secondary.

TRAINING POLICIES

While the necessity for maintaining a high level of demand for labor is clear, we must also recognize other approaches to full employment. One such approach is to train unemployed workers to fulfill unsatisfied demand. As every freshman economist knows, supply and demand forces operate in the labor market. Hence, to many observers it seems as logical to adapt supply to demand as to proceed the other way around. Indeed, training programs for unemployed workers enjoy much greater acceptance than policies designed to expand and redirect labor demand toward the poor. What accounts for their popularity and how effective are they?

Regardless of what level of unemployment exists, there are always job vacancies. Help wanted ads continue to appear even in periods of high unemployment. People move from job to job with great frequency, creating a kind of musical chairs situation in the labor market. In addition, there are always businesses either expanding or contracting, thereby creating or eliminating available jobs. Thus, at any point in time some jobs are vacant and employers must advertise that fact. How fast those vacancies are filled depends on how many workers are looking for jobs and what their talents are. Where millions of workers are unemployed (in 1971) for example, vacancies are quickly filled. In periods of lower unemployment (such as in 1967-1968) employers must wait longer and look further before obtaining needed labor.

Almost as important as the number of available workers are the skills they possess. If employers are seeking skilled craftsmen, millions of unemployed day laborers will contribute little to the fulfillment of job vacancies. Skills possesed by job-seekers must bear some resemblance to the requirements of available jobs. Nevertheless, it should not be concluded that an existing mismatch of job requirements and skills of the unemployed constitutes an insurmountable barrier to full employment. On the contrary, rarely is a worker hired who is ready to perform on the job with no orientation or training. Employers can and do provide available workers with needed skills. Government programs to train or retrain the unemployed can provide the same service.

Even though private employers frequently engage in some form of orientation or training, they seek to keep training expenses to a minimum. They much prefer to hire persons who are already skilled and experienced, but that option is not always available. As unemployment levels fall, fewer unemployed workers are available. Those who are not yet hired are likely to possess fewer skills. The amount of training employers will have to provide thus varies inversely with the level of unemployment. If aggregate demand is strong, however, they will incur the added expenses willingly. The dynamics of the situation were described in the appendix to Chapter 3.

Government programs to train the unemployed have a slightly different orientation. To some extent, they merely relieve private employers of the burden and expense of training. This may be done by providing training directly or by subsidizing the training efforts of private industry. But training programs directed at the poor have an additional objective: they seek to improve the competitive position of the poor in the labor market. Although the two training functions overlap, they have very different implications. Training designed to create skills in demand leads directly to increased employment; training designed to increase the competitive position of the poor serves to redistribute existing unemployment.

The number of government training programs has mushroomed since the early 1960s, and their annual enrollment now exceeds one million persons (see Table 12.1). Just a sampling of the major programs includes: Area Redevelopment, Job Corps, Manpower Training and Development, Neighborhood Youth Corps, Operation Mainstream, JOBS, Work Incentive Program, Special Impact, Community Work and Training, and New Careers. The number and variety of existing efforts clearly preclude a detailed examination of each. Instead, we will concentrate on two major manpower programs and simply indicate how other programs differ in orientation or impact.

TABLE 12.1   Enrollment in Federal Manpower Programs, Fiscal Year 1970

Program	Enrollment
Manpower Development and Training (MDTA)	221,000
Neighborhood Youth Corps (NYC)	482,100
Operation Mainstream	12,500
Public Service Careers	3,600
Concentrated Employment Program (CEP)	110,100
Work Incentive Program (WIN)	92,700
JOBS	86,800
Job Corps	42,600
Total	1,051,400

Source: U.S. Department of Labor, *Manpower Report of the President*, 1971 (Washington, D.C.: Government Printing Office, 1971).

The MDTA Program

The first full-scale government training program was established in 1962 under the Manpower Development and Training Act. Persistently high rates of unemployment in the period 1958-1961 coupled with fears of advancing automation led many observors to conclude that a basic mismatch existed between men and jobs. The only way to approach fuller employment, it seemed, was to provide the unemployed with the new skills demanded by advancing technology. Accordingly, Congress provided for a national effort to retrain displaced and unemployed workers in new skill areas.

The Manpower Development and Training (MDTA) program provides two basic kinds of training. Approximately half of the program's participants are enrolled in institutionalized training courses. These courses offer classroom instruction in specific vocational skills and provide remedial education and work orientation services where needed. Work orientation basically consists of advice on how to apply for a job, what to wear and say, and how to act while on the job. In the early stages of the program, participation was limited to a maximum of twelve months, but enrollees may now continue their training activity for up to two years. When their training is completed, the public employment service (the United States Training and Employment Service) offers assistance in locating a regular job.

The other half of MDTA participants are engaged in a very different kind of training program. Rather than learn skills in classroom settings, these enrollees are given instruction in actual job settings. In fact, employers are asked to hire these enrollees on a provisional basis and provide the on-site training necessary for job performance. The government compensates the employer directly for his training costs rather than provide the training itself. Known originally as the on-the-job component of MDTA, or MDTA-OJT, this program dimension is now referred to as JOBS-Optional.

The potential significance of MDTA training to expand individuals' job opportunities is clear. With more and higher occupational skills, workers should be able to command steadier employment and higher wages. This potential is apparent to workers, as evidenced by the fact that over 250,000 persons participated in MDTA during 1971. Unfortunately, however, that potential is not always realized. There is no guarantee of a job to a person who completes MDTA training. Its success, therefore, depends on how well the training course reflects current manpower needs and how many similar workers are seeking employment.

For individuals who participate in the JOBS-Optional program, eventual job placement is much more promising. The employer himself selects those workers he will train. Thus, it is reasonable to suppose that the employer intends to incorporate trainees into his regular work force when training is completed. Actual experience shows that nine out of ten such trainees are retained.

The impact of MDTA on unemployment and poverty is not easy to assess. MDTA clearly does contribute to the elimination of poverty when it provides an unemployed or low-skilled worker with new skills or a better job. However, it is not always possible to isolate the particular significance of MDTA in this process. Many MDTA participants may have acquired jobs and skills on their own, making MDTA superfluous. This is a very strong possibility in the case of participants hired and trained under the JOBS-Optional component. Private employers seek MDTA trainees only when they require more labor. Hence, it seems reasonable to conclude that the government is paying employers for a hiring and training function they would have performed anyway. If this is true, then very little independent contribution is attributable to MDTA.

This criticism of MDTA is especially relevant to the poor. Because private employers choose their own trainees, a sharp difference emerges between institutional and on-the-job trainees. The best MDTA participants are taken into private employment, while the least qualified—and thus the most needy—are assigned to classroom vocational instruction. This process of *creaming* leaves many of the poor unemployed or earning low wages at the end of their training. In recent years, 30 percent of MDTA trainees from public assistance backgrounds, that is, the poor, have remained unemployed after course completion.

Another major flaw in the MDTA program is its inability to assist the working poor. Over four million individuals were poor in 1970 because the family head worked all year round at substandard wages (see Chapter 4). Certainly these persons could benefit from the occupational upgrading which MDTA promises. It is ironic that so few can afford it. Institutional MDTA trainees receive only limited living allowances during their course of instruction. Hence, low-income workers, already severely impoverished, must incur further losses while enrolled in MDTA (for up to two years!). Families at the margin of subsistence simply cannot afford it.

It would be unfair to conclude that MDTA is wholly ineffective. On the contrary, it does provide needed training and placement services. It helps bridge the gap between labor supply and demand. Moreover, demand for MDTA services continues to run high, indicating that the unemployed perceive positive benefits from participation. The stated criticisms are intended only to highlight the inherent limits to the program and its tendency to exclude the most desperate of those in need.

The WIN Program

The Work Incentive Program, or WIN, focuses more specifically on the neediest. Like MDTA, the WIN program offers institutional training in a number of occupations. Unlike the former program, however, it serves only those who are receiving public assistance. Program participation is specifically limited to adult recipients of AFDC assistance, a restriction that gives WIN certain distinguishable characteristics. First of all, participation in the program is legislated as mandatory for all AFDC recipients. This provision resulted from the widespread conviction that welfare recipients seek to avoid employment (see Chapter 7). Second, and more positively, the program attempts to provide the supplemental services necessary for successful program completion. These range from day-care services and work orientation to medical examinations, transportation allowances, counseling, and job placement. Thus, the program offers a unified package of services designed to move people from welfare to employment.

Most of the actual training provided WIN enrollees takes place in institutional settings. After a series of aptitude tests and counseling sessions, a new WIN enrollee indicates which skill he wants to pursue. If this choice is approved, arrangements are made with training institutes or schools to enroll the individual in appropriate classes. At the completion of training, he returns to WIN, where an effort is made to place him on a job.

Because of WIN's link to welfare, there are no financial barriers to program participation. WIN enrollees continue to receive the same public assistance they had prior to entry. In addition, they are provided an incentive payment of $30 a month and a transportation allowance. Thus, no one need incur a financial setback to obtain WIN training.

There are other obstacles to successful course completion, however. Because WIN is limited to adult AFDC recipients, the vast majority of participants are women. Women suffer special handicaps in the labor market due to child care responsibilities, limited experience, and outright discrimination. In addition, welfare mothers have to contend with frequent breakdowns in transportation and child care arrangements and must overcome particularly restricted educational and occupational backgrounds. As a consequence, they have difficulty remaining in the program and in obtaining employment if they complete training. Less than one-fourth of those who enter the program end up with a job, and even then, the jobs do not provide enough income to afford financial independence. Very few WIN graduates actually leave the welfare rolls.

The failure of the WIN program to place enrollees on jobs is not due to faulty program design. There is little more that a manpower program can do, short of actually creating a job. It must be recognized that welfare mothers have the least prospects for employment. They will not be hired until all those who are more qualified have been employed. Within this context, the WIN program can be deemed successful if it provides supplemental income, satisfaction, and improved skills while the job search continues.

PUBLIC SERVICE EMPLOYMENT

It was suggested in Chapter 7 that underdeveloped skills or education are not a prime cause of poverty. It was argued instead that education and training credentials simply render an individual more competitive in the job search. Credentials provide a person with early access to job vacancies, but they do not guarantee that such vacancies will exist. The experience with government training programs tends to support this view. For the most part, training programs are unable to place people on jobs unless labor market conditions warrant. If there are no jobs waiting when training is completed, the net effect of training is to create a slightly more skilled pool of *unemployed* workers. Training programs are not able to significantly increase employment, particularly when unemployment is rampant.

Frustration with the results of government training programs has led most observers to an obvious conclusion—that more jobs must be created. Expanded labor demand, not improved labor supply, appears to be the surest and fastest way to reduce unemployment and poverty. To a large extent, the government's responsibility to create jobs is recognized in the Full Employment Act of 1946; the government pursues this responsibility by implementing the fiscal and monetary policies necessary to expand aggregate demand. But manipulation of aggregate demand is not the only, or always the most efficient, method of job creation. An alternative is for the government to directly employ those who seek work.

Public service employment, then, is a very special kind of job creation. It involves the government directly in the employment process. It gives the government explicit control over what will be produced and who will be employed to produce it. At times this control may be advantageous; public services are not well provided for in the market context. Even though all taxpayers anguish over the lack of sanitation, transportation, education, protection, and recreation services, few are willing to pay for them. Nor can these public services be provided and paid for on an individual basis.[1] Accordingly, there is an output void which can be filled only by explicit government provisions.

The control that public service employment bestows over the structure of demand can also be used to advantage. Generalized aggregate demand policies, such as tax cuts, have widespread impact, some of which may be undesirable. Public service employment programs, on the other hand, can channel new labor demand to those areas or population groups most in need. Hence, maximum impact can be achieved with minimum disruption elsewhere in the economy. This advantage is especially important when unemployment rates are low and unemployment is geographically or demographically localized.

Public service employment, then, may fulfill two objectives: it may provide needed services and expand employment opportunities. How well it fulfills these objectives depends on how much money is allocated for this purpose and how well those funds are spent. The Emergency Employment Act of 1971 provided for a maximum of 200,000 jobs over a period of two years. While that number was not insignificant, it represented only a small dent in the ranks of the unemployed, who, at the time, numbered over 5 million. The Works Progress Administration (WPA) of the 1930s employed about 2 million individuals at any given time.

It is unfortunate that the concept of public service employment instinctively produces an image of make-work activity. People continue to think of the WPA as a major leafraking force. Even the president and the Congress themselves beneficiaries of public service employment—are prone to distinguish between "real" work and public service jobs. Yet, the WPA constructed 651,000 miles of roads, 16,000 miles of water lines, 35,000 public buildings, 11,000 recreation facilities, and much more. What relatively little leafraking did take place was the consequence of hasty implementation rather than a dearth of public needs. Today the situation is no different. There is an

---

[1] This dilemma of public goods, or *externalities*, is discussed in most recent economics textbooks.

abundance of useful and needed work to be done, and well-designed programs can do it. We might start by cleaning up our air and water.

What is, perhaps, equally curious about the make-work accusations is that they are applied only to public service employment. Very few people wonder or care whether a stockbroker, psychologist, or college professor does any "real" work. Indeed, we pay farmers enormous sums to avoid real work. Yet when the spotlight turns to the employment of poor persons, the public takes on a special concern for the nature and content of the work performed. Not only is such concern ill-founded, it also implies an inequitable double standard. There is no justification for subjecting the output of the poor to any more scrutiny than that to which we subject the output of the affluent.

Another misapprehension about public service employment is that it requires government to do all the hiring. This was done in the 1930s, but it is not the only approach possible. Where the government perceives that a service can be provided usefully, it may contract with private firms to carry out the actual hiring and production activity. The federal government can just as easily pay the Boeing Company to build sewage treatment plants as to build aircraft frames. This approach cuts right across the distinction between public and private employment. It may also render public service employment programs more acceptable politically. The government can even channel public service funds through community organizations, thereby reaching a higher proportion of those in need.

A COORDINATED APPROACH

The possibilities for converting public jobs into private employment highlight the basic interdependence of the three routes to fuller employment and economic security. Aggregate demand policy, training programs, and public service employment are not mutually exclusive alternatives. Instead, they must be perceived and implemented as complementary dimensions of a single, coordinated manpower policy. High aggregate demand reduces the need for, and improves the outcomes of, training programs. Public service employment has the same effects. Each approach makes the others more effective.

To some extent, two or more of the manpower approaches are combined in a single program. Take the WIN program, for example. While billed as a government training program, WIN incorporates aspects of public service employment. Program activities require the talents of caseworkers, counselors, and trainers, all of whom are performing needed public services. In addition, many graduates of the program become coaches or counselors themselves or are employed as aides in other government programs. Hence, the WIN program not only offers training but provides new job slots as well. Expenditures on the program also tend to expand aggregate demand. Other programs, among them the Neighborhood Youth Corps and the Public Service Careers program, operate in similar fashion.

In attempting to assess the potential effectiveness of employment policies for eliminating poverty, then, one must perceive the whole of manpower activity. It must be recognized that no single approach will bring about full employment or eliminate poverty—at least not without enormous social costs. Government training efforts illustrate the point most vividly. Government training programs enrolled over one million individuals in 1970, at a federal cost of well over a billion dollars. Nevertheless, they failed to make a significant dent either in unemployment or poverty. Restrictive fiscal and monetary policies undercut all other manpower efforts.

The critical role of aggregate demand policies in a general manpower policy is underscored by another consideration. Training and public service employment programs necessitate large and direct federal expenditures. Many dimensions of fiscal and monetary policy involve no such outlays. Prevailing attitudes toward government expenditure are unlikely to yield training and public service employment programs of sufficient size to overcome the deficiencies of inadequate aggregate demand policies.

The end product of a coordinated employment policy should be an abundance of jobs—jobs that provide decent wages and advancement opportunity. The benefits of such jobs are as obvious as is the necessity for them. They will provide the incomes necessary to lift families out of poverty, to keep them together, and to give them promise of a secure future. Their benefits will reach to the children of the poor, who will have the means and incentive for staying in school. Employment policy has the potential, then, of minimizing both present and future poverty.

SUMMARY

The major components of employment policies are fiscal and monetary actions, training programs, and public service employment. While each of these components has its own character and purpose, they are all interdependent. No one component can succeed without support from the other two. At the same time, effective action in any one area enhances the potential for success in the others. One reason government manpower policy has not been more effective in the past is that these components have been viewed more as alternatives than as complements.

Government training programs have a short but well-funded history. Nevertheless, they have failed to fulfill their objectives. They are founded on the premises that good job vacancies exist and that the poor can be equipped to fill them. The Work Incentive (WIN) program of 1969 to 1971 reflects the degree to which this premise has been accepted. Every conceivable effort, including compulsory enrollment, was undertaken by WIN to prepare welfare recipients for work, but the program was not able to overcome the obstacles of slack aggregate demand and an absence of large public service employment opportunities. Training did not lead to jobs because jobs did not exist. Other programs have had the same experience, succeeding only in conjunction with broader manpower policy.

Public service employment has been regarded as the unwanted stepchild of employment policy. It suffers from distorted memories of the 1930s and widespread fears of make-work and government expansion, and yet, public service employment is a vital and necessary component of manpower policy. Not only does it create more jobs, but it can fulfill important public service needs. Moreover, the performance of these public services can be undertaken by the private sector with government financing, thus breaking down the distinction between private and public work. Nevertheless, public service employment programs continue to be viewed as a desperate approach to employment expansion.

Coordinated and comprehensive manpower policies could sharply diminish existing and future poverty. Jobs—in abundance and of good quality—are the most needed and most permanent solution to the poverty problem. Enlightened employment policy can provide them.

REFERENCES

PRESIDENT'S COMMISSION ON INCOME MAINTENANCE, *Poverty Amid Plenty*. Washington, D.C.: Government Printing Office, 1969.

SCHULTZE, CHARLES L., EDWARD R. FRIED, ALICE M. RIVLIN, and NANCY H. TEETERS, *Setting National Priorities: The 1972 Budget*. Washington, D.C.: The Brookings Institution, 1971, Ch. 9.

SUNDQUIST, JAMES L., "Jobs, Training, and Welfare for the Underclass," in *Agenda for the Nation*, Kermit Gordon, ed. Washington, D.C.: The Brookings Institution, 1968.

THUROW, LESTER C., *Poverty and Discrimination*. Washington, D.C.: The Brookings Institution, 1969, Ch. 4.

TOBIN, JAMES, "Raising the Incomes of the Poor," in op. cit. Kermit Gordon, ed.

U.S. DEPARTMENT OF LABOR, *Manpower Evaluation Reports, Nos. 6 and 8*, April 1966 and December 1968. Washington, D.C.: Government Printing Office, 1966, 1968.

U.S. DEPARTMENT OF LABOR, *Manpower Report of the President*, April 1971. Washington, D.C.: Government Printing Office, 1971, Ch. 2.

WILCOX, CLAIR, *Toward Social Welfare*. Homewood, Ill.: Richard D. Irwin, Inc., 1969, Chs. 17 and 18.

13 Equal Opportunity Policies

Earlier chapters have documented the disadvantaged status of minority groups in America. Not only do such groups command fewer resources now, but they have less chance to acquire resources in the future. They have less opportunity to attain higher educational levels or even good quality schooling at lower levels. Even with appropriate educational credentials, they are not permitted to make maximum use of their attainments in the labor market. Such discrimination—both in schools and in the labor market—creates institutional barriers between men and jobs. Those barriers, in turn, alter both the size and composition of the poverty population.

In Chapter 10, a distinction was drawn among three different categories of discrimination. These were: present market discrimination; prior market discrimination; and nonmarket discrimination. Social policies may be directed toward the elimination of any one or all of these categories. At the same time, however, we must recognize that each form of discrimination may require a different kind of policy adaptation. Furthermore, the potential of each kind of institutional policy to reduce poverty varies considerably.

The necessity for adaptive policy is easily illustrated. Consider, for example, the alternatives of eliminating present discriminatory practices or eliminating the effect of prior discrimination. There is no way to forbid discrimination that has already taken place. Consequently, efforts to combat previous discrimination must focus on the effects of that discrimination. Such remedial policies take many forms, including government training programs to provide skills and education earlier denied; and public service employment to create new and improved job opportunities. But the potential of such actions is limited. As long as discriminatory practices continue, the need for remedial action will grow. Hence, more effective policy must focus on current discriminatory practices.

In seeking to combat current discrimination, government bodies have many weapons at their disposal. To some extent, discrimination can be reduced by illuminating the nature and sources of prejudice. More direct action may include outright legal prohibitions, withdrawal or redirection of government funds, or public disclosure of discriminatory actions. Governments may choose to use all of these approaches or none of them. It may also choose to engage in actions that foster discrimination. The focus of this chapter is on the extent to which government bodies are either abetting or combatting discrimination in schools and jobs.

EQUAL EMPLOYMENT OPPORTUNITY POLICIES

Public concern with the employment status of black workers came to the forefront just prior to World War II. Frustrated with their inferior employment status in a generally depressed labor market, black workers threatened to march on Washington, D.C., in the spring of 1941. To forestall that march, President Roosevelt issued an executive order creating the first federal Fair Employment Practices Committee (FEPC). The stated purpose of the FEPC was to provide the machinery necessary to enforce the general provisions of the Thirteenth, Fourteenth, and Fifteenth Amendments to the Constitution, amendments which were thought to forbid discrimination in the labor market. The FEPC was to monitor and correct any such discriminatory practices.

The power of Roosevelt's FEPC was extremely limited. Nevertheless, it confronted persistent and decisive opposition in Congress. Congress twice dismantled the FEPC, finally burying it in 1945. While Roosevelt's FEPC never had a chance to function effectively, its members, nevertheless, saw great potential for meaningful action. In their final report, the FEPC staff claimed that racial discrimination in employment could be ended if and when the federal government took decisive action.

No further equal employment opportunity action was taken until 1951. At that time, President Truman created a committee similar to the old FEPC. That committee, too, had few powers and continued to exist quietly throughout the eight years of the Eisenhower administration. It was not until President Kennedy's executive order of March 7, 1961, that federal equal employment opportunity intentions began to appear serious.

According to President Kennedy's executive order, the federal government assumed specific responsibility to "promote the full realization of equal employment opportunity." The government pledged not only to eliminate discrimination within its own agencies and departments but to assure equal opportunity in all private firms that performed work for the federal government. Failure to eliminate discrimination, the government warned, would result in the termination of federal contracts. This threat was the first real power such a committee attained. An Office of Federal Contract Compliance (OFCC) was established to carry out the executive order.

A parallel move toward equal employment opportunity took place in Congress shortly afterwards. The historic Civil Rights Act of 1964 incorporated provisions to forbid discrimination in the labor market. Title VII of that act explicitly outlawed discrimination by corporations, unions, or any other labor market participants. The enforcement of that prohibition was delegated to the newly created Equal Employment Opportunity Commission (EEOC).

Because the enforcement machinery and effectiveness of the EEOC and the OFCC differ greatly, it is necessary to consider them separately. The Equal Employment Opportunity Commission has only limited enforcement power. It is directed by Congress to "endeavor to eliminate any discriminatory employment practice by informal methods of conference, conciliation, and persuasion." It may not impose sanctions, issue cease and desist orders, nor even make public the fact that discrimination is being practiced. It depends largely on the goodwill of the offender to bring about equal employment opportunity once a complaint is filed. Punitive or remedial action is rarely sought through the courts, and until recently it required the initiative of the victims of discrimination. But in 1972 the EEOC itself gained congressional authorization, for the first time, to initiate court action to halt discriminatory practices.

The potential effectiveness of the EEOC is still weakened, however, by its procedural orientation. Before the EEOC can take any action at all, it must receive a sworn complaint from an individual. Once the complaint is received, the commission seeks to determine whether the allegation is reasonable. If the complaint appears well-founded, the commission then approaches the offending employer, union, or employment agency for "conference, conciliation, and persuasion." If conciliation is not attained, the complainant and the EEOC may seek redress in the courts.

This dependence of the EEOC on individual complaints has several drawbacks. First of all, it is tremendously expensive and time-consuming to review and process each complaint (the EEOC successfully completed only 300 conciliations in its first three years!). Second, an aggrieved person has little incentive to report discriminatory actions. The complaint procedure subjects an individual to potential union or employer retaliation, costs him much time and money, and yields little practical benefit. At best, a complaining individual is apt to gain employment or promotion with a chastened and possibly resentful employer. Much more effective action would be possible if the EEOC had the power to initiate broader investigations and seek more comprehensive resolutions.

Stronger powers of initiative and enforcement are available to the Office of Federal Contract Compliance. The OFCC may, itself, initiate investigations to determine whether discriminatory practices exist. It may also impose sanctions, such as contract termination, where discrimination is discovered. Furthermore, OFCC may require employers to take "affirmative action" to remedy past discrimination. These sanctions may be applied to all businesses that sell or service products to the government. Thus, the potential power of the OFCC is as vast as the government's position in the economy. In 1970, over 30 percent of the labor force was potentially subject to the sanctions of the OFCC.

While the potential power of the OFCC to eliminate discriminatory practices and rectify past injustices is great, that power is rarely used. Politics are partly to blame. An employer beset by the OFCC always has recourse to other authorities. Should he command the attention and sympathy of congressmen or other executive offices, OFCC sanctions may be suspended. Bureaucratic interests also undermine the OFCC's power. The Department of Defense, for example, regards weapons procurement as more vital to its mission than guidelines for equal opportunity. Hence, it may devote relatively little attention to compliance with OFCC edicts and may even inveigh against contract cancellations that threaten orderly procurement. Accordingly, the power of the OFCC remains on paper. As yet, no contract has been terminated or cancelled to enforce equal opportunity.

A more affirmative kind of action has been taken by the government with regard to the nation's labor unions, especially the construction unions. As we saw in Chapter 10, blue-collar unions have the potential to provide many black workers with immediate remunerative employment. In addition, the government is a major force in the construction industry, purchasing up to one-third of total output, and could exert considerable leverage to break down discriminatory barriers. In pursuing such an effort, the Nixon administration tried to establish guidelines for minority recruitment in the building trades. The first attempt, in Philadelphia, proposed to raise the proportion of new black recruits from 5 percent in 1970 to 25 percent in 1975. That attempt and later "Philadelphia plans" elsewhere have not been successful, however. Unions have tremendous political strength and do not like interference. Furthermore, the slack economy of the early 1970s has stirred job fears among unionists. Faced with the prospect of unemployment, union ranks solidify against the threat of increased competition. The government has also been unwilling to carry out threats of contract termination, which would also cause losses for employers.

While the short history of federal activity in the area of employment rights is not encouraging, it has not been wholly without impact. The enactment of legislation and the issuance of executive orders are important, even if they are not religiously enforced. They at least establish the principle that discrimination is not acceptable. They also lay the groundwork for stronger enforcement powers later. From this perspective, federal equal employment policies appear to be a timid beginning rather than an outright failure.

EQUAL EDUCATIONAL OPPORTUNITY POLICIES

Government policy in the field of equal educational opportunity is more difficult to characterize than in the field of employment opportunity. Politics and bureaucracy again take their tolls, of course, and there is, again, much complacency and inertia. What renders this subject especially complex, however, is the degree to which equal educational opportunity responsibilities are shared by different levels of government. Educational policy has traditionally been a prerogative of the separate states. The federal government provides less than 10 percent of all educational expenditures and administers no schools. Consequently, it has less power to create equal opportunity in the schools. It cannot terminate contracts or open new job slots as it may do in the labor market. It must instead rely on, and cooperate with, the states and the courts to abolish discrimination in the schools.

The most obvious form of discrimination in the educational system is school segregation. While discrimination can take place even in the absence of segregation, not even a pretense of equal opportunity is possible so long as segregated schools are maintained. The Supreme Court itself made this observation, as we saw in Chapter 9. To what extent, then, are governmental bodies endeavoring to abolish segregation?

De jure v. De facto Segregation

A distinction is commonly made between two kinds of segregation. The first, *de jure*, refers to a situation where blacks and whites are legally constrained to attend separate schools. The second, *de facto*, refers to a situation where school segregation results, not from edict, but from circumstance. Such a case occurs where blacks and whites live in different neighborhoods, thereby making school integration difficult.

While the distinction between *de facto* and *de jure* segregation is often useful, it does have unfortunate consequences. It creates a distinction that few victims of discrimination can appreciate. As Judge J. Skelly Wright noted in a 1967 ruling on District of Columbia schools: "Racially and socially homogeneous schools damage the minds of all children who attend them . . . whether the segregation occurs in law or in fact." The distinction between *de jure* and *de facto* also gives rise to a false aura of innocence. *De jure* segregation is commonly seen as the consequence of evil intent, while *de facto* segregation is seen as the innocent byproduct of socioeconomic forces—especially in the housing market. Such a view obscures the fact that government bodies can and do set the pattern for much *de facto* segregation. Segregation of the schools is rarely, if ever, a completely natural and unplanned circumstance.

Governments have two kinds of effects on *de facto* segregation. They may directly affect residential housing patterns, thereby enlarging or diminishing the foundation for *de facto* segregation; or they may alter the distribution of schools within established housing patterns, thereby facilitating or obstructing greater integration of the schools.

Housing Patterns

To a large extent, existing residential patterns are the outcome of millions of individual housing decisions, but free choice is not the only force operative in the housing market. The government, through its building and loan programs, has also participated in the establishment of segregated neighborhoods, and thus, must bear a significant responsibility for the *de facto* school segregation that results from neighborhoods isolated by race and class.

The Federal Housing Authority (FHA) has been a major factor in the housing market since its creation in 1938. It had a particularly important role in establishing the housing patterns of the post-World War II housing boom, patterns that still predominate today. The power of the FHA to alter housing choices lies in its ability to insure or guarantee loans on residential construction. FHA support oftentimes determines whether a house can be purchased, at what location, and at what cost. A measure of its influence is easily grasped. In 1965 alone, the FHA, together with the Veterans Administration, insured or guaranteed some $150 billion in mortgage loans, providing money for more than 15 million housing units. During the housing boom of the late 1940s and 1950s, the FHA helped finance one-third of all new housing. Today's suburbs are, in large part, the product of FHA financing.

Given the power of the Federal Housing Authority in the housing market, its ability to foster or contain segregation is clear. For the most part, it has chosen to encourage and extend rigid racial and class segregation. The FHA Underwriting Manual of 1938 declared that "if a neighborhood is to retain stability, it is necessary that properties shall continue to be occupied by the same social and racial groups." Agency valuators, considering whether or not to make FHA loans, were warned to protect against "inharmonious racial groups." The FHA even composed and distributed a model racially restrictive covenant, prohibiting "the occupancy of properties except by the race for which they are intended." The FHA deemed it necessary and proper that it create and maintain racially and socially homogeneous neighborhoods.

In 1962, President Kennedy issued an executive order on equal opportunity in housing, which brought to an end the explicitly segregationist practices of the FHA, but that order came too late and has too little force. The new FHA policy of nondiscrimination is limited largely to new housing. Thus, the established patterns of housing segregation are virtually unaffected. Furthermore, FHA loans now cover less than 20 percent of new construction. Of even greater significance is that the issuance of FHA guarantees still depends on the decisions of private lenders. FHA loan insurance is available only to those persons who are eligible to get loans from private banks. Thus, FHA policy reflects the racially and socially restrictive practices of most commercial lenders.

Poor families, of whatever color, are further handicapped by the Federal

Housing Authority's focus on middle-class families. Because FHA loan applicants must be eligible for commerical loans, FHA insurance and guarantees benefit few, if any, poor families. As a consequence, middle-class families get loans quickly and cheaply, while the poor are confined to overpriced and inadequate housing.

Federal efforts designed explicitly to improve the living conditions of the poor have likewise failed to promote residential integration. Public housing projects are a vivid example. Public housing is almost always located in the poorest areas and most often segregated by race. Thus it tends to intensify racial and economic isolation. The U.S. Commission on Civil Rights reports that, of the quarter of a million public housing units built in the nation's 24 largest metropolitan areas, only 76 units have been located outside the central city. The result is not only residential segregation but *de facto* segregation of schools as well. The commission has cited some illustrations:

> In San Francisco, for example, six projects totaling more than 2,300 units, each predominantly Negro, are grouped on one piece of land called Hunter's Point. The schools in the area that serve the housing projects all are more than 90 per cent Negro. In Cincinnati, two nearby projects— Lincoln Court and Laurel homes—total almost 2,300 units. Together the projects are 99.7 per cent nonwhite, and house 2,616 school-age children. Schools serving the development, many of them built specifically for that purpose, are all predominantly nonwhite.

> The most extreme example, perhaps, is Robert Taylor Homes, a project in Chicago. Opened in 1961-62, it contains 4,415 units, 75 per cent of them designed for large families. Of the 28,000 tenants, some 20,000 are children. The entire occupancy is Negro and schools were built in the area to serve the project alone. Indeed, classes for lower grades are conducted in project units, by agreement between the school board and the housing authority, as a way to relieve overcrowding in the nearby schools.[1]

While the federal government cannot be held responsible for all *de facto* school segregation, it is clear that its housing policies have encouraged racial and economic isolation. The government's housing policies have also intensified popular prejudice and fear, thereby further obstructing the attainment of residential and school integration.

School Patterns

While public and private housing decisions have created a foundation for school segregation, residential patterns alone do not maintain segregated schools. School authorities have broad discretion in defining the number and nature of

---

[1] U.S. Commission on Civil Rights, *Racial Isolation in the Public Schools* (Washington, D.C.: Government Printing Office, 1967), pp. 37-38.

school boundaries to be superimposed on residential patterns. Hence, local school authorities have the power to combat the segregation that exists in housing. Once again, however, this power has often been employed to intensify rather than to combat racial and economic isolation.

The power of local school authorities to encourage or resist school segregation resides in a variety of public decisions. Housing patterns alone do not define neighborhoods, much less school zones. Instead, the definition of a neighborhood is partly determined by the decisions of where and how to locate public schools. The number of schools to build, their size, and their geographic location are all decisions that help to shape neighborhoods. Building one large school between racially segregated housing areas, for example, does more to promote school integration than constructing two separate schools within racially homogeneous communities. Also important for the pattern of school integration is the number of grades to be served by each school and the actual specification of attendance zones. These decisions, too, can abet or overcome residential segregation.

To a large extent, of course, existing school patterns reflect historical, rather than current, decisions. This fact does not exonerate school authorities from responsibility, however. Residential patterns are continually changing and schools are continually being built or rezoned. Hence, school authorities have discretion to alter the distribution of pupils or facilities and to counteract past decisions. They have broad latitude to promote or impede integration as they see fit. Unfortunately, they have often chosen either to neglect the potential for integration or, worse still, to purposefully extend segregation. Local school authorities have used the following tactics successfully to achieve precisely these results.

Gerrymandering. Gerrymandering refers to the purposeful restructuring of school attendance zones to foster school segregation. It is the oldest, simplest, and most blatant tactic available to local school authorities. Its visibility, however, has led to a decline in its use, especially where court suits have arisen. The Hawthorne Elementary School in Kansas City provides a rare illustration. There, black families began to expand westward into the school zone of the previously all-white Hawthorne School. School authorities managed, however, to keep integration just beyond the reach of black children, simply by moving school lines westward as fast as black families moved into the area.

More often than not, effective gerrymandering is accomplished in conjunction with new school construction. The Sawyer Junior High School in Cincinnati is a more typical case. Prior to 1962, two junior high schools, Ach and Withrow, served pupils in that city's western area. Ach was 92 percent black, Withrow 58 percent white. To relieve overcrowding, a third school, Sawyer, was opened in 1962. As Figure 13.1 illustrates, Sawyer Junior High was located at the boundary between white and black residential areas. While this location could have been utilized to expand integration, it was employed for opposite

FIGURE 13.1 Gerrymandered School Zones (Source: U.S. Commission on Civil Rights, *Racial Isolation in the Public Schools.* Washington, D.C.: Government Printing Office, 1967, p. 49)

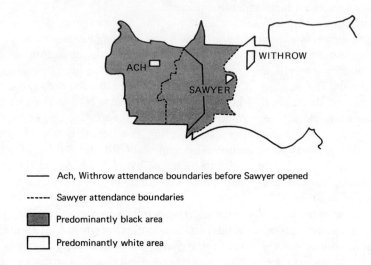

——— Ach, Withrow attendance boundaries before Sawyer opened

----- Sawyer attendance boundaries

▮ Predominantly black area

▯ Predominantly white area

purposes. The attendance zone for Sawyer was designed to extend only to the west, incorporating only black residences. As a result, Ach ended up 99 percent black, Sawyer 98 percent black, and Withrow 83 percent white. Such is the power of school authorities to create *de facto* segregation.

Optional Zones. A tactic not far removed from gerrymandering is the use of optional attendance zones. An optional zone is a limited geographical area in which students are permitted to choose the school they will attend. In effect, optional zones are a more subtle and flexible tool to achieve either greater integration or segregation. Two illustrations cited by the U.S. Commission on Civil Rights convey the potential of this tool. In San Francisco, an optional zone existed for two decades between the Geary Elementary School, predominantly white, and the Emerson School, predominantly black. During that time, the residents of the optional zone were mostly white. By 1960, however, the great majority of the zone's residents were black. Continuation of the option thus threatened to enable black children to attend the white-majority Geary School. In 1961, the option was rescinded; residents of the zone were, thereafter, included in the attendance area of Emerson. Racial isolation was enforced.

In the South, *free choice* provisions are the counterpart of optional attendance zones. Students are permitted or required to state a preference for the schools they wish to attend. Priority is given to those preferences, however, that are based on residential location, established school ties, or other correlates of race. Just how free choice can operate as a subterfuge for purposeful

FIGURE 13.2 Optional Attendance Zones (Source: U.S. Commission on Civil Rights, *Racial Isolation in the Public Schools.* Washington, D.C.: Government Printing Office, 1967, p. 53)

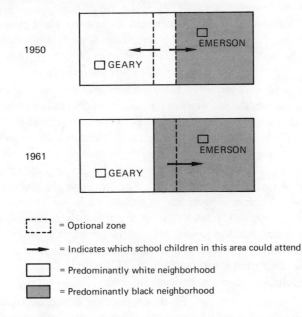

segregation was illustrated in Atlanta. Its Kirkwood School was all-white but located in an area becoming all-black. Free choice provisions required that some blacks be permitted to attend Kirkwood. To forestall integration, however, the superintendent of schools sent a letter to the parents of Kirkwood pupils, notifying them of the impending influx and reminding them of their free choice options. The parents responded promptly. Kirkwood, which had been all-white in 1964, was all-black when it reopened in 1965. All the white children had transferred elsewhere.

School Construction. As noted earlier, the selection of a school site can have tremendous impact on the pattern of school segregation. Schools located within all-white or all-black residential areas solidify racial isolation. Schools located in fringe areas have the potential—if not subsequently gerrymandered—of accelerating integration. Unfortunately, site selection all too often conforms to segregationist practices. Of the 371 schools newly constructed in 16 cities from 1950 through 1965, over 80 percent opened nearly all-white or all-black.

San Francisco's Hunter's Point community has already been mentioned as an example of federally financed residential segregation. The same area illustrates another dimension of school construction that can be manipulated for racial purposes, namely, school size. The abrupt influx of families into the Hunter's Point area necessitated more classroom space. To acquire that space, three of Hunter's Point's predominantly black schools were enlarged to a capacity of 1,000 pupils each. At the same time, however, a new school, Fremont, was constructed within an adjacent white area. The Fremont school, however, provided space for only 450 pupils. Hence, it could not handle any of the overflow from Hunter's Point. The decision on school size reinforced existing segregation. Fremont retained its all-white character.

Grade Structure.   Even when faced with established school locations and size, school authorities are not powerless to alter racial attendance patterns. One extremely subtle but very effective means for overcoming these obstacles is to redefine grade structures. Enlarging the number of grades a school will serve has the effect of shrinking its attendance zone. On the other hand, schools that serve only a few grades must reach out in all directions to include a sufficient number of pupils. The Meigs School in Nashville illustrates how the technique can be employed. Most Nashville schools are organized on a 6-3-3 or an 8-4 grade pattern. The Meigs School, however, is an exception. It is located in a small black area and is structured to serve grades one to twelve. It is the only school in Nashville so structured, and it was all-black in 1965. The Dunbar Junior-Senior High School in Lexington, Kentucky, and the J. N. Ervin School in Dallas have been structured similarly and for the same purpose.

Busing.   Visions of masses of white children being bused into black ghettos stir the fears of most white parents. Such visions obstruct an oftentimes reasonable and expedient solution to established segregation patterns. Anxiety is also expressed for the stamina of children who must be bused daily to their classrooms. What is seldom realized is that busing of children to school is a common phenomenon in the United States. In recent years, for example, over one-third of all public school children rode buses to school. Most are bused simply because such transportation is most convenient. Others are bused to distant schools to relieve overcrowding at schools nearer by. Still others are bused to extend and enforce racial segregation.

The cities of San Francisco and Cincinnati again offer convenient illustrations. The Anza Elementary School in San Francisco was built in a white area about eight blocks from the predominantly black Golden Gate Elementary School. At the same time, classrooms at Golden Gate were overcrowded and pupils were being bused fifteen blocks to another school. Yet, when Anza was completed, its enrollment was nearly all white. Black pupils from Golden Gate continued to be bused to the more distant Pacific Heights School.

Cincinnati school authorities were even more blatant. There, black students were bused out of a predominantly white area to a nearly all-black school 5.5 miles on the other side of Cincinnati. The explanation for busing focused on overcrowding, yet there was available space in closer schools, schools with predominantly white enrollments. The U.S. Commission on Civil Rights asked local school authorities to explain Cincinnati's unusual busing pattern. The response is as illuminating as it is evasive:

> ... the neighborhood—the concept of relationship of having children attend the school that is in the immediate proximity of the school, those closest to it. Now in this particular case all we did different from that is we picked them up and moved them some place else for a school, but in terms of parents we also tried to get the parents to maintain this relationship rather than dividing them up, into five different places and splitting them in five different spots. That's the only difference.[2]

In other words, the school board felt it necessary to keep all the black students together, regardless of where or how they attended school.

The Neighborhood School Concept

The question of busing—especially when it is proposed for purposes of facilitating integration—touches a very sensitive nerve in most Americans. Busing is almost always perceived as a direct threat to the cherished notion of a neighborhood school. Even the Cincinnati school board felt obliged to defend its peculiar busing arrangement on the basis of the neighborhood school concept. It is worth reflecting for a moment, then, on what a neighborhood school really is and why it is so revered.

Neighborhood schools are usually deemed desirable for two reasons. They are close to home and thus conveniently accessible. They also serve to foster community cohesiveness. Children who reside close together and attend a common school have more opportunity to interact and are thought to establish more enduring relationships. These two benefits, proximity and social integration, are the mainstays of neighborhood school support.

What is curious about arguments for neighborhood schools is not their potential benefits but their historical perspective. Arguments against economic or racial integration usually proceed from the assumption that integration is destroying the neighborhood school. There are two problems with this perspective. First of all, children have, historically, travelled quite far to school and continue to do so. More proximate schools have resulted from increasing population density rather than from an increased awareness of any "neighborhood" benefits. One could also question whether this higher density actually has fostered better community and personal relationships. Second, we have already demonstrated that there is considerable flexibility in defining a neighborhood school. School attendance zones themselves can create neighborhoods, and deliberate manipulation of school zones can even affect residential choice. Families will want to live near the schools they know they can attend.

Neighborhood schools, then, are not historically sacrosanct. They may not even be the most desirable. As they are now conceived, they serve two specific

[2] U.S. Commission on Civil Rights, *Racial Isolation in the Public Schools*, p. 56.

goals. It would not be completely alien, therefore, to broaden our objectives. Schools could be structured to promote a sense of community in a larger and integrated society rather than to promote cohesiveness in a narrower and often isolated residential tract. Indeed, the narrow neighborhood concept has been repeatedly sacrificed to other social objectives. Every major city, for example, has at least one citywide school reserved for students of outstanding ability. In these cases, productivity and individual development are deemed more important than neighborhood cohesiveness. No one has argued that the attending students are in any way deprived. A high percentage of white parents send their children to distant private schools for exactly the same reasons. And finally, society has all too often demonstrated a willingness to subordinate neighborhood socialization to the goal of racial segregation in the schools. Neighborhood schools are deemed inviolate only when integration threatens.

Fiscal Disparities

The preceding illustrations are not intended to imply that all school authorities are racist. There are scores of administrators—at local, state, and federal levels—who are dedicated to the goal of equal educational opportunity. Instead, the examples cited are designed to illustrate the potential that exists for altering patterns of school segregation. All of these techniques could be employed to reduce segregation as well as to intensify it. That they continue to be employed more for the latter purpose is discouraging but still subject to change.

However, even where school authorities are predisposed to promote equal educational opportunity, that objective is not always attainable. One enormous obstacle to the attainment of equality is the pattern of school financing. Black children tend to live in the inner city, while white children live in the suburbs. In some cities—for example, Washington, D.C. (71% black), Newark (54%), East St. Louis (69%), Atlanta (51%), Cleveland (59%)—the racial isolation between city and suburb has reached extreme proportions, creating not only a geographic obstacle to integration but a financial one as well.

Local communities continue to provide the bulk of their own school resources. In 1970, the federal government supplied only 6 percent of all educational expenditures, the state governments contributed 41 percent, while local governments provided the remainder. This means that the quantity and quality of educational resources in a community depends largely on the ability of the local populace to pay taxes. In substantive terms, this means that wealthier white enclaves in the suburbs can provide educational opportunities for their children that few cities can ever hope to match. In the state of California, for example, per pupil educational expenditures range from $407 in poor communities to $2,586 in wealthy communities. In New York, the range is from under $500 to over $1,500.

It is easy to see how such exaggerated disparities arise. In the suburbs, the ratio of property values to school age children is far higher than in the cities. Indeed, population density is ten times larger in urban ghettos than in surrounding areas. This means that residents of the city must support far more school children per square mile than people in the suburbs. Furthermore, the wealthier residents of the suburbs are better equipped to support public schools. They have the property and income on which school revenues depend.

The economics of local school financing encourages school districts to attempt to maximize their tax base while minimizing enrollment size. That is, they seek to include the wealthier and exclude the poorer, especially those with many children. The results are staggering. The city of Big Creek, California, has $306,077 of assessed property per pupil, while the city of Olinda has a scant $3,698. This leads to a lower tax rate for those most able to pay, an outcome of great benefit to the wealthier but of great disadvantage to the poor.

Given the nature of school financing, suburban communities have a tremendous incentive to insulate their school systems from the poor. They have little desire to impose higher tax rates on themselves to provide more educational opportunity for others. In some communities, wealthier neighborhoods may even seek to incorporate independent school districts to dispose of responsibilities they already share. This tactic has taken on special significance as the courts have ordered opportunities to be equalized within, but not across, school districts.

To some extent, state and federal governments attempt to equalize the educational inequalities between richer and poorer communities. The Elementary and Secondary Education Act of 1965 is an example of such an attempt. Under this act, the federal government distributes approximately $1 billion a year to the poorest schools, but even this infusion of funds is not adequate to the task. Over $73 billion was spent on education in the 1970-1971 school year, and wealthier communities continue to command a disproportionate amount of those resources. The most absurd and distressing statistic of all is, perhaps, this: the wealthiest schools are twice as likely as the poorest schools to have free milk or food programs. Poor schools are denied such benefits because they cannot afford cafeterias or extra personnel.

The subject of school financing highlights several important dimensions of the educational opportunity issue. The localized nature of school financing, for example, provides an independent motive for segregation. Even persons who harbor few racial prejudices are not immune to self-interest. On the contrary, most people seek to minimize their tax burden while providing well for their own children. Thus, they seek to exclude poor children, many of whom are black, from their school systems. This exclusionist tendency illuminates again the close ties of racial and class discrimination.

The class discrimination inherent in existing patterns of school financing has recently become a major judicial issue. In August, 1971, the California

Supreme Court acknowledged that fiscal disparities between school districts "makes the quality of a child's education a function of the wealth of his parents and neighbors." Ruling that such discriminatory treatment violated the Fourteenth Amendment of the U.S. Constitution, the court declared the state's entire system of financing public schools to be unconstitutional. That landmark decision is certain to lead to further judicial action, possibly even to a U.S. Supreme Court ruling.

SUMMARY

Equal opportunity policies can help eliminate poverty in two ways: they may provide access to educational credentials; and they may dismantle artificial barriers between men and jobs. Access to educational credentials is important to the extent that it opens new employment opportunities or redistributes existing ones.

The federal government's effort to create equal opportunity in employment has not met with much success. Black workers continue to suffer inordinate levels of unemployment and to be relegated to undesirable jobs. A major reason for this continuing discrimination lies in the nature of government efforts. For decades, the federal government has had the power only to exhort employers to create equal employment opportunities. It was not until the early 1960s that the government acquired some meaningful powers to enforce its proclamations. The Office of Federal Contract Compliance may terminate contracts of discriminatory employers, while the Equal Employment Opportunity Commission may facilitate legal action. Those powers have been used rarely, however, and then only as a threat. Political, bureaucratic, and economic interests continue to impede the attainment of equal employment opportunity.

In the educational system, equal opportunity has been just as elusive. Local and state governments have not demonstrated a consuming ambition to open school doors to all. On the contrary, they have often employed a variety of manipulative techniques to forestall school integration for as long as possible. The localized nature of school financing also creates a tremendous incentive for wealthier and whiter communities to exclude poorer and blacker children from their schools. Federal authority to alter the pattern of segregation resides primarily in the power to bestow or withdraw funds under the Elementary and Secondary Education Act. But the amount of funds involved is relatively small and the political pressure to maintain their flow, great.

REFERENCES

BENSON, CHARLES S., *The Cheerful Prospect*. Boston: Houghton Mifflin Company, 1965.

JACOBS, PAUL, *Prelude to Riot*. New York: Random House, Inc., Vintage Books, 1967.

NATIONAL ASSOCIATION OF INTERGROUP RELATIONS OFFICIALS, *Public School Segregation and Integration in the North*. Washington, D.C.: National Association of Intergroup Relations Officials, 1963.

NATIONAL COMMITTEE FOR SUPPORT OF PUBLIC SCHOOLS, *School Finance: A Matter of Equal Protection?* Washington, D.C.: National Committee for Support of Public Schools, 1970.

NATIONAL EDUCATION ASSOCIATION, *Financial Status of the Public Schools*. Washington, D.C.: National Education Association, 1971.

U.S. COMMISSION ON CIVIL RIGHTS, *Federal Civil Rights Enforcement Effort*. Washington, D.C.: Government Printing Office, 1970, Ch. 2.

_____ , *The Federal Civil Rights Enforcement Effort–Seven Months Later*. Washington, D.C.: Government Printing Office, 1971.

_____ , *Freedom to the Free: A Century of Emancipation*. Washington, D.C.: Government Printing Office, 1963.

_____ , *Jobs and Civil Rights*. Washington, D.C.: Government Printing Office, 1969.

_____ , *Racial Isolation in the Public Schools*. Washington, D.C.: Government Printing Office, 1967.

WILCOX, CLAIR, *Toward Social Welfare*. Homewood, Ill.: Richard D. Irwin, Inc., 1969, Chs. 10 and 11.

IV Summary and Conclusions

14. Directions and Prospects

14 Directions and Prospects

Recognition of the fact that 25 million Americans remain poor has led to two simple questions: (1) Why are so many individuals poor; and (2) what policies will eliminate their poverty? The preceding chapters have provided much of the background material necessary to resolve these questions. This concluding chapter attempts to summarize the salient impressions of our inquiry and offer policy suggestions.

THE CAUSES OF POVERTY

The most popular diagnoses of poverty focus on the personal characteristics of those who are poor. The poor are thus viewed as less able, less motivated, overly reproductive, too aged or sick, or otherwise handicapped. By inference or declaration, they are thus assumed to be responsible for their own impoverishment. This view of poverty is reinforced by conventional statistical profiles of the poverty population. Very high percentages of the poor *are* in families that are aged, or female-headed, or large, or prone to sickness and disability.

There are two critical weaknesses in these demographic theories of poverty, however. Not all of the poor fit one or another of the various categories of misfits. Indeed, the largest single demographic group among the poor consists of traditional male-headed families, most with a father working full time all year round. But the weakness of demographic theories involves more than just narrow horizons; these theories also suffer from shortsightedness. Even those poor families who manifest distinctive demographic traits, such as broken homes, are not necessarily poor because of those traits. On the contrary, for the most part the aged poor were poor before they were aged, broken poor families were poor before they split up, large poor families were poor when they were smaller, and sick poor families were poor even when they were well. Thus, theories of poverty causation that are based only on observations at a single point in time

187

fail to perceive the dynamics of impoverishment. They confuse association with causality.

A broader, more dynamic perspective on poverty is achieved by focusing on the relationship of people to the labor market. For the most part, it is a person's relationship to the market that determines his economic, and even social, status. One immediate advantage of this perspective is that it draws attention to two critical questions: (1) What forces determine how many good income earning opportunities are available; and (2) what forces determine who will obtain those opportunities? The myopic perspective of demographic theories of poverty encompasses only the second question. It assumes that good jobs are always available in sufficient quantity. But they are not, as history has repeatedly shown, and as we have again witnessed in the escalating unemployment rates of the early 1970s. To understand why so much poverty exists at any point in time, we must consider and resolve the first question. The answer to the second question tells us primarily how that poverty will be distributed.

In seeking to resolve the first question, we have put a heavy stress on the importance of aggregate economic policies in determining the extent of poverty. We have suggested that the number of available jobs is a phenomenon over which individual members of society have very little control. Similarly, they have little control over what kinds of jobs will be available or where they will take place. These decisions are made, instead, by the interplay of labor market forces, among which government fiscal and monetary decisions are often the most decisive. Accordingly, we conclude that collective social decisions in the area of economic policy—especially those concerning the extent and structure of the demand for labor—are responsible for much poverty.

We should not conclude, however, that all available income-earning opportunities are taken. Even in relatively prosperous times, some families will break up, others will become sick or disabled, and some may even choose not to work. Hence, even with prolonged full employment, not all families will participate fully in the economy. Some disequilibria between the number of available jobs and potential workers do arise from demographic forces, and we must include them as independent causes of poverty where appropriate. Family breakup rates high among these factors, with age and disability slightly less important. Their cumulative importance at present appears to be relatively small, however.

The third general set of causes are those related to discrimination, both in the schools and in the labor market. Minority groups and the offspring of the poor are not given an equal chance to acquire productive skills nor to use those skills in the labor market. Hence, racial and class discrimination have significant impact on both the distribution and extent of poverty. As long as discrimination persists, we may predict that the children of the poor and blacks will dominate the ranks of the poverty population. Even in a relatively prosperous economy, discrimination tends to create artificial barriers between workers and jobs, leaving some individuals poor. We may estimate that discrimination is responsible for a significant share of all poverty and that it is the foremost determinant of the distribution of low incomes.

In assessing the causes of poverty, then, we may make the following generalizations: (1) labor market forces are primarily responsible for the extent of poverty, with demographic handicaps and discrimination of secondary importance; and (2) the distribution of poverty is determined by patterns of discrimination and demographic characteristics. Because available knowledge and statistics about poverty and discrimination are not complete, there is room for argument on the exact size of each relationship. Nevertheless, the broad outlines of causality are clear enough to provide the necessary perspective for public policy approaches.

POLICY DIRECTIONS

An understanding of the causes of poverty gives clear direction to the formulation of required public policy. To eliminate poverty, we must first expand the number of decent job opportunities and make them available to all. Professor Harry Johnson of the University of Chicago has summarized the point well: ". . . in the absence of a policy of raising the demand for labor to the stretching point, ad hoc policies for remedying poverty by piecemeal assaults on particular poverty-associated characteristics are likely to prove both ineffective and expensive. The most effective way to attack poverty is to attack unemployment, not the symptoms of it."[1]

To reduce unemployment and poverty, the government has several options available. First and foremost, it must seek to maintain a high level of aggregate demand by the judicious use of fiscal and monetary tools. In addition, it must give special consideration to the structure of demand those tools stimulate. Aggregate economic policies have identifiable impact on different areas, industries, and labor market groups. Accordingly, it is the responsibility of government policy makers to select that mix of public actions that maximizes impact on the unemployed and poor, while minimizing dislocations, such as inflation, elsewhere.

Concomitant with the thrust toward full employment, government agencies must make a determined effort to equalize educational and employment opportunity. This will not only further reduce poverty and inequity, it will also make the attainment of full employment easier and less expensive.

Finally, the public must assume responsibility for those who are temporarily or permanently unable to participate in the labor market. Adequate income support must be available, both to alleviate hardship and to reduce

[1] Harry G. Johnson, "Poverty and Unemployment," in Burton Weisbrod, ed., *The Economics of Poverty* (Englewood Cliffs, N.J.: Prentice-Hall, Inc., 1965), p. 170.

intergenerational deprivation. Greatest priority should be placed, however, on reducing the need for public assistance to a minimum.

Viewed against this policy framework, recent public antipoverty activities do not appear well directed. Only rarely has there been a sustained and determined effort to reach full employment, and even at those times, policy decisions stopped short of considering the structure of aggregate demand thereby created. Instead, public antipoverty activity has, for the most part, been a bread and circus kind of affair. We have allotted—grudgingly, to be sure—huge sums of money to feed, clothe, and house the poor, in the hope, perhaps, of achieving social tranquility. At the same time, we have subjected the poor to a kaleidoscope of training and education activities, holding out false promises of job opportunity. Yet we have done close to nothing to create the job opportunities that are our most pressing need. Some recent experiences are worth reflection.

Welfare Reform

At the end of 1970, there were nearly 14 million individuals receiving, in the aggregate, nearly $10 billion of public assistance. Translated into tax dollars, this means that the average nonpoor individual in the United States contributed over $50 in 1970 to provide the poor with income maintenance. Still more tax money was appropriated to provide housing and food subsidies. While these amounts are a small fraction (under 5 percent) of all government expenditures, they are large enough to stir public anguish. Indeed, the cry for welfare reform has been strident.

In Chapter 11, we reviewed the character of recent welfare reforms. Generally, they incorporate many important and necessary improvements in our system of income maintenance. Unfortunately, they also threaten to add more punitive conditions to the receipt of assistance. What concerns us here, however, is not the substance of those reforms but the policy priority they have been assigned. President Nixon indicated on several occasions that he attached highest priority to welfare reform. The Ninety-second Congress followed the president's lead and made welfare reform the first order of business in 1971.

The problem with welfare reform's high priority is that it threatens to impede more meaningful and permanent poverty remedies. Public interest in poverty issues dissipates easily. Welfare reform thus threatens to satisfy the need for action. There is grave danger that it will be regarded as a solution to the problem of poverty and that other remedies will be neglected.

Education and Training

Perhaps the second ranking area of public concern is the field of education and training. Administrative and congressional spokesmen continue to exhort the young to stay in school and the unemployed—especially those on welfare—to undertake further training. Appropriations to expand government training programs, WIN and MDTA, for example, are rarely denied, and political support for educational outlays is easy to muster. Congressional support for the Family Assistance Act depended partly on the inclusion of fairly vigorous training requirements.

No general case against educational and training expenditures has been presented here. Again, the focus is only on the appropriateness of those expenditures as antipoverty tools. The issue is important because educational and training programs gather much of their support on the basis of their reputed antipoverty effectiveness. What we have sought to demonstrate is that this belief bears very little resemblance to the causal roots of poverty. Lack of training or education, by itself, is not a very significant cause of poverty. Thus, programs to provide more education and training are not particularly well suited to reduce the incidence of poverty. What impact they have is dependent on manpower policies generally. The limited potential of educational advancement to eliminate poverty has been underscored by a recent report of the U.S. Commission on Human Resources and Advanced Education: the commission found that 25 percent of all college graduates are already overtrained for the jobs available.

Manpower

Recent public actions in the area of manpower policy best illustrate the mistaken direction of current antipoverty efforts. The single most important observation of this book is the causal significance of aggregate demand policies for the incidence of poverty. High unemployment and sluggish economic growth are the most certain and forceful agents in perpetuating poverty. Nevertheless, public policy in the early 1970s can be characterized as a deliberate return to the slower growth and higher unemployment rates that characterized much of the 1950s. Two recent decisions illustrate the direction of public policy.

From the first day it took office, the Nixon administration expressed grave concern for the movement of prices and the threat of accelerating inflation. To restore price stability, the administration curtailed growth in government expenditures and increased the cost of borrowing. The effects of these actions were soon felt. Unemployment rates jumped from a low of 3.5 percent in early 1969 to over 6 percent in 1971. The number of persons in poverty increased at the same time. What is particularly distressing about this movement is that it was not necessary. The security of millions of individuals was hastily sacrificed without even considering viable policy alternatives. Selective actions to quell inflation while maintaining employment were rejected out of hand. The presidential veto of the 1970 manpower bill typified the administration's perspective.

By the end of 1970, the number of unemployed persons had already surpassed 5 million. In the November congressional elections, it became painfully obvious to many elected officials that some new manpower policy directions were necessary. In response both to economic necessities and public demand, the Congress passed a $9.5 billion manpower program. Its key provisions authorized the immediate funding of public service employment jobs. Congress was, in effect, conceding that more direct and forceful action was necessary to restore employment. President Nixon, however, vetoed the bill, arguing that public service was dead-end employment and bore no resemblance to real jobs. Only after sustained popular and congressional opposition did Nixon finally sign a second bill, the Emergency Employment Act of 1971. He again stressed, however, the need to make all such new job opportunities transitional in character. Welfare could be permanent, employment only temporary.

Equal Opportunity

Recent activity in the area of civil rights has been sufficiently publicized to require little restatement here. Basically, it has been a question of the courts leading and the executive branch timidly enforcing. We cannot yet claim that we have provided equal opportunity for all, white and black, rich and poor.

It is important to realize that even complete enforcement of civil rights legislation will not lead to equal status for whites and blacks. Even if all racially-based barriers to achievement fell tomorrow, blacks would continue to be handicapped by past discrimination. Black school children would still be far behind their white peers in educational attainments. Equal opportunity to attend college would thus still exclude most blacks. In the labor market, too, the enforcement of nondiscrimination would be of relatively little use to a man who has been denied twenty years of training and experience. The elimination of racial discrimination would narrow racial differences in education and income, but the process would be excruciatingly slow.

To achieve equal economic status between whites and blacks, then, we must do more than enforce equal opportunity; we must also compensate for the heritage of previous discrimination. This means providing compensatory education and training. It also means providing preferential opportunities. Black school children with fewer attainments will have to receive special consideration, while job requirements, in terms of qualifications, experience, and credentials, will have to be set aside for many black workers.

CAUSES, ATTITUDES, AND POLICY

While present policy directions are not well suited to achieve equality or eliminate poverty, there is some prospect for future change. Both the nonpoor and the poor are becoming increasingly frustrated with policies that provide more income maintenance and fewer opportunities. Moreover, there is a growing acceptance by the general public of new policy orientations. A recent poll showed that only 32 percent of the population favor a guaranteed income. By contrast, 79 percent support the concept of a guaranteed job. The *Harvard Business Review* also reports that close to half of all business executives recognize the need to provide preferential opportunities for black workers.

While public attitudes are not yet fully compatible with what is known about the causes of poverty, they are clearly ahead of policy. This is the great source of optimism. To the extent that public attitudes shape antipoverty strategies, then, we may anticipate new policy directions. To reach our goal of eliminating poverty we must bring public perspectives still closer to the causes of poverty and compel public policies to catch up.

Index